CHALLENGES TO AMERICA: United States
Foreign Policy in the 1980s

Volume 4. Sage International Yearbook of Foreign Policy Studies

CHALLENGES TO AMERICA

United States Foreign Policy in the 1980s

edited by

Charles W. Kegley, Jr.

Department of Government and International Studies
University of South Carolina

Patrick J. McGowan

School of International Relations/
Department of Political Science
University of Southern California

Sage Publications   Beverly Hills / London

For information address:

SAGE PUBLICATIONS, INC.
275 South Beverly Drive
Beverly Hills, California 90212

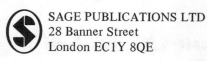

SAGE PUBLICATIONS LTD
28 Banner Street
London EC1Y 8QE

Printed in the United States of America

Library of Congress Cataloging in Publication Data

Main entry under title:

Challenges to America.

(Sage international yearbook of foreign policy studies ; v. 4)
References cited throughout text.
1. United States--Foreign relations--1945-
--Addresses, essays, lectures. I. Kegley,
Charles W. II. McGowan, Patrick J. III. Series.
JX1291.S25 vol. 4   [JX1417]   327'.07'2s
ISBN 0-8039-1121-1   [327.73]   78-14745
ISBN 0-8039-1122-X pbk.

FIRST PRINTING

CONTENTS

PREFACE

The appearance of Volume 4 marks the advent of a new format for the *Sage International Yearbook of Foreign Policy Studies*. Given the *Yearbook's* editorial goal of encouraging systematic studies of the causes and consequences of foreign policy behavior in the hope of facilitating the development of a cumulative field of inquiry, it was perhaps inevitable that the contents of the previous editions were marked by their *diversity*. Contributions were sought that addressed the major methodological, conceptual, and substantive problems confronting systematic foreign policy research and theory building; and the diversity of such analytic problems resulted in volumes which, while fulfilling their primary aim, were nevertheless broad and eclectic in scope.

To enhance the focus of subsequent editions, while appealing to a wider readership, it was the mutual decision of the editors and publisher that these goals would be met best by structuring each volume around a single theme, in an effort to make the impact of each issue greater than the sum of the individual chapters. Consequently, this fourth volume inaugurates a foreign policy *Yearbook* series focused on specific aspects of foreign policy.

The issue examined in the present volume focuses on an important theoretical problem in foreign policy research, namely, how foreign policies are shaped by the kinds of environments (and changes in those environments) encountered by national actors. To probe the linkages that may exist between a state's foreign policy and its domestic and international environments, we might well inquire how changes in environment are related to, and may precipitate, changes in policy. This volume places special emphasis on emergent properties of the global system which stimulate shifts in nations' behavior toward that external environment. In seeking to address this set of theoretical questions, our approach is rationalized by the conviction, expressed by Harf, Hoovler, and James (1974:246), that "the preoccupation of scholars with variables internal to a nation at the expense of external factors has hindered the development of theories of foreign policy."

However, given the primitive state of theory about the manner in which environmental changes exert an impact on the foreign policy of states, the effort to construct a definitive theory about this linkage, valid across time and space, is undoubtedly premature. The question raises many difficulties regarding methodology and data. In order to get a handle on the problem, therefore, this volume focuses attention on a particular "case-for-analysis" (Kegley and Skinner, 1976), the United States. We have asked our authors to explore the nexus between environmental change and foreign policy response by examining some long-term (secular) trends which are likely to present special problems to U.S. society and foreign policy as we move into the next decade. Each identified trend is posited to pose a current or potential threat of some sort to the United States, and to call for a U.S. foreign policy response; and each article assesses the probable consequences of a secular challenge and/or examines the impact which the trend is likely to exert on future U.S. foreign policy. While such investigations are incapable of producing findings necessarily valid for other kinds of foreign policy actors, they nevertheless manage to contribute to theory construction by generating, collectively, a series of propositions about the external sources of foreign policy which may be tested in other research settings. In this case-specific manner a tentative but hopefully meaningful first step toward the development of more universal positive theories of foreign policy behavior has been taken by deriving hypotheses, amenable to verification, that constitute the building blocks of more powerful empirical theories. Some of the assumptions underpinning this focus are elaborated in the introductory chapter, which attempts to put the book into theoretical perspective while providing, in a synthetic fashion, an assessment of the overall impact of what can be learned from a reading of the assembled chapters.

While the shift to a thematically focused volume constitutes a major change for the *Yearbook,* editorial continuities are far more pervasive and should not be obscured. It should be emphasized and made clear by the contents of this volume that the *Yearbook's* editorial policy remains committed to the convictions that analyses of foreign policy should be grounded in the empirical traditions of the social sciences; that analysts of foreign policy should be attentive to the methodological implications of their subject and its research; and that the development of systematic foreign policy studies as a field of inquiry itself is a worthwhile objective deserving conscious and active support.

As evidence of this latter commitment, Volume 4 contains a bibliography of recent foreign policy studies designed to keep readers abreast of emergent research developments in our field of investigation. Moreover, *Yearbook* editorial policy continues to reject methodological orthodoxy and to encourage the integration of divergent approaches. Indeed, the *Yearbook* considers the publication of case studies, qualitative and quantitative comparisons, logical treatments, descriptions, and normative prescriptions as all appropriate. Remaining intact is the view (McGowan, 1973:14) that the kind of studies sought are scientific studies, but that

> Scientific studies of foreign policy are not wedded to a particular research technique like content analysis, survey research, or archival research. Scientific studies of foreign policy are not necessarily allied to any given political ideology. This approach can be used to defend the status quo and to attack it. Comparative studies of foreign policy do not presuppose a single type of research design; they may be cross-sectional, diachronic, or longitudinal. They may look at many cases statistically, or compare a few cases qualitatively, or even examine a single case in order to generate more general hypotheses or to explain why the case in question does not fit an already established pattern (Lijphart, 1971). Scientific studies of foreign policy can use as independent or dependent concepts measured attributes of units ranging from key individuals through regional and international systems. The single unifying feature of systematic studies of foreign policy is their attempt to derive, validate, and evaluate general explanatory sentences about foreign policy.

It is this type of research that we continue to seek to publish in this *Yearbook*.

Other editorial precedents of the *Yearbook* remain preserved as well. The contributions to this volume, like those of previous editions, demonstrate (a) a concern about the way multiple methods might be combined to address the questions studied; (b) an interest in the paradigmatic controversies pervading the field; (c) an au courant familiarity with, and desire to illustrate the applicability of, new techniques of data analysis in the study of foreign policy; and (d) a sensitivity to the problems involved in investigating phenomena pervaded by contingency and indeterminacy, which is manifest in the authors' cautious attitude toward the amount of confidence that can be placed in research findings, and the extent to which those findings are reliable and generalizable to other spatial and temporal settings. In addition, the present contributions (like contributions to previous editions of the *Yearbook*) take cognizance of the need to substantiate descriptions with evidence, and to show a concern with the way discerned trends may be measured objectively. Particular attention has been placed on the collection and presentation of replicable data pertaining to American foreign policy behavior and its sources; indeed, this edition presents the field with a number of data sets pertinent to the study of foreign policy behavior previously unavailable in print. Especially noteworthy here are Small and Singer's expansion of the Correlates of War Project data set on the incidence of internal and external war, the CACI research team's (Abolfathi, Hayes, and Hayes) compilation of crisis data bearing on U.S. foreign policy, as well as Holsti and Rosenau's presentation of survey data pertaining to the foreign policy opinions of American elites. These data sets, it is submitted, are of sufficient variety and scope to constitute, in themselves, valuable resources in the field. The careful analysis and original index construction that other contributors make with derivative foreign policy data entails an important set of materials as well.

The traditional aim of the *Yearbook* to be as *international* as possible in authorship has in no way been jettisoned. But we are disappointed that the present volume includes no articles written by citizens of countries other than the United States. This is explained (but not excused) in part by the nature of the subject matter for this edition, by time constraints involved in manuscript acquisition, and by the fact that virtually all proposed submissions for this volume came from scholars residing within the United States. But scholarly work on United States foreign policy by others would be most welcome and healthy as a corrective to the ethnocentric nature of much research on foreign policy (a tendency which the present contributors have consciously—and we think successfully—guarded against). We remain particularly interested in encouraging submissions to future volumes of the *Yearbook* from authors resident outside the United States.

A final objective of the *Yearbook* deserves emphasis. This is the desire to present not only descriptive and explanatory studies, but also papers that deal with the *prediction* and *evaluation* of foreign policy behavior. Predictive and evaluative studies have been largely absent in previous editions of the *Yearbook* (McGowan, 1974:11; 1975:10-11), to our disappointment. But this deficiency has been rectified significantly in the present volume, wherein *all* the contributions engage, in one way or another, in research conducted in the predictive mode; moreover, many of the articles analyzing past and future American foreign policy are couched in a manner which explicitly permits evaluative conclusions to be drawn. Thus the need for more and better predictive and evaluative studies of foreign policy in the field has been partially met in these pages.

As editors, we must acknowledge our debts to and appreciation for those who have made the continuation and viability of the *Yearbook* possible. Foremost thanks must go to Sage Publications for the faith and support they have shown for the venture, and for their willingness to revive the volume under the new format. In particular, the editorial and administrative assistance of Don Brittain, Betsy Schmidt, and Nancy Cushing Jones of Sage, and of Elizabeth Evatt, should be singled out for exemplary service. We are also greatly appreciative of the creative efforts made by the authors whose chapters follow. All are prolific—indeed, many would say eminent—contributors to the field of foreign policy research, and we are very fortunate to have been able to attract their skills to this project and thereby bring together under one cover such informed, rigorous, and provocative opinion about the future of American policy. In addition, our colleagues on the Editorial Board continue to assist greatly in facilitating the conceptualization of the *Yearbook* and in ensuring quality contributions. Finally, the support and loving atmosphere created by our wives, Pamela and Frouzandeh, contributed immeasurably to our efforts in preparing this book for publication.

Charles W. Kegley, Jr.
Columbia, South Carolina

Patrick J. McGowan
Los Angeles, California

June 15, 1978

REFERENCES

HARF, J.E., HOOVLER, D.G., and JAMES, T.E., Jr. (1974). "Systematic and external attributes in foreign policy analysis." Pp. 235-249 in J.N. Rosenau (ed.), Comparing foreign policies. Beverly Hills, Cal.: Sage.

KEGLEY, C.W., Jr., and SKINNER, R.A., (1976). "The case-for-analysis problem." Pp. 303-317 in J.N. Rosenau (ed.), In search of global patterns. New York: Free Press.

LIJPHART, A. (1971). "Comparative politics and the comparative method." American Political Science Review, 65:682-693.

McGOWAN, P.J. (1973). "Introduction." Pp. 9-25 in P.J. McGowan (ed.), Sage international yearbook of foreign policy studies, I. Beverly Hills, Cal.: Sage.

——— (1974). "Preface." Pp. 7-12 in P.J. McGowan (ed.), Sage international yearbook of foreigh policy studies, II. Beverly Hills, Cal.: Sage.

——— (1975). "Preface." Pp. 7-11 in P.J. McGowan (ed.), Sage international yearbook of foreign policy studies, III. Beverly Hills, Cal.: Sage.

Chapter 1

ENVIRONMENTAL CHANGE AND THE FUTURE OF AMERICAN FOREIGN POLICY: AN INTRODUCTION

CHARLES W. KEGLEY, JR.
University of South Carolina

PATRICK J. McGOWAN
University of Southern California

The United States is in trouble, or so it would seem from sampling opinion in the nation's media or in its streets. The apparent ubiquity of potential crises and ominous trends throughout the world has engendered a consensus that the welfare and security of the nation are precarious, and that the future may not be bright. The sense of urgency and free-floating anxiety that seems to pervade public opinion about the future stems, it may be submitted, from more than mere paranoia or temporary disenchantment. Concern for the future stems as well from a general cognizance that American society and the entire world are undergoing profound change, at ever accelerating rates, and that these changes have generated a whole host of problems and issues which are likely to be persistent, and which comprise potential obstacles and serious threats to basic national values. Long-term changes beyond the nation's borders, as well as within the United States, present challenges to the ability of the United States to adapt to the demands of a rapidly transforming environment. It may not be hyperbole to suggest that, in the absence of such adaptation, "the difficulties of today seem destined to become the nightmares

13

of tomorrow" (Falk, 1975:2). Less apocalyptically, it seems safe to contend that the destiny of the United States appears less manifest today than at any time in recent memory.

To identify some of the most significant trends in the contemporary world system which pose challenges to the United States, and to assess and prescribe what the American foreign policy response to these trends will and should be like as we move into the next decade are the basic objectives to which the essays in this *Yearbook* are addressed.

The appropriateness of conducting a general review of priorities beyond the water's edge is, of course, beyond question. Such evaluation and planning are always essential to any nation wishing to avoid being a rudderless ship of state in the hazardous and turbulent waters of international affairs. But a strong case can be made that the present is especially timely for a major rethinking of the foreign policy of the United States. The trauma and hypnotic effect of the disastrous Vietnam experience and the tragedy of Watergate, both episodes of the nation's experience which diminished its ability to attend to and assess the future accurately (Gregg and Kegley, 1971), have begun to recede from memory. The present more "normal" period permits the nation to re-evaluate its priorities and to probe the probable consequences which any redefinition of the national interest would entail. Moreover, the emergence of new developments in the environment external to the United States, touching myriad threads in the fabric of world politics, provides a sobering catalyst to a major rethinking of the foreign policy of the country. The complexity, number, and severity of contemporary world afflictions invite—indeed, demand—that plans to cope with these emergent problems be devised. It is thus no accident that the Carter campaign strategy in 1976 was centered on the pledge to address and actively confront a plethora of (impossibly large?) challenges rising from the external environment, previously neglected, that now command attention and necessitate adaptive solutions. Nor is it coincidental that emergent international problems have stimulated extensive debate about the prospects for coping with such problems among both policy makers and the public (e.g., Markel and March, 1976; The Council on Foreign Relations' "1980s Project"). This *Yearbook* comprises a related yet different effort to deal analytically with the many diverse and interacting factors which will shape the contours of the world role of the United States in the years to come.

If the pursuit of this endeavor is rationalized in part by its alarming timeliness, it is also derived from the assumption that such a research effort is neither analytically intractable nor policy irrelevant. Our authors share the conviction that the problems assessed are amenable to analytic treatment capable of yielding meaningful understanding. And they share the expectation that the research findings may generate results of use to the policy maker in anticipating the future and coping with its threats. These twin assumptions deserve brief discussion.

In the first instance, one might well question the wisdom of any attempt to deal with the future and operate in the predictive mode. Prognostication is always a hazardous undertaking. In this case prognosis is exacerbated in no small part by the incredibly large number of variables, all interacting and in flux, which one must take into account in order to anticipate variations in the future foreign conduct of the United States, and in the global system of which it is a part. It is little wonder that astrologers are more at home with the future than social scientists, although it must be the latter, not the former, whose advice and counsel we seek.

However, the difficulties inherent in charting the future of American foreign policy and the international system should not dissuade us from making the effort. It is the considered judgment of the contributors to this volume that what is probable, possible, and desirable in the foreign policy of the United States in the near future may be (and should be) examined intelligently now.

Inevitably, the approach to prediction taken in the articles assembled here derives from authors with different specializations, different assumptions, and, happily, from different methodological persuasions. This is appropriate, because in each case the authors have tied their approach to the peculiarities of the particular trend or aspect of international relations that is their focus. But what is more revealing, and instructive, are the commonalities of the various studies. Most noteworthy here is the fact that every predictive study published in this volume addresses the future by reference to the past. While the future may be more important than the past—if only because we may still be able to exercise some control over it—the past *cannot* be totally banished from our inquiry. It will, as Professor Klingberg's chapter demonstrates, be present in the form of national heritage and prevailing tradition, predisposing the nation and its officials to act in a manner consistent with socially sanctioned customs; it will be present as national style, unconsciously affecting the way Americans respond to events and peoples beyond the nation's borders; and it will be present as a legacy of commitments entered into, opportunities missed, and mistakes made. Hence the past, or at least our images of the past, will have a significant impact, all our authors assume, on how the United States behaves as a nation in the future.

Moreover, from an analytic standpoint, it would be imprudent to ignore the immediate past in our desire to free the future from its paralyzing grip. We must study what has already happened if we are to discover what will happen, for it is only from history that we can extract some of the clues necessary to predict the probable conditions of the years ahead. The requisite attribute of a good prophet, it would seem, is to have a good memory. And indeed, in their efforts to project and prescribe the future course of American foreign policy, the contributors to the *Yearbook* have followed this advice, whether implicitly or explicitly. By looking at the past in order to foresee the future, they are asserting their acceptance of one of the methodological cannons of social science expressed by Leibniz in the 18th century: "The present is big with the future, the future might be read in the past, the distant is expressed in the near."

But as competent social scientists, the authors of these essays are sensitive as well to the limitations of deriving predictions exclusively from existing trends. They would all agree that projections are not predictions, and that forecasting by the mere extrapolation of known trends is dangerous (if for no other reason than the dubiousness of assuming that what has been will continue to be). The authors thus all take care to caution us about the tentativeness of prognostic conclusions emanating from trend projection. But these cautions remind us, again (McGowan, 1975b:10), of the continuing need in the field for the development of well-articulated theories of foreign policy and international relations from which usefully specific predictions could be made. The problem is, and remains, a pressing one in systematic foreign policy research.

This leads us to consider the second, related assumption which underlies much of the work presented in this volume. It is the belief that systematic foreign policy research can contribute findings of use to policy makers in their efforts to wrestle with emerging foreign policy challenges and to enhance their nation's survival capabilities. We think these articles have managed to support this thesis by producing a number of findings highly pertinent to any attempt to modify one's external environment and bring into being preferred future worlds. But equally revealing is the light these articles shed on the limits of our knowledge. They demonstrate the pressing need for the further development and refinement of theory and, in short, for major knowledge breakthroughs. They tell us how far we must travel if we are to gain control over our destinies. In particular, the contributions made by these assembled studies are valuable not only for what they tell us, but for what they fail to tell us. They remind us of how much work is still required if world-scale problems of vast proportions are to yield to successful solutions. They tell us as well of the need for dynamic modeling, if we are to contend with the continuation of global trends, already in progress, which show promise of stretching to extremes beyond imagination. The questions raised by these articles are as important as the answers provided and the solutions proposed.

An implication of these studies, collectively, is that they raise anew questions about the capacity of the United States to control its own fate. Indeed, the authors' findings suggest that there may be definite limits in the capacity of the United States, or for that matter any nation, to control, let alone respond as desired, to the radically new emergent conditions and challenges in the contemporary external environment. As a whole, the studies suggest that the ways American foreign policy makers are likely to respond to long-term changes in its external environment are not sources for optimism. It can be argued (Kegley and Wittkopf, 1979) that, paradoxically, the United States might be constrained by its very strength. As a superpower, the U.S. finds its freedom of choice curiously restricted by its own increasing involvement in the international system it has done so much to shape. Then, too, the sheer size and attributes of its internal political system may be said to diminish the maneuverability and adaptability of the nation's external behavior, making foreign policy change difficult and slow. In this context, Deutsch's (1968:27) analogy of a superpower to an elephant are sobering:

> A charging elephant can smash down a large obstacle, but he cannot thread a needle. Indeed, he cannot make a right-angle turn within a three-foot radius. The greater the brute power, mass, speed and momentum of the elephant, the harder it is for him to control his own motions, and the less precise his control becomes.

The conclusions of the studies published here tend to lend credance to this interpretation, indicating as they do that the problems of overcoming policy inertia and continuity are vexatious, and that efficient foreign policy modification and adaptation to the demands of external pressures have been, and may continue to remain, the exception rather than the rule.

This reasoning forces us to consider more carefully the interplay between foreign policy change, on the one hand, and environmental change, on the other. To what extent are fluctuations in features of domestic society associated with variations in a nation's foreign policy behavior, and in what sense and under what conditions may alterations in the international environment promote shifts in policy? What linkages, in short, might be specified between the environment of states and their orientations toward that environment? Unfortunately, theory on this problem is not developed. But a reading of the literature suggests a number of observations and propositions which shed some insight into the nature of the general problem, and inform us in a tentative way of how we might profitably think about the relationships between a nation's foreign policy and its domestic and international environments. Such an assessment should enable us to put the individual chapters into better perspective by showing how properties of the United States case described therein fit into this more general body of thought.

ENVIRONMENTAL CHANGE AND FOREIGN POLICY RESPONSE

From the traditional perspective, a focus on the international sources of foreign policy constitutes a conventional interpretation enjoying a wide following. Indeed, it is not difficult to find many analyses which place this conception of foreign policy at the center of inquiry. For instance, Lentner (1974:51) virtually defines foreign policy as "the coping of a state with its environment," whereas Berkowitz and Bock (1965:x) define national security policy "as the ability of a nation to protect its internal values from external threats." These conceptions stem from an analytic tradition, going back at least to Thucydides, that stresses the linkage between the international political environment and internal politics. That tradition is reaffirmed often by policy makers themselves; recall, for instance, former Presiden.t Richard M. Nixon's 1973 U.S. "State of the World" message, which argued, "In January 1969, America needed to change the philosophy and practice of its foreign policy. Whoever took office four years ago would have faced this challenge. After a generation, the post war world had been transformed and demanded a fresh approach" (cited in Wilcox, 1976:43). Or recall former President Gerald R. Ford's reminder to us that "at no time in our peacetime history has the state of the nation depended more heavily on the state of the world." These perspectives all derive from a "systemic" viewpoint of foreign policy teaching "that the first requirement of a viable foreign policy is a sensitivity to international systemic sources of danger and an American accomodation with the world environmental structure of power and influence of which every nation is but a part" (Levy, 1975:21).

This organizing proposition resides at the core of a number of other additional theoretical foci in international relations research. For instance, general systems theory operates from the working premise that a given part (i.e., "sub-system," national actor) will function differently depending on the attributes of the whole (i.e., "system," international environment) to which it belongs. Corollary propositions posit that the environmental circumstances in which actors exist and find themselves are partial determinants of the actor's behavioral response to its environment; that the manner in which environmental contexts change, and the rates at which those changes occur, are important explanatory variables of an actor's behavior; and that, therefore, characterizing the environments within which subsystemic actors must exist, monitoring the manner in which subsystems themselves change, and specifying the causal connections and interdependencies between subsystem and environment are the primary research goals. Such a system theory view, when applied to the study of foreign policy behavior, has an enviable record of demonstrating how outside events and external trends may become connected with one another in such a way as to necessitate general changes in the performance of units comprising the system.

Somewhat derivatively and analogously, foreign policy research had benefitted from the emergence of a theoretical orientation which looks at foreign policy as "adaptive" behavior. The seminal work of Rosenau (1970a; 1970b; 1971a; 1974), as elaborated and further developed by McGowan (1974a; 1974b) and Thorson (1974), among others, has led to the emergence of what may be termed an "adaptation" paradigm. This paradigm derives from a rather long and successful tradition of identifying and describing features of international environments and associating these with the adaptation behaviors and survival strategies of national units. The central question asked from this viewpoint is "how and why organisms adapt to their environments" (Rosenau, 1974:4); foreign policy is conceived therefore as "the authoritative actions which governments take—or are committed to take—in order either to preserve the desirable aspects of the international environment or to alter its undesirable aspects" (1974:6). Because the national adaptation paradigm assumes, as a central axiom, that "variation in the performance of essential structures internal to the actor is not independent of variations in the types and rates of change in the actor's environment" (McGowan, 1974b:30), it conforms to theoretical traditions which stress the interactions between a nation and its international environment, and which see foreign conduct as a response to forces beyond a nation's borders. And of course this perspective dovetails with, and may be seen as a catalyst to, the development of theories of foreign policy which focus on "linkage politics" (e.g., Rosenau, 1969b; Wilkenfeld, 1973) and which examine the processes by which nations exchange various properties with their international environments, transform these in accordance with the characteristics of their peculiar internal systems, and export behaviors back into the external environment (thereby serving to transform it).

The attractions for thinking of foreign policy and its sources in these terms are many. For instance, who would deny that at least part of the variation in a country's foreign policy behavior is accountable by the number and kind of acts that are directed to it by other actors in its external environment? Who, indeed, would fail to appreciate the potential role that international treaties, membership in international organizations, or involvement in alliances (especially entangling ones) play in shaping a nation's conduct abroad? And who might claim to construct a comprehensive theory of foreign policy which failed to include the distribution of influence and power in the system, or a nation's position in its pecking order (status hierarchy), as explanatory variables? The mere raising of these questions forces us to acknowledge that what occurs abroad may often exert an impact on the kinds of behavior a nation initiates beyond its territorial jurisdiction. Consequently, the external environment must be considered in any theory which seeks to explain and predict the foreign conduct of states.

But beyond such organizing principles, what analytic prescriptions can be offered that might enhance our efforts to understand better the linkage between environmental change and foreign policy response? How might we most profitably move beyond the common observation that the state of the world affects the condition of the United States and create more refined, specific theories relevant to the relationship between external circumstances and the foreign policies of nations? This area of inquiry, as we have noted, is shrouded with ambiguity. But a number of recommendations suggest themselves which we might do well to consider in attempting to build theories of foreign policy change. Some of the observations which might guide us in the future, and which have guided the research presented in the following chapters, deserve discussion here.

If, in comparative inquiry, description and classification logically precede explanation and prediction (McGowan, 1975a), then a crucial task that must be confronted at the outset involves describing, conceptualizing, and building typologies of various kinds of "external environments." To what phenomena do we refer when we speak of the external environment of a state, and how might we best proceed with the important task of characterizing alternate environments within which states might find themselves? This task is rendered especially difficult by the complexity of the international environment and the large number of variables which pertain to it. By convention, the external environment is used to refer to the condition of the global environment beyond the border of a state and to include *all* variables which relate to the kind of community the state lives in and to which it reacts (e.g., Kegley and Wittkopf, 1979; Rosenau, 1971b:109). This variable cluster is thus general and highly aggregated, including *everything*, presumably, that happens outside the territorial jurisdiction of a nation.

Despite the persistent tendency of researchers to use the terms "external environment" and "international system" interchangeably, it has become increasingly appreciated by some that to distinguish between the two facilitates inquiry. Differentiation has been shown to not only aid conceptualization and pretheorizing, but also to affect research results and the kind of inferences that might be drawn from empirical analyses (Harf, Hoovler, and James, 1974). Definitions vary, but many (Harf, Hoovler, and James, 1974; Rosenau, 1974) seem to agree that *systemic* properties are those characteristics belonging to the entire global system (e.g., the amount of alliance aggregation or war evident at any one point in time) which perforce are shared by all nations in the system; these may be contrasted usefully with the *external environment,* which, as a subset of the international system, entails only those potential influences not within the borders of a *particular* nation. Each nation would thus, according to this conception, possess its own external environment, comprised of such features as the unique relationship the nation under consideration enjoys or suffers with another nation (e.g., U.S.-U.S.S.R. interactions). It might be useful for future research to be attentive to these distinctions, and to remain alert to the possibility that external source variables might be treated in alternative ways. Awareness of the distinction should refine theory by encouraging us toward greater sensitivity to the contextual conditions under which research findings may be expected to hold. For instance, the "systemic" impact on U.S. foreign policy exerted by the number of alliances in operation among all nations throughout the globe might be quite different than the "external" impact exerted by the alliances to which the United States is a party. This awareness guides the inquiry of the essays in this volume.

From still another conceptual vantage point, investigation of how and when changes in a state's external environment may be shown to provoke changes in that state's foreign policies requires the theorist to inquire into the process by which such linkages materialize (Rosenau, 1972). It is not sufficient for us to posit a simple "environmental imperative" which crudely assumes that as external conditions vary, that variation automatically generates changes in the foreign policy of a state. It cannot be assumed that the external environment has deterministic powers capable of defining the future course of a nation's policies. To understand how the external environment influences foreign policy change requires that we explore the internal policy-making processes by which global inputs are converted into adaptive shifts in foreign policy.

This observation draws our attention, inevitably, to the pivotal role played in the conversion process by the official decision makers who are responsible for formulating foreign policy. It is people, after all, who make foreign policy; and what decision makers decide ultimately determines continuity and change in foreign conduct. Cognizance of this "fact" must lead us to look at how decision makers *perceive,* or fail to perceive, changes in the external environment. The distinction between "the 'psychological milieu' (the world as the actor sees it) and the 'operational milieu' (the world in which the policy is carried out)" (Jervis, 1976:13) is crucial here. Concrete reality cannot be said to "determine" how any national actor behaves; it is rather how the world appears to decision makers, how policy makers perceive their environment, that ultimately triggers foreign policy response. An external variable undergoing even extreme variation will not invite a foreign policy response, it would seem, unless that problem is recognized and acted upon.

This would suggest that consideration of foreign policy decision-making, and especially the variables that affect the ability of decision makers to recognize external threats, must be placed into any theory which hopes to account for the impact of environmental challenge on foreign policy response. "Challenge" is a subjective variable, residing in the eye of the policy-making beholder; if not perceived, it cannot be said to affect directly behavior.

However indisputable (obvious?) this reasoning, it should not drive us to an exclusive concentration on the perceptions of decision makers in our efforts to build more powerful explanatory theories of foreign policy. It may all happen in the minds of decision makers (at least initially). But this does not mean, some would argue, that external conditions—and variations within those conditions—regardless of how they are defined by policy makers, fail to play any kind of independent role in shaping the foreign policy of a nation. For from a longer temporal perspective, we would do well to recall that external variables help to define the limits of the possible by restricting what can be done in foreign policy; they preclude certain options and reduce the utility of others; they operate to bind decision makers in a chain of constraints, to render highly improbable the perception of particular kinds of alternatives, and to tie decision makers' hands in taking certain policy initiatives. The external environment, in a large number of ways, defines the boundaries of power and serves as a source of policy continuity by narrowing the range of viable choices. It is the attributes of a nation's external environment, regardless of how they are perceived, which delineate the fine line between the possible and the probable in foreign conduct. A review (e.g., Kegley and Wittkopf, 1979) of recent American diplomatic history suggests that these environmental constraints may be particularly potent in the case of the United States.

A variant of the preceding interpretation would argue that we might be well advised to return to Rosenau's (1975) conception of the international environment as one of several *sources* from which foreign policy may emanate. This conception is appealing because it avoids the deterministic and causal connotations implicit in many frameworks by suggesting that external variables (in interaction with internal ones) serve as "stimulants" for foreign policy adaptation. They operate as sources, and not causes, of foreign policy change, when they undergo sufficient variation to create pressure and opportunities for—as well as inhibitions against—that change. Note that this interpretation does *not* argue that developments abroad *cause* policy changes at home. The authors of the essays printed here tend to operate from a conception of the external environment as a "source" of American foreign policy, in that they shy away from drawing the kind of inextricable linkage between the state of the world and the state of the nation which contends that American foreign policy is somehow "dependent" on circumstances emerging abroad.

The preceding observations lead us to a final analytic prescription to consider in efforts to wrestle with the nexus between environmental change and foreign policy response. Fortunately we are not necessarily asked to evaluate the impact of any and every attribute of the environment in predictive analyses of foreign policy behavior. As previously noted, the variety of potential environmental stimuli is staggering. But we need not feel obligated to describe the physically objective external environment of a nation, and changes in all dimensions of that environment, in its totality. In this regard, Rosenau has argued (1970a:360-370) that this environment need not comprise everything external to the acting unit, but only those variables that are "salient" with respect to a nation's essential structures. Thus, analysis might well focus on *selected* environmental variables. And of course the choice of explanatory variables should be influenced by the aspects of a nation's behavior that one is seeking to predict; whether a nation is acting toward its total external environment (e.g., by giving foreign aid through a multilateral assistance agency) or toward just one other actor should make a difference in the choice of factors considered. This selectivity is evident in the kinds of explanatory factors the authors of this volume have chosen to focus on in their particular chapters.

With these analytic prescriptions in mind, a brief set of propositions about the conditions under which environmental factors might be potent in predicting foreign policy behavior may be proposed. These should be regarded as "working hypotheses" designed to guide future research, and amenable in principle to subsequent testing, rather than empirically verified findings.

Included in any such inventory of hypotheses must be the proposition that the environmental factors most deserving of treatment (that is, probabilistically the most potent in accounting for foreign policy behavior) are those which are undergoing the most rapid variation. The *rate of change* in any environmental condition may be interpreted as an indicator of its potential influence over the foreign policy of states. Alternately stated, this proposition contends that the more a particular environmental variable changes, the more influential it is likely to become; fast changing variables are the most important. Thus variables in extreme states, manifesting dramatic fluctuation, will in general be more powerful as predictors than those undergoing modest or incremental change. It is for this reason that it is probably no accident that the contributors to this volume have chosen to focus on properties of the U.S. external environment that are currently undergoing dramatic change. Instructively, the exceptions to this generalization are those essays concentrating on more slowly changing external conditions, but conditions that, while evolving incrementally through cumulation and accretion, have nevertheless culminated in producing a transformed international environment (seemingly overnight) for the United States. The "sudden discovery" of resource depletion and of international interdependence are examples of long-term environmental trends whose impact and importance were not appreciated until they reached critical proportions. The process of arriving at that condition may have been well underway for a long time, but was not deemed relevant until the situation reached a point where it was perceived as a problem. Rosenau (1969a:74) cites as an example of this latter phenomena the fact that "the world's population explosion has long been smoldering, [but] it did not become part of the global environment until its potential danger came to be perceived by those in high political offices." It might be postulated that those perceptions did not occur until population growth hindered policy goals like economic development, thereby commanding attention.

A second set of factors affecting the influence of external change are the national attributes of the country under consideration. All states should not be expected to react similarly to the same external stimuli. The type of nation may be assumed to affect the nature of the relationship it enjoys—or suffers from—with its environment. The type of country, in short, may be assumed to affect the predictive potency of various external source variables. Generally speaking it is quite plausible to argue, with Rosenau (1975), that the international environment exerts a greater causal impact on small, less modern states than on large, modern ones. This interpretation would contend, with considerable justification, that the foreign policy of a superpower such as the United States would be shaped less by external factors than would those of a mini-state. But with the advent of nuclear weapons, the emergence—however temporary—of conditions of bipolarity, and, increasingly, of international interdependence, the argument can also plausibly be made (e.g., Hoffmann, 1962:692-764) that superpowers may be as vulnerable, if not more so, to external pressures than small states. Regardless of one's theoretical preference on this issue, the proposition that different types of national societies will relate differently to their external environments is difficult to reject. The number of such national attributes that might be profitably considered is of course large. Deutsch's (1966:10) suggestion that totalitarian states "carry out much more consistently their attempts to cut down their linkages to their external international environment" is exemplary of the kind of hypothesis that might be usefully pursued in this class of factors.

This reasoning draws our attention to yet a third consideration: how the domestic policy-making environment of a state "fits" into theoretical attempts to understand the impact of external change on foreign policy.

Inclusion of this cluster of variables would seem to be crucial to the development of theory. After all, it is within the domestic policy-making structure of a society that the occasion for decisions, representing opportunities for foreign change, arise; and the dynamics of a country's foreign policy machinery undoubtedly affect how well that nation copes with challenges stemming from changes in the international environment. The disappearance of a meaningful distinction between domestic and foreign policy in the contemporary era renders consideration of the domestic political environment crucial to the predictive task; no longer is it safe to construct theories that see foreign policy derived exclusively from circumstances external to a national actor. Domestic politics shape the foreign policy options that are open to societies; affect the levels of resources available for external use; and influence greatly states' ability to cope effectively with external threats to core values. Because foreign policy today can rarely be insulated from domestic politics, the characteristics of national policy systems must be treated as explanatory factors.

The environmental-foreign policy linkage can also be hypothesized to vary with the type of international issue. That is, the degree to which a nation's foreign conduct is influenced by environmental factors may be said to be affected by, and vary with, the nature of the "issue-area" (Rosenau, 1967). Here, for instance, it may be contended that the environmental impact will be great when the United States deals with military-security issues, whereas the area of general economic policy will be relatively less affected by external influences and relatively more affected by domestic factors. What this example illustrates is that the extent of environmental influence over foreign policy may often be contingent upon the nature of the issue under exploration. O'Leary's (1976:321) suggestion, that the ascribed importance or "salience" of a particular international issue to a national actor is a crucial variable to be considered in attempts to predict foreign conduct, constitutes an important insight.

Still another potential factor affecting the potency of environmental influences on foreign policy might be considered: the extent to which particular types of "situations," but especially conditions of crisis, may serve as intervening explanatory variables. Attention is drawn here to efforts to refine foreign policy theory by typologizing categories of foreign policy situations, and then assessing the extent to which specific kinds of foreign policy responses might be related to the kind of situation in which a national actor finds itself. The rationale of this theoretical departure stems from the desire to make more specific kinds of predictions about future conditions. But it stems as well from the conviction that particular environmental settings can be linked empirically with certain kinds of foreign policy responses. That is, a number of foreign policy decisional commonalities can be discerned as responses to certain kinds of stimuli emanating from the external environment. Much of this effort has focused on crisis situations as environmental influences on foreign policy, with a considerable research payoff (see Hermann, 1972). This indicates that international crises, as types of situational variables, constitute circumstances under which environmental factors possess particular predictive potency. Part of the reason for this is that crisis situations may present special opportunities for policy innovation.

Finally, and certainly more cautiously (but not exhaustively, to be sure), we may postulate that the impact of the external environment on foreign policy may vary with *time*. Here a curious paradox may be noted: that nations appear relatively invulnerable to the influence of enduring, long-term environmental trends in the immediate, day-to-day making of policy; but over time these secular stimuli appear to exert a profound impact, prompting (forcing?) a foreign policy accommodation to them. Indeed, how is it that countries which are able to resist environmental pressures so successfully in the short-run are so unsuccessful at managing resistance in the long-run? In this context, Kegley and Wittkopf (1979) have observed that:

> the United States finds its policy inexorably molded by the necessity of adjusting and accommodating itself to the demands of a changing world. Such adaptation cannot be postponed indefinitely, even by a superpower, without dire consequences. On a day-to-day basis, the pressures might be slight, but over time they are profound. What happens abroad does matter, as do evolving developments. Cognizance of this imperative was taken by President Carter when he noted that "a new world calls for a new American foreign policy."

It is suggested that environmental stimuli may operate as powerful foreign policy inputs in the long-run, despite their often weak influence in the short-run. Of course, it might be wise to qualify this hypothesis with a counterproposition, namely, that the opposite may be true for weak states. Indeed, small states, and especially those which find themselves in dependent relationships with more powerful states, may be greatly vulnerable to external pressures on a disagreeably routine basis.

Certainly other ideas about the conditions under which environmental change may be regarded as especially important in predicting foreign policy will be identified in subsequent efforts at theory building. The hypotheses that have been presented about how nations respond to environmental change inform us of some of the assumptions that have guided the research of the following studies. They are meant to serve as an introduction to some of the theoretical reasoning that underlies the chapters, as well as the organization of this book itself. But the discussion just presented not only attempts to put

the book into perspective, it also invites us to review some of the major
additional insights about environmental change and foreign policy response
that can be gained from reading the studies we have included. Let us turn
now to introduce these important additions to the foreign policy literature.

CHALLENGE AND CHANGE IN AMERICAN FOREIGN POLICY: A LOOK AT THE FUTURE

Those attentive to the contours of contemporary international life seem to
agree that the United States is challenged, as we move into the last quarter of
the 20th century, by threats from abroad and from at home. The sense of
malaise and urgency is pervasive; but there seems to be little agreement about
the nature, magnitude, or source of the challenges. Although there has
certainly been much debate about the existence and severity of present
afflictions, a consensus viewpoint can hardly be said to have emerged.
Opinions range from those wishful thinkers who deny that contemporary
trends pose a serious threat to the nation, to alarmists who predict that, if
emergent developments continue unabated, the inevitable consequence will
be a crushing of the human spirit, mass poverty and starvation, and possibly
national extinction. Opinion about how to deal with and perhaps even rectify
perceived problems is, needless to say, equally divided.

If we are to exercise effective control over the future, we must, at a
minimum, be able to anticipate its evolving nature and devise strategies and
means for affecting its course. The authors of the following essays collectively
seek to contribute to these goals by attempting to monitor major trends in
America's external environment and by evaluating current and potential U.S.
policies for coping with these challenges. Inevitably, the authors have had to
focus attention on selected problems affecting the capability of the United
States to meet environmental threats. The collective treatment provided by
the volume is thus necessarily partial. Many candidate problems have been
ignored, but happily the authors have chosen to address a variety of major
issues. As a collection, the essays thus manage to cover the major exigencies
of our time, the challenges which are generally recognized. Let us introduce
some of the themes addressed here, noting in the process what they tell us
about the manner in which environmental pressures may provoke foreign
policy response as the United States moves into the 1980s.

Part I of the *Yearbook* contains two provocative essays dealing with the
probable nature of America's future response to global challenge. The first
(chapter two), by Professor Frank L. Klingberg, examines the existence (and
evidence supporting it) of a cyclical pattern in the American posture toward
the world beyond the water's edge. This study revises, elaborates, and extends

a classic predictive study published by Dr. Klingberg (1952), which demonstrated how America's foreign policy orientation may be a function of cyclical attitude swings in the national temperment. The work which precedes this study constitutes one of the few investigations in the foreign policy literature whose predictions have withstood the test of time. If the past record can be a safe guide to the future, Professor Klingberg's research suggests that another reevaluation and reorientation of American foreign policy can be anticipated in the near future. Indeed, the study surveys the evidence that such a mood reversal regarding American involvement in world affairs may already be underway (with President Carter as a symptom and catalyst). If so, the existence of such a periodicity in American foreign policy over 200 years suggests how powerful internal variables might be in affecting external conduct. The propositions derived from this query also raise penetrating questions about the role the U.S. can be expected to play in meeting the global challenges of the 1980s.

Professor Klingberg's speculations serve as a useful introduction to chapter three, which investigates empirically some hypotheses about the ability of the United States to adapt its foreign policy to the demands posed by the external environment. Focusing on the challenges posed by crisis activity in the international system, Drs. Farid Abolfathi, John J. Hayes, and Richard E. Hayes examine the capabilities of the United States to manage crises and prevent their escalation into foreign policy failure. Again, our readers are provided with an original data set from which patterns in the past crisis behavior of the U.S. are inferred. These data measure the frequency of crises in the international system during the 1946-1976 period, the variety of actors involved, and the modes employed by the U.S. to cope with those crises involving extraordinary military management activity. The empirically informed conclusions are illuminating and sobering. They suggest that "globalism" remains very much a center piece of U.S. foreign policy as the U.S. has not only increased steadily the number of actors with whom it experiences crisis relations; it has also not curtailed the penchant for "police" activities, and indeed shifted from the containment of communism toward involvements emanating from a more general desire for global stability. Increasingly, these activities have included a military component. The authors warn that a continuation of these trends is likely to place the United States in opposition to many of the dynamics which will characterize the coming decade. But these dangerous tendencies need not necessarily culminate, the authors conclude, should a number of available crisis management options be exercised.

Part II shifts attention, against this backdrop, to consider a number of specific challenges facing the United States. Chapter four examines the most deadly challenge facing nations, the problem of force in international relations. Failure to meet the threat of foreign aggression, or to control its magnitude and dispersion, can result in the loss of life, and, less commonly, of national sovereignty. War thus comprises the ultimate adaptive challenge in foreign policy. The study by Professors Melvin Small and J. David Singer deals with long-term global trends in the frequency, duration, and extent of war in the international system. Conducting a major expansion of the data in their important Correlates of War (COW) Project (e.g., Singer and Small, 1972), published in these pages for the first time, their article not only gives us a systematic longitudinal inventory of war over a very long time frame (from 1816 to the present); it also displays quantified indicators of intrastate wars (which continue to threaten to breed interstate wars). Analysis of the trends delineated permits the authors to explore their implications for future American foreign policy, and to derive some important empirically grounded policy prescriptions about the manner in which the United States might deal with these developments in the coming decades.

Two chapters consider the increasingly important economic setting of American foreign policy. Professor Charles F. Doran introduces the problem of economic challenges in chapter five by exploring a whole congeries of threats that derive from the rapid depletion of resources and energy in the United States. Empirically showing the extensive and growing degree to which American resource needs are supplied by foreign sources, Professor Doran provides an incisive analysis of the implications of these environmental challenges as the U.S. enters the 1980s.

Chapter six, by Professors James A. Caporaso and Michael D. Ward, examine closely the exponential growth of international interdependence. Utilizing some creative new measurement procedures, the authors are able to demonstrate how radically transformed the present international environment is from those that immediately preceded it. Nowhere is this more true than in the degree to which the fates of nations have become increasingly tied in a web of interconnections. Nations today are linked in an extraordinary number of transnational, multilateral, and supranational ties. These enhance greatly the extent to which nations composing the international system, including even superpowers such as the U.S., have become dependent on, and vulnerable to, developments occuring abroad. This has led to the rapid deterioration of the boundary between domestic and foreign circumstances today. The two go hand in hand. While one can debate the direction of causation, one cannot deny the association. Welfare abroad breeds prosperity at home; and recession in the U.S. is related to depression elsewhere. It is not necessarily an exaggeration to suggest that everytime the U.S. sneezes, other parts of the world catch cold. Revealingly, the opposite is also becoming true.

The U.S. finds itself a "penetrated" national actor, dependent on the world beyond its borders for resources and prosperity.

As Caporaso and Ward demonstrate, the growing external penetration of the United States (i.e., its dependence on the system of which it is a part) has not only promoted the growth of U.S. foreign collaboration to steer and facilitate these relationships, it has also intensified efforts by the U.S. to protect its welfare through military defense. The disutility of responding to economic challenges by military means is cogently demonstrated by the authors.

Another very important political trend in the contemporary external environment of the United States is the rise of both Japan and the European Community as significant—and powerful—actors in the international system. This development has, potentially, revolutionary implications. In a penetrating and exhaustive review, Professor Werner J. Feld (in chapter seven) describes the emergence of this development and analyzes the myriad repercussions that might be expected of it in the future. He also provides us with a probing evaluation of the policy choices available to the U.S. in response to this challenge and opportunity posed by traditional allies.

Finally, Part II concludes by considering another environmental trend shaping the international system of the next decade: how people living abroad view the U.S. as a country and how they assess America's foreign policy. Dr. Alvin Richman has compiled (chapter eight) an original data set that taps trends in foreign attitudes toward the United States. These trends show that the American image is under increasing attack. This suggests that the U.S. must attempt to meet the challenges of the 1980s in an external environment that is not necessarily favorably disposed toward it (although a residue of good will remains, even in the aftermath of Vietnam). Interestingly, Dr. Richman's study is able to show that foreign attitudes toward the United States are not related to the attitudes of those same respondants toward the Soviet Union.

Examining the future of American foreign policy from yet another perspective, Part III looks at the close nexus that currently obtains between internal trends and external developments. Here two studies examine some ways in which variations in the American domestic setting may affect the nation's ability to cope with challenges posed by emergent international trends.

One of these crucial internal factors influencing the probable future response of the United States to external challenge is the nature of the opinions held by elite American policy influentials. Previous evidence suggests that the attitudes of opinion leaders, and shifts therein, are instrumental in promoting change, and lack thereof, in American external behavior. We are pleased to be able to make available the illuminating and rigorous investigation of this topic by Professors Ole R. Holsti and James N. Rosenau. Probing extensive survey data they gathered about foreign policy opinion change among American leaders in the post-Vietnam era, the authors are able to provide us (chapter nine) with a large number of predictively potent hypotheses about the future course of American foreign policy. Undoubtedly these attitudes will exert an impact on how the U.S. will adjust—or fail to adjust—to the foreign problems confronting the nation.

Finally, Professor Charles F. Hermann employs his analytic skills to consider some of the attributes of the U.S. foreign policy-making machinery which invariably affect the ability of the country to cope with international problems. More specifically, the rise of "bureaucratic government" and the domination of bureaucratic decisional styles on foreign policy-making processes are critically assessed in chapter 10. This trend, as Professor Hermann persuasively demonstrates, carries with it implications for the way the U.S. is likely to adapt to foreign challenges that are less-than-reassuring. The study concludes with a number of incisive insights into the way bureaucratic procedures of decision-making may diminish rather than enhance the flexibility, creativity, and responsiveness of American foreign policy to threatening international circumstances.

While these essays attack what we feel are some of the basic challenges confronting the United States in the coming decade, they do not purport to provide exhaustive coverage (although they do touch tangentially on many related problems). Certainly other emergent properties of the American external environment deserve focused attention as well. Any thorough inventory of international threats to the nation, for example, would have to include such trends as shifts in the Soviet-American strategic balance; the crisis of the international monetary system; the rise of international terrorism; the erosion of cohesion in the American alliance system; the adjustments required by the advent of a multipolar world and concomitant disappearance of bipolarity; the prospect of nuclear proliferation and continuation of arms trade throughout the world and consequent militarization of the global environment; or the deterioration of the ecology of planet earth. Added to these should be consideration of the implications of exploding population on an over-crowded world; hunger and mass famine; the growing disparity between the world's rich and the world's poor, and the resultant challenge posed by the North-South debate; the continued expansion of world trade in conjunction with the historically high and exacerbating American balance-of-trade deficit; the opportunities and challenges posed by regional integration and the expansion of international organizations worldwide; and the continued denial of human rights throughout most of the world and the erosion of democratic institutions seemingly everywhere. Indeed, the possible foreign policy agenda of the United States for the 1980s would appear to be (hopelessly?) large, as the nation is challenged by numerous pressing problems both abroad and at home. The seeming incoherence of the Carter administration's initial foreign policy efforts to confront many of these issues at once may be explicable by the sheer number and diversity of problems that command attention. They may additively be beyond the capacity of any administration to manage. But the future will be shaped in part by the way the United States responds to these challenges.

It is the conviction of this *Yearbook's* authors that an effective response— and the possibility of avoiding being victimized by the future—must begin with an understanding of the nature of the problems that beset us all. The *Yearbook* hopes to have taken a step toward that understanding, and toward a better awareness of the forces that shape foreign policy, by presentation of the essays published here.

REFERENCES

BERKOWITZ, M., and BOCK, P.B. (eds.) (1965). American national security. New York: Free Press.

DEUTSCH, K.W. (1966). "External and international political relationships." Pp. 5-26 in R.B. Farrell (ed.), Approaches to comparative and international politics. Evanston: Northwestern University Press.

――― (1968). The analysis of international relations. Englewood Cliffs, N.J.: Prentice-Hall.

FALK, R.A. (1975). A study of future worlds. New York: Free Press.

GREGG, R., and KEGLEY, C.W., Jr. (1971). "An introduction to future directions in American foreign policy." Pp. 1-13 in R.W. Gregg and C.W. Kegley, Jr. (eds.), After Vietnam. Garden City: Doubleday-Anchor.

HARF, J.E., HOOVLER, D.G., and JAMES, T.E., Jr. (1974). "Systemic and external attributes in foreign policy analysis." Pp. 235-250 in J.N. Rosenau (ed.), Comparing foreign policies. Beverly Hills: Sage.

HERMANN, C.F. (ed.) (1972). International crisis. New York: Free Press.

HOFFMANN, S. (1962). "Restraints and choices in American foreign policy." Daedalus, 91, 4(Fall):668-704.

JERVIS, R. (1976). Perception and misperception in international politics. Princeton: Princeton University Press.

KEGLEY, C.W., Jr., and WITTKOPF, E.R. (1979). American foreign policy: Pattern and process. New York: St. Martin's.

KLINGBERG, F.L. (1952). "The historical alteration of moods in American foreign policy." World Politics, 4 (January):239-273.

LENTNER, H.H. (1974). Foreign policy analysis. Columbis, Ohio: Charles E. Merrill.

LEVY, R. (1975). Nearing the crossroads. New York: Free Press.

MARKEL, L., and MARCH, A. (1976). Global challenge to the United States. London: Associated University Presses.

McGOWAN, P.J. (1974a). "Adaptive foreign policy behavior." Pp. 45-54 in J.N. Rosenau (ed.), Comparing foreign policies. Beverly Hills, Cal.: Sage.

——— (1974b). "Problems in the construction of positive foreign policy theory." Pp. 25-44 in J.N. Rosenau (ed.), Comparing foreign policies. Beverly Hills, Cal.: Sage.

——— (1975a). "Meaningful comparisons in the study of foreign policy." Pp. 52-87 in C.W. Kegley, Jr., et al. (eds.), International events and the comparative analysis of foreign policy. Columbia, S.C.: University of South Carolina Press.

——— (1975b). "Preface." Pp. 7-14 in P.J. McGowan (ed.), Sage international yearbook of foreign policy studies, III. Beverly Hills, Cal.: Sage.

O'LEARY, M.K. (1976). "The role of issues." Pp. 318-325 in J.N. Rosenau (ed.), In search of global patterns. New York: Free Press.

ROSENAU, J.N. (1967). "Foreign policy as an issue-area." Pp. 11-50 in J.N. Rosenau (ed.), Domestic sources of foreign policy. New York: Free Press.

——— (ed.) (1969a). International politics and foreign policy. New York: Free Press.

——— (ed.) (1969b). Linkage politics. New York: Free Press.

——— (1970a). The adaptation of national societies. New York: McCaleb-Seiler.

——— (1970b). "Foreign policy as adaptive behavior." Comparative Politics, 2 (April):365-389.

——— (1971a). "Adaptive strategies for research and practice in foreign policy." Pp. 218-245 in F. Riggs (ed.), A design for international studies. Philadelphia: American Academy of Political and Social Science.

——— (1971b). The scientific study of foreign policy. New York: Free Press.

——— (1972). "The external environment as a variable in foreign policy analysis." Pp. 145-165 in J.N. Rosenau, V. Davis, and M.A. East (eds.), The analysis of international politics. New York: Free Press.

——— (1974). "Comparing foreign policies." Pp. 3-22 in J.N. Rosenau (ed.), Comparing foreign policies. Beverly Hills, Cal.: Sage.

——— (1975). "A pre-theory of foreign policy." Pp. 37-47 in W.D. Coplin and C.W. Kegley, Jr., (eds.), Analyzing international relations. New York: Praeger.

SINGER, J.D., and SMALL, M. (1972). The wages of war. New York: Free Press.

THORSON, S.J. (1974). "National political adaptation." Pp. 71-114 in J.N. Rosenau (ed.), Comparing foreign policies. Beverly Hills, Cal.: Sage.

WILCOX, W.A. (1976). "The foreign policy of the United States." Pp. 36-56 in J.N. Rosenau, K.W. Thompson, and G. Boyd (eds.), World politics. New York: Free Press.

WILKENFELD, J. (ed.) (1973). Conflict behavior and linkage politics. New York: David McKay.

PART I:

AMERICA'S RESPONSE TO CHANGES IN THE

INTERNATIONAL SYSTEM: THEORIES AND EVIDENCE

Chapter 2

CYCLICAL TRENDS IN AMERICAN FOREIGN POLICY MOODS AND THEIR POLICY IMPLICATIONS

FRANK L. KLINGBERG
Southern Illinois University at Carbondale

Among the questions that might be raised about American foreign policy in the 1980s are the following. In this presumed neo-isolationist period, can the United States be expected to withdraw further from involvement in world military, political, and economic affairs? What kind of world leadership could the U.S. be expected to demonstrate? Notwithstanding America's military commitments, would the U.S. be able to respond decisively to a direct military challenge against one of its allies or in some other critical area? Would it make a difference if such a challenge occurred at the beginning or near the end of the decade? Are there other types of challenges which could stimulate a major American response? Would the American people be further attracted to a foreign policy approach based on moral principles, justice, and human rights, or would such a policy be seen as unrealistic? Will the President and Congress, the government and the people, be able to establish a new general consensus on foreign policy in the 1980s? Will the U.S. be capable of responding positively to a possible call by other nations for her world leadership?

It is the thesis of this chapter that probable answers to these questions can be given on the basis of presumed cyclical trends[1] in dominant American psychological moods, which have in the past seemed to shift quite regularly

EDITOR'S NOTE: This paper was first submitted for review in October 1977. The version published here was received February 1978.

and to set limits on policy decisions. Leaders appear most effective when their policies reinforce these dominant moods.

These cycles in moods (general attitudes, strong feelings) have been evident in three primary areas or dimensions of American life—namely, the international, the cultural, and the political. Foreign policy is affected directly by the first, and indirectly by the other two.

The *international* mood studied here is the alternation between "introversion" and "extroversion"; the *cultural* mood shows a tripartite succession of rationalism, realism, and idealism; and the *political* mood has an alternation between emphases on "liberty" (individual, local, or group rights, leading to a considerable measure of disunity) and "union" (more cooperation and unity).

Leaders may try to strengthen or reinforce the dominant moods, or seek to prevent them from going to extremes; if they oppose the trends too strongly, they would normally be replaced. The basic interests of the United States need to be defined and sought under these shifting public moods and changing conditions.

This theory of moods is designed to supplement other theories, with the particular aim of giving a broad perspective on the whole development of American foreign policy.

THREE TYPES OF MOOD CYCLES

The International Cycle

The chief alternative moods in the history of American foreign policy have been "introvert" and "extrovert." During a dominant extrovert mood, the nation has been willing to support direct pressure, often military, on other nations to gain its ends. During a dominant introvert mood, there is a tendency to concentrate on domestic matters and to reduce military and political actions abroad (normal economic and cultural involvement would be expected to continue). Rather clear examples of introversion and extroversion are the periods, respectively, between the World Wars (1918-1940) and after World War II began (1940-1967). A study of the development of

TABLE 1. THE INTERNATIONAL CYCLE

Period	Introvert	Extrovert
I	1776–1798	1798–1824
II	1824–1844	1844–1871
III	1871–1891	1891–1918
IV	1918–1940	1940–1966(67)
V	1966(67)–	

American foreign policy as a whole shows such an alternation was the norm ever since 1776 (Klingberg, 1952)[2] –suggested dates are shown in Table 1.

The shifts normally occur over a six- to eight-year span, but the date given seems to be the middle of such a period and contains certain specific events which dramatize the change. The whole movement is spiral in character, with the U.S. becoming more deeply involved abroad during each extrovert phase, followed by a relative plateau or modest withdrawal. During the introvert plateau there is time for consolidation of gains in territory or world influence, for domestic rehabilitation, and for preparation for the coming extrovert challenges or desires. The process has enabled the U.S. to develop from a small nation into a great world power while maintaining commensurate internal strength (likewise vital to its external power position).

Each period, combining an introvert and an extrovert phase, has been devoted largely to a particular problem: I, building *independence* while reducing European threats; II, responding to the challenges of *slavery* and *Manifest Destiny;* III, becoming an *industrial world power;* IV, meeting the special *crisis for world democracy;* and V, apparently being challenged to lead in establishing a *stable world order.* By the end of each period in the past, the problem seems to have been solved, at least for the time being.

During the extrovert phases, foreign policy becomes recognized as vital to the security or expansion of the nation, and presidential leadership is widely supported, particularly during critical developments. During the introvert phases, with foreign policy believed to be less important and with fewer overt challenges from abroad, Congress would be expected to reassert its constitutional prerogatives, while ethnic and other interest groups would bring special pressure to bear.

The beginning of the cycles is dated at 1776 with the length of the international phases apparently related to the years in an average "political generation" (when political leaders are most influential, as from 35 to 60 or 40 to 65) of about 25 years. The extrovert phases, averaging 27 years, might be a little longer than the introvert phases, 21 years, because of the more dramatic character of foreign involvement.

The shifts from one mood to another could be prompted by the following pressures: (1) the possible abuse (or extreme use) of a mood-policy; (2) possible failures of long-continued policies; (3) the arrival of a new ambitious political generation, possibly accompanied by a reaction on the part of youth; (4) the rise of critical problems in the "opposite" direction (such as domestic problems near the end of an extrovert phase, or special foreign challenges near the end of an introvert phase); (5) America's freedom of expression for the opposition, and the country's unique geographical position as a great power.[3] The alternating approaches were established deeply in America's origins: a desire for separation, and a desire to expand territory or influence. A special social contribution of the alternation may have been to keep each mood from going to extremes—either to deep isolationism or to unchecked imperialism.

All but two of America's wars were fought during the extrovert phases, and these two were begun near the close of extrovert phases. The American Revolutionary War began in 1775, and a major invasion of Canada was attempted, but by 1776 the war became a defensive operation fought on American territory. The direct military phase of the war in Vietnam was begun in 1965; by 1966 and particularly 1967, internal opposition to the war had mounted to a pronounced degree. The magnitude of the opposition may be explained in part by the changing mood of the American people after over a quarter of a century of deep world involvement, as well as by the nature and location of the struggle on the other side of the earth.

The occurrence of the Civil War during an extrovert period appears paradoxical. In a sense, the existence of slavery had led to the virtual rise of two countries inside the Union, and both North and South may have turned the extrovert mood against one another—the South to expand slave territory, and the North to conquer the South. Even so, the Lincoln Administration was able to play a significant extrovert role in world affairs during the Civil War (especially in relation to Britain and France, and toward China and Japan).

It is also important to note that Western Civilization has shown a somewhat similar alternation between phases of relative international quiescence (introvert) and international dynamism (extrovert). Other nations, even if totalitarian, show tendencies to turn, say, to introversion, as Russia did from 1918 to 1940 or China did from 1966 to 1977. Challenges to the U.S. from abroad could be expected to be a special stimulus or catalyst for a shift to American extroversion at a time when the mood may be beginning to change anyway.

The Cultural Cycle

The cultural cycle seems definitely to have involved Western Civilization as a whole, if not the world. As mentioned above, the United States has faced different types of challenges during the five periods since 1776. In Period I (1776-1824), the Western world experienced three major revolutions (the American, French, and Latin American) and three world wars (American Revolutionary, French Revolutionary, and Napoleonic). In this age of power politics and ideological division, the United States followed a *realistic* policy, using military force or pressure to attempt to remove European (British, French, Spanish, and Russian) power from this hemisphere insofar as possi-

TABLE 2. THE CULTURAL CYCLE

Motivation	Cycle I	Cycle II
Age of Enlightenment (Reason)	1729–1776	1871–1917(18)
Power Politics (Realism)	1776–1824	1917(18)–1966(67)
Consolidation (Idealism)	1824–1871	1966(67)–

ble. The world did not again enter such a time of world-shaking revolutions and world wars until 1917-1918, with power politics again in the saddle.

It is noted that an "Age of Enlightenment" (or "Reason" or *rationalism*) preceded each of these revolutionary phases, and that a period of consolidation, molded in part by a renewed *idealism,* morally and spiritually, followed this first revolutionary phase. The periods would then be dated as shown in Table 2 (Klingberg, 1970).

In the "Age of Enlightenment," economic, educational, and scientific factors tended to dominate; wars were limited in character, and fought for specific economic gains (economic imperialism). In the subsequent periods of power politics, ideological divisions became more evident, and world wars (hot and cold) were fought for goals of ideological conquest, while realism moved toward irrationality in the pursuit of national power or pride. In the third period of consolidation (1824-1871), there was an effort to establish more justice internally and more self-determination externally, leading to civil wars (France, U.S.A., China) or struggles devoted to gaining independence or national unity (Belgium, Greece, Italy, Germany), while a relatively stable international order was being established.

It is also noteworthy that the whole of Cycle I (1729-1871) was devoted to the establishment of a dominant new political and international system in the Western world–namely, democratic (middle class) nationalism. For the U.S. this meant the building of an independent federal republic based on the principle of liberty. The new *idea* was first developed, which resulted in a period of bitter *struggle* between supporters of the old and new, and finally ended in a *consolidation* of the new synthesis. The three periods show characteristics delineated by Hegel and Freud (as interpreted by Lasswell, 1949), as shown in Table 3.

TABLE 3. THE CULTURAL CYCLE: HEGEL AND FREUD

Theme	Hegel	Freud
Preparation (Reason)	Thesis	Ego
Struggle (Power)	Antithesis	Id
Consolidation (Justice)	Synthesis	Superego

Cycle II (since 1871) was probably precipitated by the expansion of the industrial revolution, which gave rise to mass production, the new laboring class, and greater world economic interdependence. The dominant theme seems to have been liberalism (concern for the welfare and dignity of the common man, regardless of race, class, or continent) and internationalism. For the United States, this became the time of rising American influence in world affairs.

The length of the different periods (about 47 or 48 years) might be related to the normal length of an active adult life; to two successive political generations which together have "solved" the challenge of the times; and to three related shifts in cultural moods of 15 to 16 years each (Oretga y Gasset (1959) pointed out this cultural shift as dependent on changes in individual lives at 15-year intervals—ages 15 to 30, 30 to 45, and 45 to 60). Following Ortega's suggestion, the first third of a *superego* period would be strongly affected by the preceding *id* period, and the last third by the coming *ego* period. The periods will differ also because of the changing technological environment.

The succession of periods would seem to be stimulated by the reaction of new generations to the previous dominant spirit. For example, rationalism reduces the earlier idealism, and moves toward realism. Realism stresses the power struggle, and tends toward irrationality and overemphasis on violence, military and police force, and false propaganda. Idealism is stimulated as a reaction against violence and the abuse of power, with restored emphases on emotions and feelings of faith, hope, and love, and with rationalism under the rising control of moral and spiritual goals.[4]

The Political Cycle

The two dominant themes in American domestic political life since 1776 have been "liberty" and "union"—the paradoxical effort to build a strong national society based on the principle of individual and local liberty. Thus, it is not surprising to detect a rather regular alternation in the dominance of these two moods, as each tends to extremes or relative failure in about three presidential terms (or, rather, 10 to 14 years). Each international phase can be divided into two halves, devoted first to liberty (with individual, group, and local pressures) and then to union (a reaction toward cooperation or centralization). The dates for these shifts may be suggested as shown in Table 4.

In the introvert phases, the effect of a dominant "liberty" mood appears to be to turn even more attention to domestic problems and differences and thus to intensify the introvert tendency; the movement toward "union" enables the nation to stand more strongly for the defense of its presumed

TABLE 4. THE POLITICAL CYCLE

Period	Phase	Liberty	Union
I	Introvert	1776–1787	1787–1798
	Extrovert	1798–1811	1811–1824
II	Introvert	1824–1834	1834–1844
	Extrovert	1844–1857	1857–1871
III	Introvert	1871–1881	1881–1891
	Extrovert	1891–1904	1904–1918
IV	Introvert	1918–1929	1929–1940
	Extrovert	1940–1953	1953–1966
V	Introvert	1966–1976	1976–

international rights, to strengthen the growing consensus for nationalism, and to begin preparation for the extrovert phase ahead, particularly in noting possible future foreign challenges.

In the extrovert phases, "liberty" would seem to promote disunity over foreign policy, as shown by the internal struggles over the new expansionist tendencies after 1844 and 1891; the shift to "union" would be characterized by a general acceptance of the new extrovert role and the probability of rather steady political or military involvement in world affairs. A unique period of "union" occurred after 1857, when only the North became vitally concerned with the maintenance and strengthening of the Union as such, particularly under the leadership of Lincoln.[5]

CURRENT TRENDS AND OUTLOOK

Since the three cyclical trends have been evident since 1776 and appear to be based on elements in human nature, social dynamics, and the length of generations, there is strong reason to expect the trends to continue. Thus, even the speed of technological change might not affect these fundamental moods and their shifts. Yet modification could occur through leadership, education, and unexpected challenges at home or abroad.

The International Cycle

During the analogous period of "consolidation" in the last century (1824-1871), the introvert phase lasted about 20 years and the extrovert 27. For purposes of discussion, let us accept these numbers for the current introvert phase, which began to be fairly clear in 1966-1967 and could then be expected to continue until 1986-1987, with the first signs of a shift toward extroversion apparent by, say, 1983.[6]

A basic point to be noted ·concerning the current introvert phase is America's continuing deep involvement in world affairs. Not only is this true in the economic area (where the interdependence of the world on energy sources such as oil is noteworthy), but also in the political-military field as shown by the continuation of America's major alliances. Furthermore, there has been a recent renewal of American concern about the Soviet Union's growing military strength (see, e.g., Schlesinger, 1976), and a resulting strong support in Congress for a high level of defense expenditures. Even foreign aid is relatively high (President Carter signed a $6.7 billion appropriation on November 1, 1977).

Yet the general trend has remained toward a retrenchment or reduction of military-political actions abroad. Between 1966 and 1969 the decision was made to withdraw from Vietnam; the year 1975 saw the end of the American role in Vietnam, Cambodia, and Laos, as Communist governments moved into control, while many American scholars and statesmen came to regard Southeast Asia generally as outside America's basic security sphere. Troops were taken out of Thailand in 1976, SEATO was disbanded (June 30, 1977), and the renegotiation of American bases in the Philippines began in 1977 (preliminary agreement was reached on November 16 for a transfer to Philippine jurisdiction and a reduction in size). Even in the vital area of Japan, President Nixon reduced American forces in South Korea by one third and President Carter announced that American land forces would be withdrawn by 1982. Ethiopia and Bahrain asked the United States to remove its bases from their countries.

Congress has taken the initiative in the retrenchment of American military power abroad. It insisted that the Ford Administration's assistance to forces in Angola be stopped (1976); a pro-Communist government, aided by Cuban troops, took over. When Zaire was invaded in 1977, very little help was given by the United States; France and Morocco gave the support which turned back the invaders. Congress had passed the War Powers Act in 1973 with the aim of limiting the President's power or inclination to involve American forces in hostilities abroad without Congressional approval. After the Turkish invasion of Cyprus in 1974, Congress, under pressure from the pro-Greek lobby, cut off most American aid to Turkey, a major anchor of NATO's defense in the east. In addition, Congress cut the number of military advisory teams abroad in 1976 and ordered all to be abolished by October 1977, except those specifically authorized by Congress. All Presidential emergency powers previously granted were ended in 1976. Administration efforts to be "even-handed" in the Middle East conflict were opposed by the powerful pro-Israeli lobby. Both Congress and the Carter Administration remain hesitant to give military help to any government which violates human rights on a broad scale.[7] Labor and some industries (such as steel) are pressing the government for protectionist measures.

Administration moves to reduce America's commitments to Taiwan, South Korea, and even the Philippines were under discussion in 1977, while closer ties were sought with the People's Republic of China, Vietnam, and Cuba. Détente with the Soviet Union remained a major goal of the Carter Administration. The controversial treaty with Panama could also be regarded as a move toward the withdrawal of American power in an area which many believe is vital for the security and economy of the United States.

Public concern with domestic problems continued.[8] Nevertheless, there was a growing recognition of the relation of international affairs to certain domestic problems, as suggested by a possible oil embargo from a new Arab-Israeli war, a change in America's huge international trade and investment abroad, and by tense race relations in southern Africa.[9] Major governmental initiatives were being devoted to promoting peace in the Middle East and Cyprus, and encouraging peaceful change in Rhodesia, Southwest Africa, and South Africa.

Another sign of introversion is seen in the widespread criticism of the United Nations, a two-year lapse in payments to UNESCO (1975-1976), and the withdrawal from the International Labor Organization in November 1977 (even though President Carter's approach to the United Nations in general has been more supportive). A unilateral decision, forced by Congress, extended America's fishing zone to a limit of 200 miles (March 1, 1977).

There is danger of extreme introversion if America should enter an economic depression (as in the 1930s) or a period of extremely high inflation, or maintain huge trade deficits; if hostility should rise unusually high in the Third World against the United States; or if difficult problems should divide America from its major allies. With deeper introversion, another Great Power might be able to move aggressively, in some significant region of the world, with impunity as far as the United States was concerned.

Many of the possible or probable types of challenges from abroad in the 1980s, which could stimulate a return to extroversion near the end of the decade, are already foreshadowed: (1) world hunger and population growth, with a Third World demand for a "new international economic order"; (2) the search for justice and equality in southern Africa, and the danger of major hostilities; (3) the crisis in energy (particularly oil), and its increasing cost; (4) the threats from international feuds to the peace of the world, as in the Middle East or Cyprus—the problem of peace-making and peace-keeping; (5) the economic and psychological burdens of the nuclear and missile arms race; (6) the potential for the expansion of Communist influence in various areas of the world; and (7) the possibility of a major military threat from the Soviet Union or China, or from a Sino-Soviet war.

The Cultural Cycle

Since 1966 or 1967, the bitter political-military confrontation between East and West has been moderated. France and West Germany first came closer to the Soviet Union and East Europe, and then the United States opened relations with the People's Republic of China and negotiated strategic arms control treaties with the Soviet Union. The period of extreme or "irrational" political, military, and ideological struggle inaugurated in 1917 was apparently ending.

Following the reduction of tension among the Great Powers, problems of alleged injustice, domestic and international, gained prominence—such as the status of three million Palestinian Arabs, the Greco-Turkish division of Cyprus, the Protestant-Catholic feud in Northern Ireland, wider awareness of the repression of dissidents in the Soviet Union, and martial law in South Korea and the Philippines. Democratic nations were encouraged by the moves toward democracy in Portugal, Spain, Greece, India, and Sri Lanka, along with some signs of the relaxation of dictatorship in Bolivia, Brazil, Chile, Ecuador, Peru, Uruguay, the Philippines, South Korea, and Iran.

A rise in American concern over the application of moral principles in political, economic, and social life was apparent; and a search for meaning in life, for deeper spiritual convictions, grew particularly among the youth. Opposition to war, the arms race, and materialism in general was widespread.

During the first third (1966-1982) of the period of consolidation (synthesis, superego), the high crime rate, corruption, immorality, and family break-up might well be laid to the harvest being reaped from the steady decline of standards, moral values, and spiritual life in the preceding two periods (ego and id). At the same time, however, publicity given to the evils of the time helped strengthen the growing reaction against them. President Carter's stress on interracial cooperation (both at home and in Africa), human rights, international justice, the goal of nuclear disarmament, and spiritual values gave impetus to the moral-spiritual renewal already evident in America. As usual, however, this idealism was mixed with a degree of realism apparently required for the protection of America and the so-called "free-world" in the face of a continued totalitarian threat.

The middle third (1982-1998) of the period of consolidation would be expected to show stronger dedication to moral-spiritual values and actions in America and in other countries, and the external challenges to come in the later 1980s could well be expected to have a strong moral, rather than military, component—as in the areas of world hunger, poverty, and race relations. A marked increase of respect toward and understanding of other nations, races, and cultures should be evidenced, if America seeks to create a new synthesis of Judeo-Christian democratic values appropriate to the "technetronic" era (Brzezinski, 1970).

The Political Cycle

The reaction to the disunity of the decade between 1966 and 1976 helped give rise to the increasing unity after 1976, dramatized that year by the spirit of the bicentennial celebration. After the rather friendly campaign and the close election, President Jimmy Carter received the support of a large majority of the American public, especially at first,[10] and symbolized a new unity between South and North. Under his leadership, the United States has supported a more positive policy on human rights, encouraged a comprehensive peace settlement in the Middle East, and taken a somewhat stronger stand in relation to the Soviet Union.

It would be expected that Americans might again, in the introvert-union phase, build a consensus on international goals and means, as well as make relatively successful efforts to solve basic internal problems. Such a result would not only be vital for America's own development, but it would restore America's image on the world scene, so that many peoples would again look to America for dynamic leadership.

POLICY IMPLICATIONS: PROBABILITIES AND RECOMMENDATIONS

In the past 60 years, for example, there have been many illustrations of the impact of the national mood on presidential policies. Woodrow Wilson in 1919 opposed the new trend toward introversion and toward a weakened sense of responsibility (id), and lost his dream of American membership and leadership in the League of Nations. Franklin D. Roosevelt bent to the strong isolationist mood in 1937, but then took measures to prepare the way for an extrovert response to an expected world crisis (evident in 1940 with the fall of France to Hitler and the subsequent "Battle of Britain"). In 1952, Harry Truman was involved in a limited, inconclusive war in Korea—the voters, in an extrovert mood, installed General Eisenhower as President with a mandate to end the war and strengthen America's military position in Asia and Europe.

Lyndon Johnson perhaps felt in 1965 that he was supporting the public desire, as well as his own personal wish, to concentrate on domestic affairs and to accept only a limited war in Vietnam, with the expectation of a quick negotiated settlement. When the new American mood toward introversion became evident in 1966 and 1967 (after over a quarter century of extroversion), with neither peace nor victory appearing to be attainable, again the voters gave to a Republican president a mandate to end the war and this time to reduce America's military-political pressures abroad. President Nixon adapted his policy gradually to the new mood by accepting withdrawal from Vietnam along with "Vietnamization" of the war, by proclaiming the "Nixon Doctrine" of retrenchment, and by opening the door to the People's Republic of China. But his Administration moved so slowly to end the war that a youth revolt threatened to break the fabric of American society.

During the introvert phase (in this superego period), when internal problems would be expected to be paramount, the United States should prove to be willing to defend its own territory and possessions (for many Americans, the Panama Canal Zone has seemed virtually a part of the national territory); to maintain a deterrent military force (but doubt about its use abroad could possibly tempt an aggressor); to seek the reduction of nuclear weapons, and of American troops abroad; to honor its treaty commitments, but with the hope that some of these might be renegotiated or legally abrogated (as possibly for the Republic of China—Taiwan) and that none of them would be challenged; to seek to bring peace in critical areas; to demonstrate cooperative leadership in the United Nations; to promote "human rights" by example and influence; to strive for a world economy which would better "prime the pump" for the developing areas and relieve natural disasters more efficiently; and to stimulate work with other nations on the common problems of mankind. President Carter already appears to have set this pattern of goals for his Administration.

Among the major alternatives for American foreign policy in the introvert phase of the 1980s are the following, with segments of the public already supporting each of the approaches: (1) anti-Communism and a military balance of power; (2) the "Fortress America" concept; and (3) liberal internationalism, as in the Carter pattern.[11] It is possible that certain elements from each of these approaches might be followed. "Liberal internationalism" would seem most likely in the present period of consolidation (synthesis, superego), which should add a special sense of individual and national responsibility worldwide. It most closely approximates the fundamental principles on which America was built, already has considerable support,[12] and is to be recommended.

If either of the first two choices should be followed, one would expect that military and ideological challenges to the U.S. would move toward a climax during the latter 1980s. The outlook for a more peaceful world should be promoted by "liberal internationalism"; yet failure to achieve the sought-for goals could even speed future turmoil and challenge—as in a possible racial war in southern Africa, a strengthened and more aggressive Soviet Union or China, widespread hunger and subsequent chaos, or intensified conflict in the Middle East.

In any case, the United States should be preparing for special world crises and challenges in the late 1980s, and for American willingness to support strong international action. Leaders in education and government have a particular responsibility to encourage young people to study foreign languages and cultures, history, and international affairs, at a time when the trend has been in the opposite direction, and to point out the probability of major American involvement in the coming decades.

After 1986, depending partly on the nature of the challenges, the U.S. could be expected to emphasize either: (1) a major military response, in terms of using or threatening military force to help lay the foundations for a stable world order; or (2) more likely in the superego period, to exercise political, economic, cultural, and moral leadership, thereby attracting wide world support and cooperation in building a more just and stable international order stressing mutual respect, freedom, and human concern. Should the challenges require a major military response, America would most likely turn in the second direction as soon as possible.

Policy leadership in the introvert phase should endeavor to prevent the introvert mood from going to an extreme.[13] A major national interest abroad should not be ignored; the world balance of power should not be allowed to be upset (a special hope in this direction lies in the possibility that the Soviet Union and China will also be dominated by an introvert mood);[14] and the common problems of mankind, as in economic development and trade, should not be so neglected that a devastating world crisis would result. An awareness of these presumed cyclical trends might help to reduce the intensity of future shifts—through a wider realization that even political-military isolation is no longer feasible, and that the application of moral ideals at home and abroad is part of a true realism, on the assumption, more commonly accepted now, that self-centered materialism is not the fundamental principle for man, individually or socially.

In the 1980s, one could expect the American public to respond to moral leadership on the world scene and to a revived sense of national and individual responsibility. Care should be taken to prevent the growth of unseemly national self-righteousness and undue pride, through a spirit of respect for other peoples, their cultures and their potential contributions.

A moderate introvert-union mood (along with lessons from the 1960s and early 1970s) should help promote a somewhat stronger spirit of cooperation between the Executive branch and Congress, with a wiser understanding of the special abilities and prerogatives of each in formulating and implementing foreign policy. Similarly, there should be better relations between the House and the Senate, the press and the Government, and public opinion and the Government, while a new foreign policy consensus is hopefully being realized.

CONCLUSION

If these historical cycles are continued (relative introversion, and a spirit of "union" and "realistic" idealism), Americans can be expected to build greater consensus in the next five years on their nation's appropriate role in world affairs for the time being. There would be continued concentration on internal problems, but with special international economic and humanitarian considerations (trade, development of third world nations, and interracial cooperation). The United States would continue its endeavors to reduce international tension, serve as a mediator in critical disputes, and promote disarmament. Considering America's current deep involvement in world affairs and over-all power, one would expect the maintenance of a sufficient military establishment for the defense of vital allies, while seeking improved relations with the Soviet Union and the Peoples Republic of China.

Two specific dangers lie ahead: (1) such strong moves toward economic protectionism that a world depression could be precipitated; and (2) the possibility of a drop in realistic alertness or political will sufficient to weaken America's key alliances with NATO or Japan, or tempt Communist expansionists to seek control of some key strategic positions.

America's historical development can be divided into grand periods (see Table 5), each devoted to one of America's three major traditional concepts (as stated and analyzed by Gabriel, 1956). The consolidation of America's world role in the third period (1966-2013?) should move *toward* its fulfillment in the 1980s—first, with the renewal of the American nation internally (during the introvert phase), while it seeks partnership with other nations;

TABLE 5. THREE GRAND PERIODS IN AMERICAN HISTORY

Dates	Principles
1587–1729	The Fundamental Law Outside of Man (on which a Protestant Christian society was built)
1729–1871	The Free Individual (on which a strong Union was established)
1871–2013(?)	America's World Mission (probably to help establish a just and stable peace)

and, second, with a vigorous response to the international challenges which should be perceived before the 1980s have ended, and lead to world moves *toward* a more stable international order.

The expectation of peace in the world would appear to depend on the creation of at least four types of international order: (1) the establishment of a stronger international *law* and better processes of peaceful change and settlement; (2) the organization of collective *force* for peace maintenance; (3) the development of the creative *spirit* of man, including loyalty to the ideal of a world community; and (4) the cultivation of international *economic relations* so that man's basic physical needs may be met and mutual prosperity increased. There is special hope that in the 1980s, in an age of synthesis and superego, these goals can be sought in a spirit of hope and faith.

If America's image becomes positive in the world by the end of the 1980s, other nations will look to America for special leadership, and the U.S. will itself seek advice and help from other nations in working toward a new moral order for mankind. The prospect of moving toward such a moral order will be a special challenge to all nations, including the United States, but especially to the totalitarian ones (where internal pressures might force some hopeful changes).

In the 1980s, civil and racial strife, and international feuds over territory may continue. The superpowers may be tempted to intervene, yet the American people will likely refrain while the introvert mood remains dominant.

Before the 1980s are ended, we may expect a spirited political struggle in America over the country's future role in the world. The likely result is majority acceptance of a special leadership role or mission for America based largely on her fundamental principles of justice for both strong and weak, liberty under law, and peaceful international cooperation as far as possible. Power politics was "in the saddle" in the "id age" (1917-1966), but the idealistic elements in the spirit of man may yet have their day in the last two decades of the 20th century.

N O T E S

1. For all types of cycle theories and their causes, see Sorokin, 1941:281-583; and 1947. A summary of possible "causes" of social cycles is given in Klingberg, 1952:260-268. See also Dewey and Dakin, 1947.

2. This article presents statistical evidence for the cycles, based on an analysis of events, the annual presidential messages, the inaugural addresses, major party platforms, and annual naval expenditures. Some of the indices of *extroversion* are: wars and military expeditions abroad; steeper slope in the graph of military expenditures; annexations of territory or acquisition of foreign bases; treaties of alliance; strong diplomatic

warnings; support of strong presidential actions abroad by Congress, the media, and the public; the normal election of extrovert presidents and Congresses; public concern with foreign policy problems (as shown in polls); relatively high international tension and challenges.

Indices of *introversion* tend in the opposite direction: normal unwillingness to use military or strong political action abroad, even in the face of significant challenges; tendency to withdraw from certain world positions and to reduce military commitments and interventions; continuing concern with international economic and humanitarian problems; restraint on presidential military and political actions by Congress, the media, ethnic or other interest groups, and the public in general; domestic problems overshadowing foreign problems in the public mind; mutual criticism between Allies; closer ties with former enemies; promotion of peace in international feuds; lower international tension and fewer challenges from abroad.

3. Dr. Jack E. Holmes (1976, 1977, 1978a, 1978b) has written a number of papers and a manuscript on a "mood/interest" theory, showing the special confrontation which normally comes between the national political-military interest and the extreme application of either the introvert or extrovert mood near the end of a phase. This stimulates the reaction to the opposite mood. He believes the dominance of American liberalism is the key to the changing moods—noting the different approaches at times of the "business-liberal" and the "reform-liberal" groups. America's basic political-military interests are defined as: (1) preventing one-nation dominance in Europe; (2) the defense of the Western hemisphere; (3) preventing one-nation dominance in East Asia; and (4) preventing nuclear war.

4. Criteria for the *id* period of struggle are regarded as: world-shaking revolutions (as the French or Soviet revolutions); world wars and emphasis on "power politics"; high tension between "super-powers" or Great Powers; intense ideological struggles; secularism, materialism, and militarism; moral decline in general.

Criteria for the *superego* period of consolidation or synthesis would be: moderation of the ideological struggle; reduction of international tension, particularly among the major powers; increased cooperation among nations; renewed emphasis on moral principles or goals (as shown in Presidential statements and decisions, Congressional actions, writers, and pools); special concern for human welfare, disarmament, and rectification of injustices (domestic, possibly producing civil wars abroad, and international, sometimes leading to limited wars among smaller powers); spiritual growth (as in the churches, ecumenical movements, new religious groups, the conversion of noted individuals); moves toward democracy and the protection of human rights; greater application of moral principles to the social, economic, and political problems of mankind.

5. A spirit of *liberty* is evidenced by special pressure from individuals, groups, and local areas in seeking their "rights," resulting in increased disunity, sharp political division, and sometimes violent action. A spirit of *union* would be shown by a decline in major political party differences; greater cooperation and sense of unity, sometimes evidenced by increased centralization; greater confidence in leadership, and normally closer cooperation between the President and Congress.

6. A number of scholars have been impressed by these introvert trends in our time; see, for example, Brzezinski, 1973 and 1976; Cohen, 1973; Free, 1973; Holmes, 1976, 1977, 1978a, and 1978b; Huntington in R. M. Pfeffer, 1968:38-41; Roskin, 1974; Russett, 1975; and Schlesinger, 1973.

7. Former Secretary Henry Kissinger, among others, has pointed out the "ominous prospect that the issue of human rights, if not handled with great wisdom, could unleash

new forces of American isolationism." There is danger, he says, of disrupting "security relationships which are essential to maintaining the geopolitical balance. If conservatives succeed in unraveling ties with nations on the left and liberals block relations with nations on the right, we could find ourselves with no constructive foreign relations at all, except with a handful of industrial democracies" (Kissinger, 1977). The Harris Survey, published on June 9, 1977, showed a 62% to 14% majority of Americans opposing U.S. backing of "authoritarian governments that have overthrown democratic governments."

8. The Gallup Poll, published on August 13, 1977, showed the public choices of the most important problems facing the country today: high cost of living, 32%; unemployment, 17%; energy problems, 15%; international problems and foreign policy, 10% (as compared to a total percent of 103 indicating domestic problems—some gave multiple responses).

9. Watts (1975) noted that Potomac Associates polling data in 1975 suggested that the trend away from internationalism might have peaked in 1975, with "internationalists" rising from a low of 41% in January 1974, to 45% in the summer of 1975, and "isolationists" dropping from a high of 21% in 1974 to 20% in 1975. He saw a new international perspective showing "signs of being based on a growing acceptance of an interrelated world, not the cold war internationalism of the U.S. as a global policeman." See also Watts and Free (1974).

10. The Harris Survey, published September 7, 1977, showed Carter had slipped to 52% overall job rating (44% negative), from a high of 69% in April (27% negative). The Gallup Poll, published November 27, 1977, showed a decline in approval of the President's performance from 75% in March to 59% in October and in November.

11. Among the authors who deal with choices for the future are Cobbledick, 1973; Crabb, 1976; and Owen and Schultz, 1976. Those who point out the possibilities of retrenchment or introversion or a more limited role for America include Baldwin, 1976; Brandon, 1973; Gilbert, 1973; Kaplan, 1975; Kennan, 1977; Lesh, 1974; Liska, 1975 and 1977; Rosecrance, 1976; Tucker, 1972; Urban, 1976; and Watts and Free, 1974. For emphasis on the need for a liberal internationalism, see Ball, 1976; Bloomfield, 1974; Brzezinski, 1970; Chace, 1973; Isaak, 1977; and Wesson, 1977.

12. The Harris Survey, published on June 9, 1977, showed a 51 to 39% majority rejecting the idea that "we should build up our own defenses and let the rest of the world take care of itself," as compared with a 52 to 44% majority in 1974 agreeing with the concept of a "Fortress America." The public felt, by 79 to 15%, that "the U.S. has a real responsibility to take a very active role in the world." But by 50 to 27%, the public opposed "the U.S. giving military guarantees to African countries which might be threatened by a communist takeover."

13. Holmes (1976) stressed the tendency of American moods ultimately to go to extremes, beyond the constraints of the national interest. He pointed out the need for improved education to present a "balanced picture" in order to try to " 'straighten out' the mood curve so that it consistently operates within a viable interest zone."

14. Even though another Great Power may also be in an introvert phase, that phase may end earlier for it than for the United States, as happened between 1938 and 1940 when Hitler moved aggressively and could calculate the the U.S. would remain quiescent.

REFERENCES

BALDWIN, D.A. (ed.) (1976). America in an interdependent world. Hanover, N.H.: University Press of New England.

BALL, G.W. (1976). Diplomacy for a crowded world: An American foreign policy. Boston: Little, Brown.

BLOOMFIELD, L.P. (1974). In search of American foreign policy: The humane use of power. New York: Oxford University Press.

BRANDON, H. (1973). The retreat of American power. Garden City, N.Y.: Doubleday.

BRZEZINSKI, Z. (1970). Between two ages: America's role in the technetronic era. New York: Viking.

——— (1973). "U.S. foreign policy; the search for focus." Foreign Affairs, V (4, July):708-727.

——— (1976). "America in a hostile world." Foreign Policy, 23 (Summer):65-76.

CHACE, J. (1973). A world elsewhere: The new American foreign policy. New York: Charles Scribner's.

COBBLEDICK, J. R. (1973). Choice in American foreign policy: Options for the future. New York: Thomas Y. Crowell.

COHEN, B.C. (1973). The public's impact on foreign policy. Boston: Little, Brown.

CRABB, C.V., Jr. (1976). Policy-makers and critics: Conflicting theories of American foreign policy. New York: Praeger.

DEWEY, E.R., and DAKIN, E.F. (1947). Cycles: The science of prediction. New York: Henry Holt.

FREE, L.A. (1973). "The introvert-extrovert cycle in national mood during recent decades." Paper presented at American Association for Public Opinion Research, Asheville, N.C., May 18.

GABRIEL, R.H. (1956). The course of American democratic thought (2nd ed.). New York: Ronald Press.

GILBERT, J.H. (ed.) (1973). The new era in American foreign policy. New York: St. Martin's Press.

HOLMES, J.E. (1976). "A mood/interest theory of American foreign policy." Paper presented at International Studies Association, Toronto, Canada, February 25.

——— (1977). "American foreign policy regarding six geographic regions: An application of the mood/interest theory." Paper presented at International Studies Association, St. Louis, Missouri, March 17.

——— (1978a). "The return of American introversion." Paper for presentation to International Studies Association, Washington, D.C., February 23.

——— (1978b). "The mood/interest theory of American foreign policy." Unpublished manuscript.

ISAAK, R.A. (1977). American democracy and world power. New York: St. Martin's.

KAPLAN, M.A. (1975). Isolation or interdependence? Today's choices for tomorrow's world. New York: Free Press.

KENNAN, G.F. (1977). The cloud of danger: Current realities of American foreign policy. Boston: Little, Brown.

KISSINGER, H.A. (1977). "Morality and power: The role of human rights in foreign policy." The Manchester Guardian Weekly, October 9, p. 17.

KLINGBERG, F.L. (1952). "The historical alternation of moods in American foreign policy." World Politics, IV (2, January):239-273.

——— (1970). "Historical periods, trends, and cycles in international relations." Journal of Conflict Resolution, XIV (4, December):505-511.

LASSWELL, H.D. (1949). The analysis of political behavior. New York: 1949, 180-194 (first published in the American Journal of Sociology, January 1932).

LESH, D.R. (ed.) (1974). A nation observed: Perspectives on America's world role. Washington, D.C.: Potomac Assocs.

LISKA, G. (1975). Beyond Kissinger: Ways of conservative statecraft. Baltimore: Johns Hopkins University Press.

——— (1977). Quest for equilibrium: America and the balance of power on land and sea. Baltimore: Johns Hopkins University Press.

ORTEGA y GASSET, J. (1959). Man and crisis (trans. from the Spanish by M. Adams). New York: W.W. Norton.

OWEN, H., and SCHULTZ, C.L. (eds.) (1976). Setting national priorities: The next ten years. Washington, D.C.: Brookings Institution.

PFEFFER, R.M. (ed.) (1968). No more Vietnams? The war and the future of American foreign policy. New York: Harper and Row.

ROSECRANCE, R. (ed.) (1976). America as an ordinary country: U.S. foreign policy and the future. Ithaca, N.Y.: Cornell University Press.

ROSKIN, M. (1974). "From Pearl Harbor to Vietnam: Shifting generational paradigms." Political Science Quarterly, 89 (3, Fall):563-588.

RUSSETT, B. (1975). "The American retreat from world power." Political Science Quarterly, 90 (1, Spring):1-21.

SCHLESINGER, A., Jr. (1973). "Foreign policy after Vietnam." Wall Street Journal, March 2, p. 6.

SCHLESINGER, J.R. (1976). "Introduction." In Defending America: Toward a new role in the post-detente world. New York: Basic Books.

SOROKIN, P.A. (1941). Basic problems, principles and methods, Vol IV. Social and cultural dynamics, 4 Vols. (1937-1941). New York: American Book.

——— (1947). Society, culture, and personality. New York: Harper.

TUCKER, R.W. (1972). A new isolationism: Threat or promise? New York: Universe.

URBAN, G.R., (ed.) (1976). Détente. New York: Universe.

WATTS, W. (1975). "New yeast in the old internationalism." New York Times, September 19, p. 35.

——— and FREE, L.A. (1974). State of the nation. Washington, D.C.: Potomac Assocs.

WESSON, R.G. (1977). Foreign policy for a new age. Boston: Houghton Mifflin.

Chapter 3

TRENDS IN UNITED STATES RESPONSE
TO INTERNATIONAL CRISES: POLICY
IMPLICATIONS FOR THE 1980s

FARID ABOLFATHI
JOHN J. HAYES
RICHARD E. HAYES
Policy Sciences Division, CACI, Inc.—Federal

This chapter examines trends in United States crisis behavior—particularly frequency of crises, U.S. objectives during crises, and actions taken by the U.S. during crises. Change over time is determined by comparing the 1956-1965 time period with 1966-1976. Three important trends are identified that, taken together, project potentially dangerous results from U.S. crisis management activities:

(1) Crises involving the threat of military action are becoming somewhat less frequent over time, but U.S. adversaries are becoming more and more diverse.

EDITORS' NOTE: This paper was first submitted for review in December 1977. The version published here was received in April 1978. The authors report that the data analyzed in this paper shall ultimately be made available for dissemination through the Inter-University Consortium for Political and Social Research at the University of Michigan.

AUTHORS' NOTE: The research on which this chapter is based was performed by CACI, Inc.—Federal under the sponsorship of the Cybernetics Technology

(2) U.S. objectives during crises are shifting from those related to the cold war policy of containing expansionist Communist countries to those related to general stability in the international arena, implying that the U.S. will find itself opposing many of the profound changes in the international arena likely to occur in the 1980s.

(3) Actions taken by the United States during crisis situations are shifting away from the use of military assistance and other forms of international aid toward a set of more direct actions characterized by exposure of U.S. military forces, implying a loss of buffer activities which reduce the probability of military clashes and involvements.

The authors assume the trend toward change and challenge of the existing order that has characterized the 1970s will continue and may accelerate in the 1980s. This assumption is not tested in this chapter, but there is a rapidly growing literature on this subject.[1] Essentially the arguments on which the assumption is based are as follows: The rapid rise in the number of nation-states in the international system, the breakdown of the post-World War II bipolar alliance system, and increasing competition over diminishing natural resources by nations with multiple and changing interests have led to trends toward increasing complexity, instability, and uncertainty in the international system.[2] Moreover, the rapid rise in Soviet economic and military power during the 1950-1970 period essentially ended the post-World War II era of U.S. economic and military dominance and facilitated the increasing militancy of less-developed countries, particularly in their economic relations with Western industrialized economies. Thus, there is a growing expectation among many students of international affairs that the future international system will experience increasing pressure from the Third World for a new international economic order and greater opportunity for Soviet military initiatives in Africa, Asia, and Latin America.[3]

If these expectations are borne out, and if the key trends in frequency, objectives, and actions of U.S. crises continue, the United States will be faced with more and more widely based challenges to its perceived national interest (defined as global stability). Where these challenges are considered serious enough to generate crisis activity, however, the United States will have fewer and fewer nonmilitary options. Hence,

Office of the Defense Advanced Research Projects Agency. Contract Number N00014-76-C-0454, monitored by the Office of Naval Research, was a part of an overall Crisis Management Program. The authors wish to express their indebtedness to Leo A. Hazlewood for the leadership and intellectual strength which he provided to the project. The views and conclusions are those of the authors and do not represent the official policies, either expressed or implied, of the Defense Advanced Research Projects Agency or the U.S. Government.

(a) There is a good chance the United States will be effectively immobilized in all but the most serious crises, and

(b) Where action is taken, there is a good chance that the United States will directly expose military forces[4] and run the risk of conflict initiation.

The challenge that is seen for U.S. diplomacy in the 1980s, then, is the creation of a national consensus about objectives in the international arena which (1) recognizes the nature of the forces for change at work in the world, and (2) provides a basis for an active policy fostering constructive change where it is in the U.S. national interest. At the same time there is need for creating new types of action alternatives (or providing the resources necessary for the use of older types) which (a) avoid the direct involvement of U.S. military forces in all but the most serious crises, (b) have strong and direct impact on the actors in a crisis, and (c) are applicable to the variety of key actors (developed and less developed, oil rich and oil poor, military and civilian ruled, great powers, regional powers, and local actors, allied and adversary) likely to be involved in future crises.

BACKGROUND: PREVIOUS RESEARCH

The research reported here is part of an ongoing effort sponsored by the Defense Advanced Research Projects Agency (DARPA) to produce information and insights about crisis management. Crisis management refers to acts (or failures to act) by governments once they have perceived a potentially threatening situation. The Department of Defense, which is often a key actor in formulating crisis management policy, has an important interest in generating an accurate record of what occurs during crises and in finding ways to improve the effectiveness of U.S. crisis management.

Over the past few years, CACI, Inc.—Federal (CACI), a private research corporation, has been under contract to DARPA to improve knowledge and understanding of crises and crisis management. A first effort produced a new definition of crises (the presence of extraordinary military management activity) of interest to the Department of Defense, and began the task of producing an inventory of such crises involving the United States since the end of World War II (CACI, 1975).[5] A second project completed that inventory process through 1976 and examined the trends in types of crises over the past 30 years and the problems experienced by the military in crisis management (Hazlewood et al., 1977; CACI, 1976). Subsequent research has focused on terrorist-induced crises (CACI, 1977a) and the development of computerized decision aids that can be used to improve crisis management (CACI, 1977b). The database has also been expanded and now includes information on 307 crises during the period 1946-1976. The data used below to discuss frequency of crises and variety of actors involved are drawn from this set of crises involving extraordinary military management activity.

DATA ANALYSIS FOR THE FULL CRISIS SET

Frequency of Crises and Variety of Adversaries

All three of the recent major efforts at examining crisis activities involving the United States have found that the frequency of crises has been lower since 1965 (Blechman and Kaplan, 1977; Mahoney, 1976; CACI, 1976). Figure 1 presents the CACI crisis frequency data from 1956 to 1976 on an annual basis. The average number of crises coded for a year in the 1956-1965 time period was 10.3, while from 1966-1976 it was 8.1 and would have been 7.2 except for the unusually high frequency (17) recorded in 1976.[6]

A variety of reasons can be advanced for this recent decrease—the decline of the cold war, the absorption of U.S. interest and resources in the Vietnam conflict and the subsequent caution on the part of U.S. leaders about foreign involvements, the gradual reduction in the size of the U.S. system of alliances, and so forth. The trend, whatever its causes, is clear.

Figure 1: FREQUENCY OF INTERNATIONAL CRISES INVOLVING U.S. MILITARY CONTINGENCIES: 1956-1976

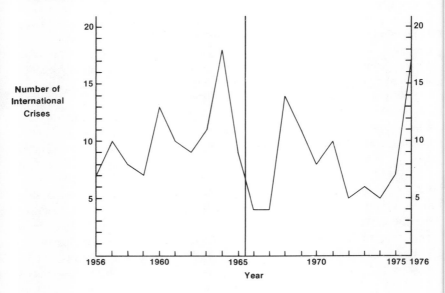

Somewhat less attention has been paid, however, to the changing nature of the actors involved in these crises. Obviously, if the cold war era is closing, there will likely be a reduction in the frequency of U.S. clashes with the Soviet Union and its allies. Figure 2 portrays the changing variety of key actors in the crises over time. Crises have been divided into four general

Figure 2: VARIETY OF KEY ACTORS IN U.S. CRISES: 1956-1976*

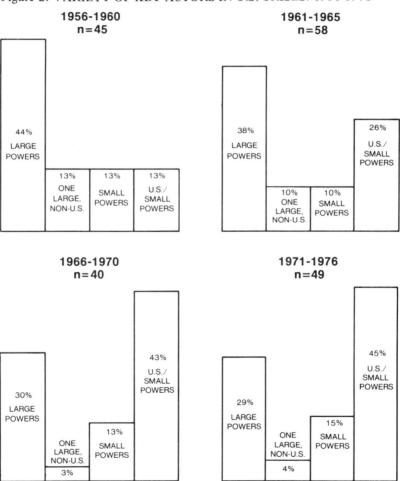

*Percentages do not total to 100% because of the presence of U.S. domestic crises and cases which cannot be classified clearly in the four categories used here.

types—those involving the United States and one or more large powers (large powers include the United States, the Soviet Union, China, Japan, the United Kingdom, France, and NATO acting as an organization), those involving at least one large power other than the United States, those involving only small powers, and those involving the United States and one or more small powers.

Examination of Figure 2 makes it clear that the percentage of crises classified as involving large powers declines somewhat over the four time periods examined (from 44% in 1956-1960, to 29% in 1971-1976) and that the decrease is not a transitory phenomenon. A small decline (from 13% to 4%) is also shown in crises involving a single, large power other than the United States. Crises between smaller powers remain at a steady 10% to 15% of the cases coded. At the same time, crises in which the United States was involved with smaller states rose dramatically (from 13% to 45%) and in a pattern suggesting that the change is not transitory. Since these smaller powers represent a wide variety of different sizes, levels of wealth, cultural heritages, levels of military sophistication, and types of government, it is clear that *U.S. adversaries during crises have become more diverse over the past 11 years.* Large power crises are still an important element in the crisis management problem, particularly because of the larger threat implied by their involvement. However, crises among smaller powers and between the United States and smaller powers have grown from a minor category to the largest single type of crisis.

The Length of Decision Time

One further observation should be made about the set of crisis cases. Traditionally, quantitative political scientists have defined a crisis as (a) severe threat to national interest, (b) surprise, and (c) limited decision time (Hermann, 1969). Considerable confusion exists about limited decision time. Many people see crises as developing and forcing decisions in a period of minutes or hours. This type of crisis can occur, particularly when strategic weapons are involved. More typically, however, there are several days during which decisions are taken. The Cuban missile crisis, for example, lasted several days. Figure 3 shows the percentage of crises that had "extended" decision time over the past two decades.[7] *Hence, no less than 38% and as many as 53% of all crises involve extended decision time.* This fact is an important element in the following arguments.

DATA ANALYSIS FOR CRISIS OBJECTIVES AND ACTIONS

Sample Selection and Coding

A sample of 101 U.S. crises between 1956 and 1976 was developed from a universe drawn from several different sources. Sampling allowed more careful coding of the data to be used. First and foremost among the sources for the crisis sample was CACI's previous research on crisis management in which crises between 1946 and 1975 were inventoried (CACI, 1975, 1976). Additionally, crises identified in two other major studies of U.S. crisis and crisis-like behavior (Blechman and Kaplan, 1977; Mahoney, 1976) were examined to expand the CACI crisis list. Unlike the crisis cases examined in CACI's research on crisis management problems (CACI, 1976), only international crises are included in the 101-case sample.

Case selection for the sample of 101 crises took into account CACI's major empirical findings on crisis behavior (CACI, 1976). Thus, crises selected for

Figure 3: DECISION TIME AVAILABLE: 1956-1976

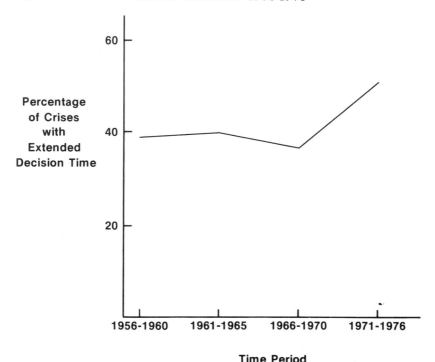

the sample were primarily politico-military because this type of incident was most commonly encountered in recent U.S. history. Major power crises were emphasized as were crises completed in less than seven or more than 30 days. Similarly, geographical locations and time of occurrence were also stressed with an oversampling of more recent (1970-1976) crises and an under-sampling of 1950s-era crises.

Data on U.S. International Crises. U.S. crises were examined for two types of data: (1) information on U.S. actions during the crisis; and (2) information on U.S. policy objectives during the crisis. Data in each of these areas were coded from public sources. An initial analysis of the quality of information on problems encountered in U.S. crises between 1946 and 1975 (CACI, 1976) suggested that public reporting on U.S. crisis behavior was adequate to permit the research team to determine whether an action or policy objective was present during the crisis. Additional study of a number of official (but unclassified) U.S. government publications, such as command histories, reports to the U.S. Congress, and annual reports by the Secretary of Defense and the secretaries of the three services, suggested that sufficient information for binary coding (that is, an action was present or absent) was available in unclassified sources.

Coding Procedures. Information on U.S. actions and policy objectives was coded for each of the 101 crises. Three of CACI's senior professional staff were used to examine historical material on the crises. After reading the available source materials on a crisis, a coder determined the U.S. actions and policy objectives and the actions and objectives of the crisis initiator. When a set of crises had been coded in this manner the three staff members jointly considered the codings before finally entering the information into the data file. During this process each coder related the events of the crisis and defended the coding made in each category. The results of this process are dichotomously coded data files for U.S. actions and policy objectives for a sample of 101 U.S. crises between 1956 and 1976. Because of resource constraints, no reliability checks were run on the data. Informed peer review was used in place of systematic reliability testing.

Research Strategy

The frequencies and cross-sectional relationships between U.S. actions and objectives in 101 crises were carefully examined. This analysis covered the 101 crises as a set. Subsets of crises were drawn to cover the date of occurrence and type of U.S. adversaries involved. Date of occurrence was examined to test for shifts in U.S. crisis behavior over time in response to changes in the international system (such as increased system complexity, greater economic interdependence, and diffusion of power throughout the system). Accordingly, the 101 crises were divided into 54 crises that occurred between 1956 and 1965 and 47 crises between 1966 and 1976.[8] Research reported here focuses on the differences between these two data sets.

U.S. Crisis Management Objectives: 1956-1976

Frequency Analyses. Table 1 shows the percentage of time in which the 30 key U.S. policy objectives were coded in the full sample of 101 crises and in the two time periods (1956-1965, 1966-1976). The first column shows that there are several objectives that occur frequently, such as protection of legal and political rights (50%) of the time), protection of military assets (40%), preserving a regime from an external threat (34%), preventing the spread of Communist influence (32%), and confirming or reestablishing prestige (also 32%).

Some insight can be gained by examining categories with the larger *changes* between the two time periods, as shown in columns 2 and 3.

(a) The category having the greatest change, inducing maintenance of a current policy, falls 19%, from 30% in the earlier period to 11% in the later one.
(b) Preserve readiness gains 19%.
(c) Preserve balance of power gains 18%.
(d) Preserve regime from internal threat and preserve regime from external threat lose 13%.
(e) Preserve or reestablish prestige gains 12%.

The objectives that changed most over the two periods are those associated with moving away from policies of containment (less involvement in other countries, more focus on U.S. global capabilities, image and role).

Patterns of Objectives. Inspection of raw frequency data, particularly where 30 or more variables are involved, is difficult and can lead to confusion. Frequently, when confronted with this problem, researchers resort to quantitative techniques for "data reduction," manipulation of available information to simplify the task of understanding the data set. This can be accomplished by eliminating all but a few variables that represent the main ideas of interest or by finding patterns in the data that aid interpretation.

The research team decided to keep the richness of the data set intact and search for patterns using a technique called factor analysis.[9] This technique identifies clusters of variables which tend to vary together. Each such cluster is called a "factor." Factors are named on the basis of variables associated

TABLE 1. FREQUENCY DISTRIBUTION OF UNITED STATES
            OBJECTIVES

	Percentage of All Crises: 1956–1976	Percentage of All Crises: 1956–1965	Percentage of All Crises: 1966–1976
Protect Legal and Political Rights	50	52	47
Protect A Military Asset	40	44	34
Preserve Regime From External Threat	34	41	26
Prevent the Spread of Communist Influence	32	31	32
Confirm or Reestablish Prestige	32	26	38
Preserve Territory or Facilities	31	35	26
Preserve Balance of Power	29	20	38
Restore Peace	28	33	21
Preserve Peace	28	24	32
Preserve, Restore or Improve Alliance	27	28	26
Improve or Rectify Difference Posture	25	28	21
Preserve Readiness	24	15	34
Preserve Regime From Internal Threat	24	30	17
Dissuade From a New Policy	23	20	26
Induce a Maintenance of a Current Policy	21	30	11
Restore Military Balance of Power	21	17	26
Prevent Spread of War	20	20	19
Assure Continued Economic Access	19	20	17
Contain Opponents	16	15	17
Restore Territorial Integrity	14	15	13
Deter Imminent Attack	13	15	11
Preserve Line of Communication	13	11	15
Preserve or Regain Control of the Sea	9	9	9
Put Down a Rebellion	9	11	6

TABLE 1. FREQUENCY DISTRIBUTION OF UNITED STATES
OBJECTIVES (Cont.)

	Percentage of All Crises: 1956−1976	*Percentage of All Crises: 1956−1965*	*Percentage of All Crises: 1966−1976*
Preserve or Regain Control of the Air	8	6	11
Restore Readiness	5	4	6
Regain Access to Economic Resources	5	2	7
Prevent Nuclear Proliferation	3	4	2
Insure Self-Sufficiency	2	4	0
Restore a Regime	1	2	0
Number of Crises	101	54	47
Average Number of Objectives Per Crises	6.00	6.13	5.87
Average Percentage of Objectives Per Category	20.2	20.4	16.6

with them. Study of the factors then allows the research team to gain insights into the data.

For example, Table 2 shows the results of a factor analysis of the full sample of 101 cases for the 30 key objective variables. Note that the top eight variables in the list are associated primarily with Factor 1, the next six with Factor 2, the next four with Factor 3, and the next three, along with "prevent the spread of war," with Factor 4. The last nine variables are not particularly associated with any of the factors—they are not part of the overall pattern located by the factor analysis.

After careful review of the patterns of association, labels or names reflecting major common concepts of each factor were assigned:

Factor 1: Containment of Communism.
Factor 2: Preservation of U.S. military capability and protection of U.S. interests.
Factor 3: Preservation of stability.
Factor 4: Restoration of control or readiness.

TABLE 2. FACTOR STRUCTURE OF U.S. OBJECTIVES IN 101 CRISES, 1956–1976[a]

| Variables | Factor | | | |
	1	2	3	4
Prevent spread of Communist influence	.69	.21	.07	.09
Preserve balance of power	.64	.22	−.08	.02
Contains opponents	.57	−.04	.18	.05
Restore military balance of power	.51	.11	.11	.28
Prevent spread of war	.46	−.16	.26	.54
Preserve regime from external threat	.46	−.14	.21	.16
Preserve, restore, or improve alliance	.43	−.04	.04	.21
Deter imminent attack	.40	.09	−.14	.35
Protect a military asset	−.19	.68	−.16	.24
Preserve lines of communication	.10	.60	−.12	−.11
Protect legal and political rights	.01	.52	−.06	.14
Improve or rectify deterrence posture	.26	.45	−.03	.23
Preserve readiness	.25	.45	−.25	−.35
Confirm or reestablish prestige	−.06	.41	−.14	−.09
Put down a rebellion	−.07	.03	.80	.05
Restore territorial integrity	.16	.14	.58	.01
Preserve regime from internal threat	.10	−.15	.48	.00
Restore peace	.30	−.12	.47	.37
Preserve or regain control of sea	−.06	.11	−.12	.50
Restore readiness	.06	.08	.05	.46
Preserve or regain control of air	.05	.11	.03	.41
Restore a regime	−.02	−.09	.21	−.04
Regain access to economic resources	−.03	−.13	−.07	−.08
Preserve peace	.25	.22	−.19	−.18
Preserve territory or facilities	.29	.24	.01	.29
Induce maintenance of current policy	.21	.05	−.14	.11
Dissuade from a new policy	.22	.06	−.21	−.26
Assure continued economic access	−.00	.09	.09	−.30
Prevent nuclear proliferation	−.07	−.22	−.06	0.1
Insure self-sufficiency	.03	.00	.04	.08
Percent variance explained	39	30	18	13

[a]Variance structure, orthogonal rotation.

The bottom line of the table, "percent of variance explained," is an indicator of the relative power of each factor in explaining the data in the set. Hence, Factor 1 is considerably stronger than Factor 4.

Here, again, interesting patterns emerge when the 21-year time span is divided into its component groups, 1956-1965 and 1966-1976. Table 3 shows the relative composition of the first factor that emerged from an analysis of the 1956-1965 data with the first factor that emerged from an analysis of the 1966-1976 data.

Table 3 indicates that the primary high loading items for the 1956-1965 crises (labeled containment by the researchers) were a variety of actions that involved deterrence, status quo, and defensive policies. In the first factor in the 1966-1976 data, however, the highest loading items involved U.S. efforts to restore peace and government stability and prevent conflict. Relative to the earlier period, containment of Communist adversaries was given less emphasis. This finding is consistent with a number of commentaries on changes in the international system during this time period. U.S. actions focused more on peace and stability over the last 10 years and less on containing communism.

Table 4 presents an overview of the complete results of the factor analyses carried out to identify the meaningful patterns in the U.S. objectives data for the two time periods. Note that preservation of stability, which was the fourth factor to emerge in the data for 1956-1965 and explained only a relatively small percentage of the variance in that analysis, jumps up to be the dominant factor in the analysis of the 1966-1976 data set. Containment drops to second place from the first to second period.

TABLE 3. COMPARING DOMINANT OBJECTIVES FACTORS FOR
            1956–1965 AND 1966–1976 CRISES

	Factor Loadings for First Factor After Orthogonal Rotation	
U.S. Objectives	1965–1965 Crises	1966–1976 Crises
Deter imminent attack	.71	.57
Preserve regime from external threat	.56	.47
Preserve territory or facility	.55	.42
Preserve or regain control of air	.54	.01
Prevent spread of war	.52	.74
Prevent spread of Communist influence	.52	.25
Preserve balance of power	.49	.26
Preserve or regain control of sea	.49	.02
Improve or rectify deterrence posture	.45	.07
Induce maintenance of current policy	.40	.17
Preserve Peace	.16	.46
Preserve regime from internal threat	−.00	.50
Restore territorial integrity	−.06	.53
Restore peace	.35	.78
Percent variance explained	41	39

TABLE 4.   MAJOR FACTORS OF U.S. OBJECTIVES

Factors of U.S. Objectives	Percent Variance Explained
1956–1965 Crises	
1. Containment	41
2. Preserve capability/ protect interests	28
3. Preserve capability/ preserve stability	16
4. Preserve stability	14
Total	99
1966–1976 Crises	
1. Preserve stability	39
2. Containment	27
3. Protect interests/ preserve capability	19
4. Miscellaneous	15
Total	90

Each of these analyses supports the same conclusion. *U.S. objectives during crises have shifted away from containment and toward maintenance of general stability in the international arena.*

U.S. Crisis Management Actions: 1956-1976

Frequency Analyses. There were 33 categories of U.S. crisis actions that were coded with sufficient precision to support analysis. The frequency of each action is shown in Table 5. The first column shows the raw frequencies. Eight actions were coded as occurring in 20% or more of the cases—employ diplomacy (74%), redeploy nonnuclear forces (31%), reaffirm an existing political/military commitment (31%), provide miscellaneous military equipment (30%), provide supplies from U.S. depots (29%), lodge protests (23%), reposition sea forces (20%), and reposition air forces (20%). Just below this 1-in-5 level is an interesting cluster of very active options—commit air support (19%), commit land support (17%), commit sea support (17%), provide military logistic support (15%), threaten nonnuclear forces (15%), and reposition land forces (13%).

TABLE 5. FREQUENCY DISTRIBUTION OF U.S. ACTIONS (PERCENTAGE)

U.S. Actions	1956–1976 Crises	1956–1965 Crises	1966–1976 Crises	Crises With Communist Adversaries	Crises With No Communist Adversaries
Employ Diplomacy	74	70	76	67	79
Redeploy Nonnuclear Forces	31	31	29	42	21
Reaffirm Existing Political/ Military Commitment	31	33	28	36	27
Provide Military Assistance (miscellaneous)	30	28	32	27	32
Provide Supplies From U.S. Depot	29	31	26	31	27
Lodge Protests	23	24	21	31	16
Reposition Sea Forces	20	24	15	27	14
Reposition Air Forces	20	17	23	36	7
Commit Air Support	19	22	15	24	14
Commit Land Support	17	19	15	16	18
Commit Sea Support	17	13	15	9	23
Provide Other Military Logistic Support	15	19	11	19	11
Threaten Nonnuclear Forces	15	19	11	11	18
Provide Military Advisory Assistance	14	19	9	18	11
Reposition Land Forces	13	7	19	20	7
Advocate/Support Peacekeeping Forces	11	9	13	13	9
Change Nonnuclear Alert Status	10	13	6	13	7
Provide Supplies From Non-military Sources	9	7	11	9	9

TABLE 5. FREQUENCY DISTRIBUTION OF U.S. ACTIONS (PERCENTAGE) (Cont.)

U.S. Actions	1956–1976 Crises	1956–1965 Crises	1966–1976 Crises	Crises With Communist Adversaries	Crises With No Communist Adversaries
Redeploy Nuclear Forces	8	2	15	18	0
Provide Training For Combat Troops	8	13	2	13	4
Mediate a Dispute	7	4	11	4	9
Other U.S. Actions	7	7	6	9	5
Provide Other Military Training	6	6	6	7	5
Commit Land Forces to Combat	5	9	0	4	5
Commit Air Forces to Combat	4	4	4	7	2
Provide Military Maintenance Assistance	4	6	2	2	5
Improve Scientific/Technical Capabilities	4	2	6	4	4
Threaten or Do Withdraw Support	3	1	4	0	5
Commit Sea Forces to Combat	3	4	2	4	2
Change Nuclear Alert Status	2	0	4	4	0
Threaten Nuclear Forces	2	0	4	4	0
Draw Down Equipment From U.S. Units	2	0	4	2	2
Number of Crises	101	54	47	45	56
Average Number of Actions Per Crisis	4.58	4.67	4.49	5.35	3.96

The actions recorded least frequently tend to be extreme moves that are used only as a last resort. Their low frequency of use reflects the reluctance of decision makers to commit themselves to extreme actions during crises. Hence, committing land, air, or sea forces to combat all appear less than 5% of the time, changing nuclear status and threatening nuclear forces only 2%, threats and actual withdrawals of support only 3%, and so forth. By contrast, the most frequent categories mainly include low risk responses that do not foreclose peaceful conflict resolution and are not likely to escalate a conflict. They are not irrevocable, but they do signal U.S. resolve and emphasize U.S. capabilities in a crisis. They are, in short, crisis management tools.

The second and third columns of Table 5 show the same data (percentage of times actions were taken) for the 1956-1965 and 1966-1976 cases in the data sample. Comparison shows several fairly strong differences between U.S. actions in these two time periods.

(a) Reposition land forces moves from 7% frequency in 1956-1965 to 19% in 1966-1976.
(b) Redeploy nuclear forces rises dramatically from 2% of the cases in the earlier decade to 15% in the later time period.
(c) Providing training for combat troops declines from 13% in 1956-1965 to a mere 2% between 1966-1976.
(d) Providing military advisory assistance decreases by a full 10% (from 19% to 9%) between the two periods.

There are a number of slightly smaller changes that suggest a pattern of reduced conflict commitment:

(a) Commit land forces to combat declines 9%.
(b) All cases of U.S. commitment of land forces occur before 1966.
(c) Provide military logistic support falls 8%.
(d) Threaten nonnuclear forces falls 8%.
(e) Commit air support falls 7%.
(f) Change nonnuclear alert status falls 7%.

Hence, there is a pattern of greater caution and less risk in the later time period as well as an apparent decline in the use of military assistance. To understand better the patterns in crises actions, the sample of 101 cases was redivided into two groups, those crises involving Communist adversaries and those with no Communist adversaries. The 101 cases had originally been chosen to overrepresent Communist adversary cases to alow this type of analysis. The last two columns in Table 5 present the percentage frequency data for these analyses.

Because of the findings regarding objectives that U.S. policy has been shifting away from containment and into situations involving the maintenance of global stability, examination of the types of actions used by the United States when confronting a Communist adversary as contrasted with a non-Communist one was considered important.

(a) The largest difference is that both nuclear and nonnuclear forces are deployed much less frequently (21% and 18%, respectively) when non-Communist adversaries are involved.
(b) Protests are lodged about 15% less frequently against non-Communist adversaries.
(c) Both land and sea forces are repositioned about 13% less frequently in dealing with non-Communist adversaries.
(d) Air support is committed about 10% less frequently when dealing with non-Communist adversaries.
(e) By contrast, sea support is used about 14% more frequently when non-Communist adversaries are involved—but a number of these codings resulted from the use of sea support forces to evacuate U.S. nationals during crises.

Perhaps most important, *the United States takes less action* (an average of less than four of the categories being coded for non-Communist adversaries, over five for Communist adversaries) *when dealing with crisis situations not involving Communist adversaries.*

Patterns of Actions. Here again, the research team was interested in locating patterns in the data. The relatively low frequency of almost all individual action variables made this an imperative part of the analysis. The overall set of actions is much more meaningful than changes in individual variables.

The results of a factor analysis of the 101-case sample are shown in Table 6. Four identifiable factors emerged:

Factor 1: Show of force based on redeployment and repositioning actions.
Factor 2: Military aid and assistance.
Factor 3: Commitment to combat.
Factor 4: Direct involvement short of combat.

The most important analysis undertaken was the comparison of factor analyses for the 1956-1965 and 1966-1976 time periods. Table 7 shows the important variables that are associated with the dominant clusters in these actions. The actions factor from the earlier time period is dominated by military aid options. The strongest factor in the 1966-1976 period contains only one aid-related component (military maintenance assistance) and has a large "deterrence" component. It is dominated by cautious actions, signaling

TABLE 6. FACTOR STRUCTURE OF U.S. ACTIONS IN 101 CRISES, 1956–1976[a]

Variables	Factor			
	1	2	3	4
Reposition Air Forces	.80	.27	-.11	-.09
Reposition Sea Forces	.64	-.05	-.06	-.04
Redeploy Nonnuclear Forces	.55	-.10	.01	.11
Redeploy Nuclear Forces	.54	.04	-.04	.23
Change Nuclear Alert Status	.51	-.11	.08	.20
Reposition Land Forces	.51	.03	-.15	-.06
Reaffirm Existing Political-Military Commitment	.32	.23	.07	.03
Provide Training for Combat Troops	.02	.70	-.06	.11
Provide Military Advisory Assistance	.11	.65	-.07	-.13
Provide Supplies From U.S. Depots	.21	.62	.00	.09
Provide Other Military Logistic Support	.16	.58	-.05	-.07
Provide Military Maintenance Assistance	-.08	.40	.06	-.05
Provide Other Military Training	.05	.38	-.11	.21
Commit Sea Forces to Combat	-.00	-.04	.74	.17
Commit Air Forces to Combat	-.05	-.05	.69	.13
Commit Land Forces to Combat	-.03	.15	.51	-.22
Change Nonnuclear Alert Status	.37	-.12	.39	.04
Commit Land Support	-.12	.21	.39	-.41
Provide Supplies From Nonmilitary Sources	.05	.17	-.02	.41
Advocate or Support Peacekeeping Forces	.36	-.03	.21	.38
Commit Sea Support	-.16	-.05	.01	-.35
Employ Diplomacy	.07	.16	-.28	.35
Improve Scientific-Technical Capability	-.09	-.05	-.03	-.31
Commit Air Support	-.18	.31	.13	-.30
Threaten Nuclear Forces	.25	.06	-.00	-.02
Threaten Nonnuclear Forces	-.02	.22	.13	.02
Draw Down Equipment From U.S. Depots	.09	.13	-.07	-.26
Provide Other Military Assistance	.08	.30	.01	.05
Threaten to or Do Withdraw Support	-.15	-.04	-.04	-.27
Lodge Protest	-.06	0.4	.09	.23
Other U.S. Actions	-.22	-.04	-.06	.12
Mediate a Dispute	.18	-.06	-.07	.13
Percent Variance Explained	37	28	21	14

[a]Varimax solution, orthogonal rotation.

actions, and actions that avoid direct involvement. *The actions involved largely include changing the location, status, and exposure of U.S. military assets to convince other actors of U.S. resolve and capabilities.*

TABLE 7. COMPARING DOMINANT ACTIONS FACTORS FOR
1956–1965 AND 1966–1976[a]

	1956–1965 Crises	1966–1976 Crises
Provide military advisory assistance	.82	−.05
Provide training for combat troops	.81	−.05
Provide supplies from U.S. depots	.68	.05
Provide other military logistic support	.50	−.02
Reposition air forces	.49	.44
Provide military maintenance assistance	.48	−.04
Provide other military training	.42	−.01
Provide supplies from nonmilitary sources	.21	.50
Redeploy nonnuclear forces	−.06	.54
Reposition sea forces	−.02	.55
Change nonnuclear alert status	−.12	.61
Redeploy nuclear forces	.27	.64
Change nuclear alert status	−	.76
Advocate/support peacekeeping effort	−.05	.83
Percent variance explained	36	43

[a]Action categories with loadings less than 0.40 in both cases are not shown.

This interpretation is strengthened when Table 8 is examined. This table compares the largest factors for the data subsets in which the United States faces a Communist or a non-Communist adversary. *The United States is more prone to become militarily involved in crises without Communist adversaries.* This pattern is clearer still when the overview of the full factor solutions for both pairs of cases is reviewed (Table 9). Over time, military aid has declined dramatically as a tool for crisis management. Cautious policies designed to provide warning of U.S. capabilities have replaced them as the most frequent crisis management tools. At the same time, the United States shows a marked tendency to become involved in direct conflict situations when the adversaries are not Communist.

Giving military aid was the dominant U.S. action prior to 1966.[10] After 1966 the United States tended to redeploy, reposition, and increase the alert status of its forces.[11] In addition to clear changes in U.S. aid policy, the switch to repositioning may come from both changes in policy and changes in clarity with which "signals" to adversaries could be transmitted. Once aid is removed, manipulation of existing forces is a logical alternative means to show concern and resolve. Moreover, as worldwide monitoring capabilities of power increased after 1966 (with the use of various types of electronic and

TABLE 8. COMPARING DOMINANT ACTION FACTORS BY TYPE OF ADVERSARY[a]

U.S. Actions	Crises With Communist Adversaries	Crises Without Communist Adversaries
Advocate/support peacekeeping force	.76	−.05
Change nonnuclear alert status	.71	.06
Change nuclear alert status	.67	−
Reposition sea forces	.65	−.05
Reposition air forces	.62	−.05
Redeploy nonnuclear forces	.51	−.08
Redeploy nuclear forces	.51	−
Mediate a dispute	.45	−.09
Reaffirm existing political-military commitment	.40	−.10
Commit land support	−.15	.40
Commit land forces to combat	−.06	.65
Commit sea forces to combat	.11	.96
Commit air forces to combat	.03	.96
Percent variance explained	34	29

[a]Action categories with loadings less than 0.40 in both cases are not shown.

TABLE 9. MAJOR FACTORS OF U.S. ACTIONS FOR SELECTED SUBSETS OF CRISES

Factors of U.S. Actions	Percent Variance Explained	Factors of U.S. Actions in Crises	Percent Variance Explained
1956−1965 Crises		*With Communist Adversaries*	
1. Military Aid	36	1. Reposition forces	34
2. Commit forces to combat	25	2. Military aid	28
3. Reposition forces	21	3. Commit forces to combat	24
4. Miscellaneous	17	4. Miscellaneous	13
1966−1976 Crises		*Without Communist Adversaries*	
1. Deterrence	43	1. Commit forces to combat	29
2. Commit military support	22	2. Commit military support	27
3. Reposition forces	19	3. Military aid	24
4. Military aid	17	4. Reposition forces	20

photographic reconnaissance capabilities), repositioning of forces was more likely to be monitored and interpreted as a crisis-related activity.

Against Communist adversaries, the United States sends signals and gestures with its forces, apparently depending on the extensive monitoring capabilities of these states to check such force positioning. Against non-Communist adversaries, the United States has more commonly committed forces in an effort to achieve U.S. objectives in the crisis. Sea and air forces are both very high-loading items in these crises.

A CHALLENGE FOR THE 1980'S

The evidence suggests, then, three important trends:

(1) There is increasing variety in the set of actors with whom the United States experiences international crises.

(2) There is a tendency for U.S. crisis management objectives to shift away from "containment of Communism" toward a more general desire for global stability.

(3) The set of actions taken by the United States during a crisis is much more likely to include military involvement when there is no Communist adversary. The United States is using military assistance less frequently and utilizing military deployments and repositionings to signal resolve and indicate potency more frequently.

In isolation, these tendencies are interesting. In combination, they are potentially very dangerous. Assuming the 1980s will be a decade of change in the international economic, political, and social order, global stability will be a goal that may place the United States in opposition to much of the dynamics that will characterize the decade. The trend toward less concern with containment and more with stability is likely to reinforce the U.S. trend toward involvement in crisis situations with a greater variety of countries, particularly smaller powers. Given these patterns, there are dangers inherent in reducing the use of assistance as a buffer, using force against non-Communist adversaries, and exposing U.S. military forces as a dominant response to crises. The result will tend to be a United States that (a) is increasingly involved in crises with lesser powers over issues of stability; (b) has reduced its options to exposure of military forces, and/or their use; and (c) must therefore choose between impotence and military involvement.

Of course, there is no reason why these trends must continue. The key to avoiding these dangerous situations would appear to hinge on a reassessment of both objectives and tools in crisis management. First, there is a need to develop a dialogue that explores the forms and rates of change which the

United States wants to encourage in the 1980s. This type of dialogue is difficult and can occur only slowly. However, until a national consensus emerges that the global arena is dynamic and that some parts of that dynamism can be beneficial to the United States, the tendency to seek stability will drive crisis management planning.

Second, and perhaps more tractable, is the need to rethink the set of crisis management options available. In Angola, the United States was effectively immobilized because of the Vietnam experience. The ideas that aid programs are self perpetuating and that military assistance leads to military involvement are certainly supported by recent history. The question of whether they are inevitably true would not seem to be so settled. Abandoning military assistance as a buffer in crisis situations and the cutoff of such aid as a lever for influence does, however, have the natural consequence of placing U.S. military assets more directly into crisis situations. Each such exposure brings a risk of conflict. Ideally, new instruments of diplomacy can be developed that will avoid the need for this military exposure and be relatively free from the pitfalls of endless involvement.

The purpose of this article is not to resolve the issue of new actions, but to point up the dangerous tendencies inherent in the pattern we see today. It is possible, however, to indicate some of the attributes of the new types of actions needed. They should

(a) Allow for reserving the direct involvement of U.S. military forces in all but the most serious crisis situations;

(b) Have a direct, strong impact on the actors in a crisis and, if possible, on the crisis itself; and

(c) Be applicable to the increasing variety of key actors that may be involved in future crises.

The finding that most recent crises have allowed extended decision time may also tell us that some of these crisis management tools may well take days or weeks to implement rather than having to be effective in a matter of hours. A major challenge for the 1980s is, then, the development of these new approaches to crisis management.

NOTES

1. See, for instance, Brown, 1973; Pranger, 1972; Sanderson and Cleveland, 1974; Bergsten and Krause, 1975; Osgood and Associates, 1973; Scott, 1969; and Cole et al., 1978.

2. In their survey of 16 recent studies of global futures Cole et al. (1978) found that in only two or three of the cases was the outlook for the future world seen as stable. The other cases generally anticipated increasing instability, conflict, and economic hardship.

3. Soviet-Cuban involvements in Africa during the mid-1970s are among the evidence supporting such an argument.

4. "Exposure of military forces" means placing them in a position where they can be attacked by an adversary with minimal warning. Except in times of war, commanders usually seek to minimize exposure.

5. Cases such as Vietnam and Korea, where the United States became embroiled in active fighting over an extended period, were usually coded as a single crisis during the period in which a decision to commit forces was made. The coding rules and procedures are detailed in CACI (1976).

6. It is not yet clear whether this 1976 figure represents a return to the higher crisis frequency which characterized earlier decades.

7. Extended decision time was defined as more than seven days.

8. Previous analyses (Blechman and Kaplan, 1977; CACI, 1976; Mahoney, 1976) indicate that 1966 was a watershed year in U.S. involvement in international crises.

9. See the technical appendix for a brief explanation of the techniques utilized.

10. U.S. military aid has declined in scope over the 1956-1976 time period. The value of U.S. military aid has increased for only a limited number of countries (such as Israel and South Korea) over the same period. Unambiguous historical support for the increased importance of deterrence is difficult to identify, however. Since the Dominican intervention of 1964, U.S. policy has involved far less actual or threatened use of force in crises. The rise of the deterrence factor after 1966 may summarize this pattern.

11. The highest loading item for 1966-1976, "advocate/support peacekeeping efforts," is coded to include actual commitment of support and the desire to support these efforts. Hence, it loads higher than any other action by including both words and deeds.

REFERENCES

BERGSTEN, C.F., and KRAUSE, L.B. (eds.) (1975). World politics and international economics. Washington, D.C.: Brookings Institution.

BLECHMAN, B.M., and KAPLAN, S.S. (1977). The use of the armed forces as a political instrument. Washington, D.C.: Brookings Institution.

BROWN, S. (1973). "New forces in world politics." In Chapter 13 of H. Owen (ed.), The next phase in foreign policy. Washington, D.C.: Brookings Institution.

CACI (1975). Crisis inventory. Arlington, Va.: CACI.

――― (1976). Planning for problems in crisis management. Arlington, Va.: CACI.

――― (1977a). Research gaps on crisis management of terrorist incidents. Arlington, Va.: CACI.

――― (1977b). Executive aids for crisis management. Arlington, Va.: CACI.

COLE, S., GERSHUNY, J., and MILES, I. (1978). "Scenarios of world development." Futures: The Journal of Forecasting and Planning, 10, 1 (February):3-20.

HAZLEWOOD, L.A., HAYES, J.J., and BROWNELL, J.R., JR. (1977). "Planning for problems in crisis management: An analysis of post-1945 behavior in the Department of Defense." International Studies Quarterly, 21, 1:75-106.

HERMANN, C.F. (1969). "International crisis as a situational variable." In J.N. Rosenau (ed.), International politics and foreign policy. New York: Free Press.

MAHONEY, R.B., JR. (1976). "American political-military operations and the structure of the international system, 1946-1975." Prepared for presentation at the Annual

Meeting of the Section on Military Studies, International Studies Association, Ohio State University, October.

OSGOOD, R.E., and Associates (1973). Retreat from empire: The first Nixon Administration. Baltimore and London: Johns Hopkins University Press.

PRANGER, R.J. (1972). Defense implications of international indeterminacy. Washington, D.C.: American Enterprise Institute for Public Policy Research.

SANDERSON, F.H., and CLEVELAND, H.V.B. (1974). Strains in international finance and trade. Washington Papers, Vol. 2, No. 14. Beverly Hills, Cal.: Sage.

SCOTT, A.M. (1969). The revolution in statecraft: Informal penetration. New York: Random House.

TECHNICAL APPENDIX: A BRIEF
REVIEW OF FACTOR ANALYSIS

Factor analysis defines a set of statistical techniques that have been found useful by scientists for analyzing large numbers of variables and observations (that is, large matrices of data).[1] The perspectives with which the researcher approaches factor analysis partly determine the interpretation of the results. In this chapter, our approach is purely *descriptive*. That is, we are interested in exploring the patterns of interrelationship among our variables to identify sets or clusters of variables that have relatively high intercorrelations. We are not interested in other more complex uses of factor analysis such as determining causality or testing hypotheses.[2]

The factor technique employed in this chapter involves three steps:

(1) Calculation of a Pearson product-moment correlation matrix of relevant variables.

(2) Defining orthogonal (uncorrelated) *factors* in terms of exact mathematical transformations based on the correlation matrix of Step 1. Briefly, this can be formally stated as follows:

$$Z_j = a_{j1} F_1 + a_{j2} F_2 + \ldots + a_{ji} F_i$$

where Z_j is the jth variable, a_{ji} is the *factor loading* of jth variables on factor i, and F_i is the ith factor.[3]

(3) Rotation of the first four factors to an orthogonal final solution.[4]

The technical names for the procedures selected are principal factoring with iteration and varimax orthogonal rotation. Principal factoring with iteration is a relatively robust technique and is one of the most widely accepted factoring methods. For our purposes, orthogonal rotation was judged most suitable because it simplified the task of examining distinct clusters of variables by maintaining the factors' independence with respect to each other.

There are many different types of statistical information that can be obtained from factor analysis. To minimize the task of the nontechnical readers, we have presented only two types of information in this chapter, factor loadings and percent variance explained. The factor loading (a_{ji}) of a variable (Z_j) represents a standardized multiple-regression coefficient of that variable with a factor (F_i). In other words, factor loadings can be interpreted as correlations (or indicators of degree of statistical agreement) of variables with the factors.

In this context, factors (F_i's) can be interpreted as hypothetical variables that define underlying dimensions or general concepts. Each factor is closely related to a subset of the original variables (Z_j's). Each factor can be assigned a name on the basis of the subset of variables that have high loadings on it. Since the values of factor loadings vary between -1 and 1, in examining the subset of variables that are closely related to a factor it is generally convenient to examine only variables with loadings greater than ± 0.30. This enables the researcher to identify rapidly the clusters of variables with intercorrelations, which constitutes our main reason for using factor analysis in this chapter.

The second type of factor analysis statistic presented in this chapter is percent variance explained. This is the percent of *total* variance explained by each factor. For a factor (F_i), variance explained is equal to the sum of its squared loadings, or

$$\sum_{j=1}^{n} (a_{ji})^2$$

and percent variance explained is

$$\frac{100}{n} \sum_{j=1}^{n} (a_{ji})^2$$

NOTES

1. More extensive, technical discussions of factor analysis can be found in Kim, 1975; Cooley and Lohnes, 1971; Rummel, 1970; and Palumbo, 1969. Among these Kim and Palumbo require the least prior technical knowledge.

2. Rummel (1970) provides the most exhaustive review of various approaches to factor analysis.

3. Note that each observed variable (Z_j) is described linearly in terms of n factors (F_i's), each of which is a linear combination of the original n variables (Z_j's).

4. Factors beyond the first four were not statistically significant (in terms of their explained variance) and were not included in the analysis.

REFERENCES

COOLEY, W.W., and LOHNES, P.R. (1971). Multivariate data analysis. New York: John Wiley.

KIM, J.O. (1975). "Factor analysis." Pp. 468-514 in Nie and Associates (eds.), SPSS: Statistical package for the social sciences. 2nd ed. New York: McGraw-Hill.

PALUMBO, D.J. (1969). Statistics in political and behavioral science. New York: Appleton-Century-Crofts.

RUMMEL, R.J. (1970). Applied factor analysis. Evanston, Ill.: Northwestern University.

PART II:

SOME EMERGENT GLOBAL

CHALLENGES TO THE UNITED STATES

Chapter 4

CONFLICT IN THE INTERNATIONAL SYSTEM, 1816-1977: HISTORICAL TRENDS AND POLICY FUTURES

M E L V I N S M A L L
Wayne State University

J. D A V I D S I N G E R
University of Michigan

An American sea captain who plied the oceans in the 1780s reported that his newly independent country was seen "in the same light by foreign nations as a well-behaved negro is in a gentleman's family" (Elliot, 1891:34). Far off the beaten track geographically speaking, the pariah republic was also far removed from the complicated diplomatic and martial games played in the

EDITORS' NOTE: This article was first submitted for review in February 1978. The version published here was received in April 1978. The data reported on in this article shall subsequently be made available to other researchers through the Inter-University Consortium for Political and Social Research at the University of Michigan.

AUTHORS' NOTE: We are indebted to Richard Stoll, Michael Champion, Thomas Cusack, and Thomas Kselman for their contributions to the data and the analysis on which the chapter rests, and for their assistance in the presentation and interpretation of the results.

capitals of the Old World. One hundred years later, the United States was still on the fringes of the major power system; reciprocal interests were marginal, and her navy was inferior even to that of Chile. In his first inaugural address in 1885, Grover Cleveland recommended the "scrupulous avoidance of any departure from that foreign policy commended by the history, the traditions, and the prosperity of our Republic. It is the policy of independence . . . the policy of neutrality, rejecting any share in foreign broils and ambitions upon other continents . . . peace, commerce, and honest friendship with all nations; entangling alliances with none" (Richardson, 1904:301).

Obviously, as the United States enters her third century as an independent actor in the international system, the scenario has changed appreciably. Today, and for the foreseeable future, she is at the very center of that system. Her political, economic, and cultural activities affect the outcome of a war in the Horn of Africa, the price of wheat in India, and the wearing apparel of teenagers in Hungary. In addition, the system is no longer dominated by a handful of Christian Majesties who spoke the same language, figuratively as well as literally. Prominent players in the game now include not only newly independent states, but liberation and terrorist groups, intergovernmental and nongovernmental international organizations, producers' consortia, and multi-national corporations. All of these actors, ranging from the superpowers like the U.S. and the U.S.S.R. to the International Office of Epizootics, participate in a highly interdependent network using sophisticated technology and weaponry that would have seemed like science fiction not only to Grover Cleveland but to Franklin Roosevelt as well.

Today's system seems so complex, the pace of activity so rapid, and the stakes so high that the first American secretary of state, Thomas Jefferson, probably exercised more control over his nation's role in the international firmament than did Henry Kissinger, with all of the advanced communications (and weapons systems) available to him. Indeed, today's diplomats may well envy that small coterie who were able to keep the nation on an even keel through most of its history without "going to the brink" or "losing" a country.

But how different *is* the international system today compared to that of 50, 100, 200 years ago? While the system is clearly larger, the technology more advanced, and the boundaries more permeable, is it indeed more complex, more interdependent, or more dangerous? Are we, as many suggest, living in an age of conflict, a century of total war, an era of violent peace (Chambers, Harris, and Bayley, 1950; Aron, 1954; Mydans and Mydans, 1968)? Is the world more conflictful than it has been; is it becoming a more dangerous place for its citizens to inhabit?

Asked by statesmen, scholars, and journalists, such sweeping questions are answered with a multiplicity of conflicting projections, often based on the conventional wisdom of the day, buttressed by an anecdote or two from history. Thus, for some, the immediate future will be unlike any other period because of the disappearance of fossil fuels; or it will see a rebirth of the balance of power system of the 1870s; or it will experience global revolution as in 1848; or nuclear Armageddon will leave a few survivors back in the Stone Age. Such projections, while sometimes insightful and imaginative, are frequently based upon the most marginal evidence and an all-too-selective recall of diplomatic history.

We propose to examine trends in war and conflict in a systematic fashion, as we seek to describe where we have been and to suggest where we may be headed. Over the past decade or so, the Correlates of War Project has collected a wealth of data on international and domestic conflict ranging back to 1816. The presentation of some of these data here should enable us to chart more precisely the trends and cycles in the incidence of international violence. We undertake this task not merely out of historical curiosity, but because a more precise description of the past is a useful first step toward intelligent extrapolations about future levels of conflict in the global community. Such a description also provides a useful basis for analyzing American foreign policy in the 1980s.

There are, of course, many bases upon which to rest our forecasts of international events and conditions. Leaving aside such dubious methods as chicken entrail or tea leaf reading, we see five basic strategies. One is what might be called the "seat of the pants scenario," popularized by such futurologists as Kahn and Wiener (1967) and deJouvenal (1967), but well known in one guise or another in the foreign ministries of the world. At bottom, this is little more than combining a bit of imagination with a large dose of the contemporary folklore, and such a forecasting strategy rests on an all too flimsy foundation. The error rate of decision makers using this "method" is manifest in a long list of battle fatalities over the centuries, as well as in many disasters of a less dramatic sort.

Slightly more systematic is the Delphi method (Helmer, 1973), which has a number of specialists respond to a forecasting questionnaire, whose results are then pooled and returned to the respondents. In light of these tabulations, the respondents are asked to revise or confirm their original forecasts to see whether two or more iterations can lead to a clear consensus. In our view, this is merely a paper and pencil version of what occurs in foreign ministries every day, and while it does tell us something about the suggestibility of the specialists (Asch, 1952), it is perhaps even more dangerous than the less formalized version because it implies some of the aura of scientific method.

Then there are forecasts resting on either man-machine or all machine simulations, and while they *could* be effective, their success depends largely on the quality of the "theory" that informs the simulation. But given the state of codified knowledge (that is, theory) in our field, it would be a mistake to place much confidence in either form of simulation at this stage. Another type of analogy to the international system of tomorrow (and simulation is one) is that reflecting our understanding of apparently similar social systems, such as business firms, economic markets, universities, or social psychological experiments. Finally, and also resting on analogy, is the forecast based on history.

This will be our strategy here, despite the dangers inherent in it. As Harold Nicolson (1961:ii) reminded a British Foreign Office planning for the post-World War II period, "events are not affected by analogies; they are determined by combinations of circumstances. And since," he added, "circumstances vary from generation to generation, it is illusive to suppose that any pattern of history—however similar it may at first appear—is likely to repeat itself exactly in the kaleidoscope of time." We are not, in other words, oblivious to the discontinuities in world history, nor are we indifferent to the frequency with which repetitive patterns begin to appear, only to be shattered by some unexpected or rare event. But we also suspect that today's practitioners and observers—like observers in every generation—exaggerate the changes that are currently under way, even as they urge the incomparability of the several epochs that have gone before.

Further, we suspect that despite a major increase in popular participation as well as dramatic technological innovations, the game of nations has changed but little since Machiavelli codified the ancient rules of diplomatic conduct more than 450 years ago. The state system ushered in after Westphalia, or at least after the Congress of Vienna, is still with us today. The national (or multinational) state remains the dominant actor in the system, despite its limited ability to meet the basic needs of its citizens, and despite the recurrent focus on varieties of subnational and extranational entities that seem to challenge the dominant role of the state. Moreover, the substance of foreign policy decision rules has remained relatively constant across time, as well as across states whose structural and cultural characteristics appear to be quite different. Thus, even though many priorities as well as strategies continually shift, the *basic* goals and decision rules of foreign policy elites continue to revolve around national survival, autonomy, and power.

At bottom, of course, the relationship of our times to those that preceded it is an empirical question that analyses such as ours ultimately address. As noted above, each generation tends to think of itself as new or revolutionary.

However, at least to date, each appears to be not only affected by and intimately linked to previous ones, but also remarkably similar to those that went before. There is, of course, always the chance that we *have* come to a major watershed in world history, and that the events of recent decades *are* so unique as to constitute the sort of systemic transformation that occurs only once or twice a millenium. Perhaps; yet it might well be that the allegedly historically unique period in our lives is over. In a recent historical overview, Wilson (1977) argues that the 1920s offer important guidance for the future. In her view, the most recent past—the Depression, World War II, and the Cold War—were aberrations followed now by a period of "normalcy" comparable to that of the Harding-Coolidge-Hoover years. Similarly, Rosecrance et al. (1974) see a close parallel between the contemporary period and a prior one, but for them the referent is that of the 1870s.

Whether or not contemporary decision makers find Wilson's parallel compelling, most do think they can learn from the past. Unfortunately, their historic memories are often too selective, if not blatantly self-serving, to produce accurate or particularly credible forecasts. For only one of many examples, May (1973) reminds us how a misreading of history led American policy makers in the 1960s to perceive another Munich in Vietnam, and each of us has a favorite horror story about how a highly selective and distorted recall of the past has contributed to one foreign policy disaster or another.

THE HISTORICAL TREND DATA

Because history will continue to be studied for guidance to the future, it behooves us to examine it carefully and systematically. To do so, certain procedures must be followed from the beginning, so that even if our interpretations and inferences are erroneous, our historical data base will at least be accurate. Crucial to such accuracy is a set of categories that are logically exhaustive and mutually exclusive, resting on a set of classification rules that are unambiguous and reliable. In other words, one must devise a set of operational coding rules so that all possible cases of a particular type are first identified, after which each is assigned to the appropriate sub-category.

In the sections that follow, we have done exactly that. We have taken three basic types of political conflict—international wars, military confrontations short of war, and civil wars—and developed explicit and operational criteria by which all possible or "candidate" cases are examined. Those conflicts that satisfy the criteria for each type are assigned accordingly, and those that do not are left aside for the moment, to be reexamined at a later date. After we summarize the results of these procedures for all three types of conflict, we will turn to an interpretation of the data and an examination of the implications for foreign policy in the decades ahead.

International Wars

To describe historical trends in international war since 1816, we must first define what we mean by international war. To qualify for this designation, a sustained military conflict had to array at least one sovereign member of the interstate system against another member, or an independent nonmember, or a colony, and result in at least 1,000 battle deaths to the system member participant(s). Excluded here are internal wars involving only one political entity, as well as those scores of internation skirmishes and exchanges of fire that resulted in very few battle deaths. From 1816 through 1977, we found 103 such wars, of which 57 involved system members on both sides (interstate wars) and 46 involved a system member in combat with either a colony or another polity that did not qualify for system membership (extra-systemic wars).[1] A more complete explanation of our coding rules and research procedures relating to wars and system membership is found in *The Wages of War* (Singer and Small, 1972).

To make more meaningful comparisons over our long time span, we will subdivide it into seven distinct periods, conforming closely to the periodization used by most diplomatic historians. For the most part, their termini are found in years following major upheavals or substantial rearrangements in the international system. Thus, we look first at the years from the Congress of Vienna through 1849, the so-called Concert Period, largely shattered by the widespread revolutions that racked the continent in 1848-1849. We then demarcate a period from 1850 to 1870, in which the international system is in a state of flux as the Italian and German states are forged with blood and iron. The third period, 1871-1890, is the Age of Bismarck, marked particularly by the Iron Chancellor's successful isolation of his enemy, France. During the fourth period, from 1891 through 1914, an alliance system develops that results in the severe bipolarization of the European system and ends in the First World War, while the years following (1919-1939) comprise the conventional interwar period.

The identification of possible break points within the past 32 years (1946-1977) is of course somewhat more difficult, given our lack of historical perspective; later generations might well view it in a manner entirely different from the way we do today. Emphasizing the tentativeness of this decision, we examine first the years from 1946 through 1965, a period that experienced the worst of the Cold War and which is bounded by the breakup of the Grand Alliance at one end and the Americanization of the war in Vietnam at the other. Finally, our seventh period covers the most recent 12 years

(1966-1977), in which the international system seems to be in considerable flux.

We have not divided our temporal domain in this manner in order to test the validity of historians' periodizations—although that might be a useful exercise. Rather, for the purposes of this chapter, we accept the reasonableness of these break points, most of which seem to have been internalized by contemporary policy makers as well as scholars. Table 1, which shows the frequency of international wars, is similar in format to the tables that follow, with the first column indicating the number of years spanned by each of the historic periods. Five of the seven periods are of relatively equal length, but the first (1816-1849) is the longest and the last (1966-1977) is the briefest. The fact that not all periods are of the same length could make comparisons awkward, but the problem disappears when we "normalize" and present our calculations in terms of annual averages, or wars per year. The second column shows the average number of nations in the system during the period, a figure that ranges from 29 to 135. Then, in columns 3 through 5, we present the number of wars begun during each period, the average number of wars begun per year, and the number of wars begun per year, per system member. Thus, the figures in columns 4 and 5 control for both the differing size of the system and the differing lengths of the periods. Our final two columns deal with *national* war involvements or the *number of nations* that participate in wars, and thus do not necessarily reflect the same phenomena reported in columns 3 through 5. It is entirely possible to experience two different sorts

TABLE 1. FREQUENCY OF INTERNATIONAL WARS, 1816—1977

	1	2	3	4	5	6	7
Period	*No. of Years*	*Avg. System Size*	*No. of Wars Begun*	*No. of Wars Begun Per Year*	*No. of Wars Begun Per Year Per Nation*	*No. of War Involve- Ments Per Nation*	*No. of War Involve- ments Per Nation Per Year*
1816–49	34	29	21	.62	.021	1.00	.034
1850–70	21	39	19	.90	.023	2.43	.062
1871–90	20	34	12	.60	.017	.85	.025
1891–1914	24	42	17	.71	.016	2.00	.047
1919–39	21	64	11	.52	.008	2.33	.037
1946–65	20	95	11	.55	.006	1.87	.025
1966–77	12	135	9	.75	.006	1.67	.012

of violent eras, one with a great many dyadic wars of perhaps brief durations, and another with a few, but very large or long, multilateral wars. Thus, in columns 6 and 7 are national war involvements per year and national war involvements per year per system member, respectively.

Because we will return to all six of the tables later in the chapter, this section will be used only for a brief introduction to each. Looking at Table 1, the first impression is that of a fairly steady decline in the frequency of international wars, going from 21 in the first period down to 9 in the final one. But when (in column 4) we average the figures to account for the differing lengths of these seven periods, the annual frequencies that emerge are clearly not indicative of any historical trend. Rather, we get the impression of a fluctuating pattern, perhaps suggesting a mild periodicity. When, however, we normalize for the number of nations in the system as well as the duration of the period, the downward trend reappears in column 5. And shifting to the annual frequency of national war involvements (as distinct from *systemic* war occurrences) in columns 6 and 7, we again find a discernible downward trend, but more fluctuating than that in column 5.

Of course, the *frequency* of international wars may not be the most valid indicator of historical patterns. More revealing may be the *amount* of war, measured in nation months (our indicator of magnitude) and in battle-connected deaths (or severity); from some points of view, the number of discrete wars is considerably less meaningful than their duration, the number of nations involved, and the fatalities that resulted. Thus, in Table 2, we find further evidence of a fluctuating pattern and again perhaps a very crude periodicity. That is, the periods that experience the most intense martial activity are generally followed by periods of somewhat less activity. When we normalize for the length of the period and size of the system (column 4), the pattern remains the same. Shifting to the severity (battle deaths) indicator in columns 5 and 6, we again see the rising levels from 1816 up through World War II, and then a dramatic decline. Notice also the temporary drop along all four of the magnitude and severity indicators during the period from 1870 to 1890. It should be emphasized that Tables 1 and 2 reflect the frequency, magnitude, and severity of wars *begun* in each period, rather than the amounts of war actually *underway*. Thus, the high magnitude and severity scores for the war in Vietnam (which began as a civil war, became an internationalized civil war in 1961, and then escalated to a full interstate war in 1965) show up only in the 1946-1965 period, when that bloody disaster began. No other period is affected by this coding rule, but it should be kept in mind.

TABLE 2. MAGNITUDE AND SEVERITY OF INTERNATIONAL WARS, 1816-1977

	1	2	3	4	5	6
Period	No. of Years	Avg. System Size	Nation Months of War Begun Per Nation	Nation Months of War Begun Per Year Per Nation	Battle Deaths Per Year From Wars Begun	Battle Deaths Per Year Per Nation From Wars Begun
1816−49	34	29	12.37	.47	9,997	359.3
1850−70	21	39	30.45	.80	37,076	998.7
1871−90	20	34	19.59	.59	18,280	564.0
1891−1914	24	42	37.82	.88	374,200	8525.8
1919−39	21	64	62.30	.98	789,400	12145.0
1946−65	20	95	67.20	.71	150,000	1579.0
1966−77	12	135	12.85	.09	9,551	70.1

Military Confrontations

Turning to a second indicator of martial activity, we now examine the incidence of military confrontations *short of war*. Here we are interested in all cases in which a system member threatens, displays, or actually uses military force while engaged in a serious dispute with another member of the system. Such actions range from verbal threats, mobilizations, and deployments, through seizures, border crossings, and bombardments.

Needless to say, the task of generating this particular data set is a formidable one. While research on *all* nation members of the system continues, we have completed our survey of the serious disputes only of the major powers.[2] These include not just confrontations between the majors themselves, but also those that minor powers were unlucky enough to engage in against majors. While this data set, then, is not quite comparable to those embracing the entire system, all of our investigations to date have shown that majors are involved in the bulk of the system's diplomatic and martial activities. Moreover, their interactions seem to set the tone for other nations' interactions during the various historic periods. Thus, we are fairly certain that major power disputes constitute a significant portion of all confrontations and that their patterns reflect those that obtain throughout the system.

The dispute data arrayed in Table 3 are a bit more difficult to interpret than those shown in the first two tables. More important than the number of confrontations that occurred in any period is the number that escalated into full scale war. Obviously, the most desirable international environment would

TABLE 3. FREQUENCY OF MILITARY CONFRONTATIONS INVOLVING AT LEAST ONE MAJOR POWER, 1816–1977

Period	1 No. of Years	2 Avg. System Size	3 Avg. No. Major Powers	4 No. of Confrontations	5 Avg. No. of Confrontations Per Year	6 No. of Confrontations Per Year Per Major	7 No. of Major Power Wars	8 Percent of Confrontations Ending In War	9 No. of Major vs Major Confrontations	10 No. of Major vs Major Wars	11 No. of Confrontations Per Year Per Nation
1816–49	34	29	5	29	.85	.17	6	21	8	0	.03
1850–70	21	39	5.5	34	1.60	.29	9	23	10	4	.04
1871–90	20	34	6	23	1.15	.19	2	6	4	0	.03
1891–1914	24	42	7.5	25	2.29	.14	7	17	17	2	.05
1919–39	21	64	6.5	51	2.43	.37	7	10	17	2	.04
1946–65	20	95	4.5	48	2.40	.53	4	8	16	1	.02
1966–77	12	135	5	24	2.00	.40	0	0	4	0	.01

be one with few confrontations and few wars. In the absence of such a prospect, however, we might prefer an environment in which confrontations continue to occur—or even increase—but in which few result in war, and our indicators are designed to pick up this distinction.

In column 3, we show the average number of major powers in the system during each period, a figure that ranges from 4.5 to 7.5, and columns 4, 5, and 6 report the number of military confrontations that occurred in each period, the average number per year, and the average number per year per major power. In column 7 is the number of major power wars, a figure that includes both major-major and major-minor wars; and this is followed (column 8) with the all-important indicator, the percentage of confrontations that escalated to war. Columns 9 and 10 are restricted to those confrontations and wars that involved major powers on both sides. The last column gives the number of confrontations per system member, reflecting the number of possible countries in the entire system with which a major power has the opportunity to join in highly disputatious behavior.

Reexamining this table, and especially column 5, we see that there have been more confrontations per year in the 20th century than in the 19th, with the Metternichian age appearing to be as crisis-free as the Austrian leader planned it to be. And this pattern holds even when we normalize for fluctuations in the number of major powers, as shown in column 6. While we are fairly confident in our data-gathering procedures, skeptics might ask whether this increase in the 20th century might not be a reporting error. After all, while a Soviet rocket rattle leaves traces in the media that cannot be ignored, perhaps our intrepid diplomatic historians have not picked up every comparable rumble emanating from Czar Nicholas I in the 1830s.

The data in columns 7 and 8 are more promising, however, and show that the probability of major power confrontations escalating into full scale war is generally lower in the 20th century than in the 19th. Indeed, since 1946, although we have averaged better than two major power confrontations per year, only four have led to war (Korea, Suez, Hungary, and Vietnam) and only one of those four involved a major on each side (Korea). And when we normalize for total system membership (column 11), our most recent period again appears to be the most pacific.

Civil Wars

If international war is not occurring more frequently or with more intensity than in the past, then perhaps the impression that we live in an age of conflict is because of the intranational wars that seem to abound in our time. Scarcely a day goes by without a news report of a bombing in Northern Ireland, a kidnapping in Argentina, or a raid in Angola. Many of these actions

CHALLENGES TO AMERICA

have international implications, since they may lead to informal political and economic involvement by other members of the system or, as in the case of war in Vietnam, full scale military intervention. Is it the incidence of civil unrest and war, then, that makes our time appear to be especially conflictful?

To answer this question, we have identified all of the civil wars experienced by system members since 1816 that resulted in at least 1,000 battle deaths per year. After a lengthy search through literally thousands of national histories, we found exactly 100 wars that met our coding criteria requirements. The severity threshold served, of course, to eliminate hundreds of coups and putsches from our purview, not to mention scores of riots, disturbances, and so forth.[3]

In Table 4, we again break down our 161-year span into several historic periods. Columns 3 and 4 offer the number of civil wars in each period, and the normalized civil wars per year, respectively. In column 5, we control for system size with civil wars per system member, and then normalize still further (column 6) with civil wars per member per year. Finally, in column 7, we show the percent of civil wars that were internationalized through the entry of an outside party on one or both sides.

Again, as with the international wars, there is no clear trend or periodicity in the civil war data, but the two types of war do seem to be related temporally to one another. Thus, we find, as earlier, the periods from 1816 to 1849 and from 1871 to 1890 to be more pacific than the 1850-1870 period separating them. And even more than with international wars, most of the

TABLE 4. FREQUENCY OF CIVIL WARS, 1816—1977

	1	2	3	4	5	6	7
Period	No. of Years	Avg. System Size	No. of Civil Wars Begun	No. of Civil Wars Begun Per Year	No. of Civil Wars Begun Per Nation	No. of Civil Wars Begun Per Year Per Nation	Percent of Civil Wars Internationalized
1816—49	34	29	12	.35	.41	.012	25
1850—70	21	39	15	.71	.38	.018	7
1871—90	20	34	6	.30	.18	.009	0
1891—1914	24	42	17	.71	.40	.017	18
1919—39	21	64	11	.52	.17	.008	18
1946—65	20	95	26	1.3	.27	.014	27
1966—77	12	135	11	.91	.08	.007	36

indicators show periods of intense civil war activity generally succeeded by periods of somewhat less activity. As might be expected, the years from 1946 through 1965 witnessed the rapid decolonization of European empires and the subsequent struggle for power within the new states, leading to many civil wars. When we control for system size (column 5), however, these years appear less warlike than the period before World War I or the span from 1816 to 1870. And while the past 12 years rank second on the number of civil wars per year, controlling for system size makes this period easily the lowest in terms of the frequency of civil wars. Finally, column 7 suggests a different story: third party intervention has been rather constant, with the low point (no interventions) during the Bismarckian period, but with the post-World War II figures even higher than that following the Napoleonic Wars.

In Table 5, we shift from the frequencies of civil war to its magnitude and severity, as we did for international war in Table 2. In columns 3 and 4 are nation months of civil war begun per year and per year per system member, and in columns 5 and 6 are battle deaths per year and battle deaths per year per system member. In general, the severity and magnitude data do not change our impressions of the amount of civil war activity in the various periods. The one glaring exception is in battle deaths during the most recent period; although the years from 1966 through 1977 rank second lowest on nation months per year per system member (column 4), they rank third highest on battle deaths per year per system member. Even more ominous is the ranking of all civil wars by severity in battle deaths (not shown here); 13 of the first 15 most severe civil wars were fought in the 20th century, eight of

TABLE 5. MAGNITUDE AND SEVERITY OF CIVIL WARS, 1816–1977

Period	1 No. of Years	2 Avg. System Size	3 Nation Months of War Per Year	4 Nation Months of War Per Year Per Nation	5 Battle Deaths Per Year	6 Battle Deaths Per Year Per Nation
1816–49	34	29	14.7	.51	2,828	97.5
1850–70	21	39	26.6	.70	135,650	3,478.2
1871–90	20	34	3.6	.10	2,200	64.7
1891–1914	24	42	11.2	.27	15,498	392.6
1919–34	21	64	14.7	.23	46,100	720.3
1946–65	20	95	55.1	.58	107,920	1,136.0
1966–77	12	135	29.5	.14	133,250	987.0

those 13 were fought since 1946, and three of those occurred since 1965 (Nigeria, Bangladesh, and Cambodia).

Our data also reveal that European states, especially in the 20th century, have not experienced as many major civil wars as nations in the Western Hemisphere and other parts of the developing world. Indeed, since 1917, only Russia, Hungary, Spain, and Greece suffered major civil wars; and since 1945, no civil war that resulted in more than 1,000 deaths per year has occurred in the Old World, unless one were to shift the 1956 war in Hungary from the international to the civil war category.

SUMMARIZING THE HISTORICAL DATA

Before we turn to the delicate matter of future levels of conflict, it is important that we try to make sense of the patterns that have obtained in the past. In the process, we might also lay to rest some of the more widely accepted notions about conflict and violence in the current international system. Turning first to these notions, we find three that enjoy wide popular support.

The most general suggests that there has been a steady upward climb in the amount of violent conflict during the past century and a half, with today's world more conflictful, violent, and dangerous than at any time since the Napoleonic or even the Thirty Years' Wars. Certainly the World Wars were more destructive than any that preceded them, and they were not only close together in time, but were followed all too quickly by the Korean and Vietnamese Wars, neither of which could be thought of as an antiseptic war of skirmish and maneuver. Nor can we overlook the incredible rise in the destructiveness and range of offensive weapons, or the dramatic increase in militant and organized dissatisfaction in every region of the world and in nations of all types at all levels of economic and political development. Another possible contribution to this general belief is that of the media; a greater percentage of political events, in more graphic form, is more widely disseminated in less time than ever before.

But let us look at the data and see whether there is "less there than meets the eye." Are we indeed operating under some serious misperceptions, or conversely, is humanity moving steadily along a road whose end looks like Armageddon? In Table 6, we assemble a number of the indicators that were first presented separately, and use them to rank the seven periods along eight distinct dimensions of conflict and then along a ninth composite rank dimension.

As we examine these figures, it is important to remember the ways in which they are normalized, and thus the "null model" against which our

TABLE 6. THE INDICATORS COMPARED BY RANK AND SCORE WITHIN EACH PERIOD, 1816–1977

Period	1 International Wars Begun Per Year Per Nation		2 Nation Months From International Wars Begun Per Year Per Nation		3 Battle Deaths From International Wars Begun Per Year		4 Civil Wars Begun Per Year Per Nation		5 Nation Months From Civil Wars Begun Per Year Per Nation		6 Battle Deaths From Civil Wars Begun Per Year Per Nation		7 Confrontations Per Year		8 Percent of Confrontations Ending in War		9 Standardized Scores
1816–49	2	.021	6	.47	6	359	1	.41	3	.51	6	98	7	.85	2	21	+.04
1850–70	1	.023	3	.80	4	999	3	.38	1	.70	1	3748	5	1.60	1	23	+.84
1871–90	3	.017	5	.59	5	564	5	.18	7	.10	7	65	6	1.15	6	6	–.51
1891–1914	4	.016	2	.88	2	8526	2	.40	4	.27	5	393	3	2.29	3	17	+.45
1919–39	5	.008	1	.98	1	12145	6	.17	5	.23	4	720	1	2.43	4	10	+.13
1946–65	7	.006	4	.71	3	1579	4	.27	2	.58	2	1136	2	2.40	5	8	–.10
1966–77	6	.006	7	.09	7	70	7	.08	6	.14	3	987	4	2.00	7	0	–.85

observations are conducted. If, for example, we assume that the "normal" amount of conflict or violence in the international system depends on the number of people on the face of the earth, or the number of nations, or the total number of subnational and extranational as well as national actors, we would normalize accordingly. Or, if, as some might suggest, our expected levels of conflict should reflect the number of possible *pairs* of protagonists, the denominator in our normalization formula would be even larger. The range of plausible null models is all too large, and we have selected the more conventional and obvious normalizing unit: the number of nations in the category under scrutiny. Parenthetically, if one chooses to generalize and compare on the basis of the non-normalized scores found in Tables 1 through 5, that, too, rests on an implied null model: that system size, population growth, or number of possible pairs, etc. should have *no effect* on the incidence of violence and conflict.

Turning, then, to Table 6, we find that the bad news has been rather exaggerated. On six of the eight normalized indicators, the latest period ranks lowest (seventh) or next to lowest (sixth) of all the periods since the Congress of Vienna. And on the standardized composite score, this most recent period is clearly the lowest in wars and confrontations with the greatest negative value; even the preceding post-World War II period is far from the most conflictful. Further, no matter how one looks at these normalized indicators, there is virtually no evidence of a secular trend—up or down—in any of the columns.

On the other hand, calculating our coefficient of concordance (Kendall's $W = .31$) suggests that the periods do have a degree of commonality. That is, those that are low on one dimension tend to be low on the others (such as 1816-1849, 1871-1890, and 1966-1977) and those that are high are generally high (such as 1850-1870).

This pattern leads us, in turn, to consider a second but different general belief that seems equally unfounded; that while international confrontations and wars have declined since World War II, civil wars have been on the rise. But columns 4, 5, and 6 in Table 6 clearly belie that impression. Not only do neither of the post-1945 periods match the 1850-1870 period in the frequency and magnitude of civil violence, but the most recent period ranks lowest or second lowest on two of these three indicators when we normalize for system size (and, of course, length of the period).

An important corollary of this finding is that the "substitutability hypothesis" is far from supported. That is, some have urged that when the nations are involved in civil wars, there will be a decline in international wars, and vice versa. The evidence points, rather, in the opposite direction, with the above-noted tendency for some periods to witness high amounts of *both* civil and international war and others to see relatively low levels of both. Apparently, then, international and civil wars rise and fall together, but whether these fluctuations are experienced by the same or different nations has not yet been determined. Nor are we prepared to say here whether the same conditions account for both.

A final generalization is similar to the previous one, and appears to be equally unfounded. It suggests that the recent past has seen a decline in only one form of international war—that between sovereign states—in parallel with a rise in imperial or colonial wars. That is, the conventional interstate war so typical of 19th century Europe has allegedly been replaced by the war of national liberation, in which a western industrial state is pitted against a third world nation whose people are either resisting the imposition of foreign control or are in the process of throwing off a previously imposed imperial yoke. This proposition stands only if some inconsistent and/or unconventional coding criteria are invoked. For example, Kende (1971 and 1977) identifies 97 wars in the period 1944-1969, but he invokes no criteria for inclusion that rest upon either a minimal number of casualties, the political status of the combatants, or the degree of combat reciprocity. These are indeed examples of armed violence, but many cannot be classified as war in the conventional meaning of the term, especially since some of the cases qualify only because of the intervention—often unopposed—of foreign forces in the domestic conflicts of third world nations. Such cases may be reprehensible, but that does not make them wars. Very similar problems arise with the classifications developed by Wallensteen (1973) in his excellent study of the 1920-1968 period, and by Bouthoul and Carrére (1976a) in their more sweeping inquiry into the challenge of war.[4]

In sum, we found no long range secular trend, and any cyclical pattern—in the precise sense of the word—is more apparent than real.[5] All three types of conflict rise and fall together, and the only clear trend involves that which may have begun with Hiroshima and Nagasaki and continues up to the present day. This latter point will, of course, be central to our discussion in the next section, where we offer some possible explanations and some very tentative forecasts.

These, then, are the patterns revealed by our systematic examination of the incidence of wars and confrontations since 1816. While these data are not only interesting in their own right, and will also play a crucial role in testing a number of theoretical models of the correlates and causes of war, our interest here is more pragmatic and immediate. But before we shift to the more interpretive and speculative mode, it is important to summarize in one place the limitations of the evidence adduced in this chapter.

While these analyses rest on a highly operational and carefully generated data base, covering the entire globe and a very long time period, they are nevertheless quite limited. The statistical tools used for this exercise were fairly primitive. More sophisticated ones might turn up patterns that have so far remained unnoticed. And our interperiod break points, while consistent with those most often used by diplomatic historians, could be deceptive. It is, for example, possible that by shifting the boundaries between conceptual, spatial, or temporal categories, we can markedly affect the number of cases falling into each, and thus, the possibility of an "unintended gerrymander" could be affecting our temporal distributions. Then there is the fact that all of our data are aggregated at the international system level, thus concealing some potentially interesting patterns at the regional and national levels of aggregation.

Finally, there is the most sensitive issue of all: the extent to which our coding rules themselves affect the results. For example, does the 1,000 battle death threshold exclude a large number of international or civil wars, and would a threshold of 500 or 750 lead to the inclusion of many more cases? On the basis of our investigations to date, the answer is negative, but one would want to examine all candidate cases as well as those that fell into the mini-war and military confrontation categories to be sure. Similarly, as we noted in discussing the data sets generated by Kende (1977) and Wallensteen (1973), one's theoretical orientation can indeed affect the content of one's classification criteria. No matter how meticulous their articulation and application, the substantive reasoning behind the coding rules can markedly shape the data sets that emerge. Hence the importance of explicit coding criteria and careful application; and we trust both have been attended to here.

INTERPRETATIONS AND CONTINGENT FORECASTS

With these methodological caveats made clear, we may more prudently turn to the kinds of forecasts permitted by the data base and the elementary analyses to which it was exposed. Bearing in mind the points made in our introduction, what forecasts, if any, are permitted by these empirical findings? First of all, there are no discernible long-range trends, and therefore little temptation to propose a simple extrapolation into the future. Are there, however, any shorter-range trends to which we might turn for guidance?

Here the evidence is relatively clear, because there is a steady if modest decline since the World War II epoch on many dimensions. Returning to Tables 1 and 2, we find fairly credible downward trends in the annual frequencies of war involvements per nation as well as nation months of war begun and battle deaths from war begun, whether we control for system size or not. Similarly, for military confrontations that involve one or more major powers (Table 3), there is a post-World War II decline in their annual frequency, as well as in those confrontations involving a major on each side. Moreover, there is the dramatic decline in the frequency with which they escalate to war, with only 8% doing so after World War II, and none since 1965.

Shifting from *inter*national violence to that found at the *intra*national level, there is also a general downward trend, but of much shorter duration. That is, the annual frequency of civil wars (Table 4) rose sharply (and not surprisingly) in the two decades following World War II, but has declined markedly in the decade since then; however, the number of civil wars that became internationalized via large-scale foreign intervention has risen. The data in Table 5 show the same pattern, with annual nation months of civil war begun, plus battle deaths from those wars, both rising after World War II and then declining over the past 12 years.

Thus, to the extent these trends of the past three decades offer grounds for prediction, we might expect that the decades ahead will show a gradual decline in the frequency and destructiveness of war. But, aside from the dangers of simple extrapolation, there is the other problem alluded to earlier: the rather rough, but visible, periodicity in these data over the entire 160-odd years. It will be recalled that on many of the indicators, the relative peacefulness of the Concert period gave way to the extreme violence of the 1850s and 1860s, followed by a general decline in martial activities in the 1870s and 1880s. Then we experienced general increases in those activities through World War I, a decline during the inter-war years, and increases again after World War II. Finally, we have the relative decline that we have already described.

In summary, we can examine the long range century-and-a-half trend and find little pattern, examine the short range trend of the past few decades and predict a continuing general decline, or examine the crude periodicity and predict an upsurge in international and civil war as the current decline "bottoms out." The point should be manifest: in war and many other social phenomena, there are indeed temporal regularities, but few of them are inexorable. As Lewis Richardson (1960) reminds us, the statistical regularities in international combat rest on the human failures of the past, and their continuation into the future rests on the assumption that people *still* will not "stop to think." Thus, any forecasts we make in this sector should be *contingent* and conditional forecasts (Singer, 1973), rather than unconditional ones.

Does it follow from this that all of our systematic research into the past is of little value for policy purposes? To the contrary, the sort of data generated and reported here can turn out to be quite valuable in the policy context, but not as the basis for any mechanical projection of trends or cycles into the future. Rather, their main value will be in the formulation and testing of alternative explanations for the incidence of global violence, which, of course, was the original purpose.[6] Thus, as our theoretical models are tested against these outcome data, and gradually become accurate enough to account for the fluctuations and distributions across time and space, we will increasingly be able to build contingent forecasts on explanatory models. And, of all the bases from which to make forecasts, the explanatory model that has been tested against both the constancies and the dynamics of history is the most reliable.

Having argued against inexorability, and suggested that the thoughtful application of scientific knowledge can help shape our future, let us at the same time recognize that certain historical processes are *not* particularly vulnerable to conscious human intervention. If, for example, the structure and culture of today's international system are appreciably dependent on decisions and accidents that occurred decades or centuries ago, some finite degree of variance in system change will be beyond our control now. But just as it is useful to know how much of our future we *can* shape, it is also useful to know how much of it lies beyond our control. While systematic (and, we hope, cumulative) research goes on, we must, of course, act on the basis of what we know now, and one of the things we know with some confidence is that a certain momentum inheres in some of the processes now unfolding in the global system. Let us, therefore, close with a brief and rather speculative discussion of such possibilities in the context of certain trends that seem to be quite vigorous today. Needless to say, we will go well beyond our data here, and many of our forecasts should be examined alongside those papers in this volume that consider similar dimensions in considerably greater depth.

One of the trends that seems particularly germane to prospects for conflict in the next decade or so is that of weapons technology. In the major power stratum, the nuclear-missile combination gives so dramatic an advantage to the offense vis-a-vis the defense that almost all concerned consider strategic war an act of madness, engaged in only by accident or in desperation. Because the exotic defenses against either the warhead or the delivery vehicle—such as laser beams or magnetic force fields—seem unlikely to modify the offense-defense ratios in appreciable ways, the downward trend in major versus major war should continue. As our Table 3 data show, the major powers do continue to go to the brink, but less and less against one another, and so far they have always managed to halt the escalation process short of war. The fact that the 20 major versus major confrontations since V-J Day have gone to neither conventional nor nuclear war (except for China's "volunteers" who intervened in Korea as General MacArthur approached the Yalu) strongly suggests that the nuclear deterrent, as clumsy and fragile as it is, seems to exercise an inhibiting effect.

Another war-inhibiting trend that seems likely to continue is that of increased interdependence, which is operating in two sectors. One is implied in the above discussion, with the major powers becoming involved in a large fraction of minor versus minor confrontations, taking on a patron-client role, and thence exercising a restraining role through the granting and withholding of military and economic assistance. Since the missile crisis of 1962, the annual frequency of minor versus minor wars has increased slightly (Table 1), but given the increased number of actors, the normalized frequency has actually declined. More important, as Table 2 indicates, there has been a rather dramatic drop in the absolute *amount* of war as reflected in nation months and battle deaths. The second sector in which interdependence seems to be inhibiting international war is that of resources and trade. The evidence is less clear here, but because most conventional wars occur between neighbors, and because proximity is usually correlated with economic interdependence (and will probably be more so in the decades ahead), this inhibitory effect may well continue for some time.

A third factor at work is that of nation-building, and while this *can* be a source of conflict—over territory, seaports, resources, and prestige, for example—the inhibitory mechanisms are far from negligible. It is, for example, one thing for third world elites to engage in "wars" of words and maneuvers, and quite another to enter into sustained military combat with a neighbor's forces; since 1816, for the major powers at least, only about 10% of military confrontations ended in wars. With the steadily rising expectations and demands for material improvement, their citizens may enjoy the drama of parades, air shows, and some judicious sabre-rattling, but there seems to be increasing resistance to heavy military spending and to foreign military adventure. The significant exception appears to be Cuba, but as something of a client state for the U.S.S.R., much of the bill is footed by Moscow. And while the Cuban economy may be headed for trouble, the convergence between expectation and performance is—for the moment—sufficient for domestic stability. More typical would be Egypt, whose elites and public show every sign of turning away from military adventure and toward domestic development.

Closely related to this trend in the third world is the decline in ideology, by which we mean the tendency to take literally the political scriptures of the various founding fathers. One consequence of this is the tendency to view foreign conflicts in more pragmatic and less Manichean terms, thus reducing the frequency with which confrontations should escalate to war. Of course, this trend began even sooner in the first and second worlds, even though it may not have been widely noticed. Just as Soviet or Czechoslovakian factory workers have been cynical about their required courses in Marxism-Leninism for several decades, citizens in the West have gradually lost their appetite for a holy war against "Godless, Communist atheism," thanks in part to their costly war involvements in Algeria, Korea, Suez, and Indochina. A particularly compelling reflection of this trend at several strata and in many sectors of the global system is the recently consummated trade pact between China and Japan. Despite the long history of conflict, exploitation, and war—as well as ideological opposition—economic realities and diplomatic pragmatism seem to have taken precedence.

Having examined these data sets, and the relatively reassuring inferences they permit, let us return to our earlier point regarding the distinction between noncontingent and contingent forecasts. Most of the above inferences are, of course, noncontingent; they essentially assume that not much will happen to interfere with a continuing decline in the frequency of warfare. But, to reiterate, it would be quite irresponsible to rest our forecasts on simple extrapolation, and even more irresponsible to suggest that a nation's foreign and military policies be based on such extrapolations.

That is, even while there seem to be several trends that promise a decreasing likelihood of war, there are certain countertrends whose portent is much less reassuring. Most dramatic of these is, of course, that of military spending. Global expenditures for preparedness stood at about 107 billion U.S. dollars (1974 prices) in 1960, at about 201 billion in 1970, and by 1975, the figure was approximately 324 billion (Sivard, 1977). Even allowing for the dramatic growth in the world's population, the per capita military expenditure rose from 35 to 55 to 81 dollars over those three time points.

An attentive observer of the U.S. foreign policy scene over the past three decades would certainly note a rather bizarre pattern. That is, the dominant line on arms control and arms reduction has essentially been that articulated by such respected analysts as Morgenthau (1948) and Kennan (1957). Starkly stated, these shrewd theoreticians held that armaments are (a) merely the manifestation of political tension; (b) that this tension is a result of unresolved "political" differences; and (c) that such tension will decline as political differences are successfully negotiated. By extension, they suggested further that (a) these political differences can be negotiated prior to any meaningful arms reductions; (b) tensions can therefore be reduced prior to arms reduction; (c) arms reductions cannot be successfully negotiated until tensions are markedly reduced; and (d) once tensions *are* reduced, arms reduction will easily follow. The events of the past three decades show that these arguments were essentially incorrect. That is, we have seen some political settlement and some tension reduction in East-West relations; this is clearly the meaning of détente. But the final and most critical assumption in this scenario has been clearly refuted. There have, admittedly, been some arms *control* agreements, but arms *reduction*—as some of us predicted long ago (Singer, 1958) and have often reiterated since (Singer, 1962 and 1970)—just could not be expected.

Why should this be? The explanation is simple, except to those who are naive enough to believe that nations acquire and add to weapons stockpiles solely in response to external threats. While that external threat is essential to the initial moves and can help keep the momentum in the later stages of an armament race, the arm-for-defense-only model is woefully incomplete. The allocation of resources to preparedness, beyond certain minimal levels, is escalatory in its effects at home as well as abroad. First of all, each increment in military expenditure enhances the credibility of those in the *opposing nation* who claim that an external threat exists, and this enhances the likelihood of increased expenditures in that nation. Second, each such increment carries with it a modest—but devastatingly cumulative—redistribution of economic power *within* the nation, thus weakening the forces of restraint and prudence. In the end, those who advocate and benefit from bloated defense budgets become the "realists," and those who oppose this kind of "realism" are classified as soft and irresponsible, if not lacking in political virility and patriotism.

The extent to which this has occurred in the U.S. and the U.S.S.R., with the burden of proof shifted from the hawks to the doves, is not readily measured, but a content analysis of foreign policy debates or newspaper editorials or discussions on defense budgets would almost certainly reflect such a shift during these past three decades. Another reflection of this overall trend might be the size and budget of governmental and private organizations engaged in research, planning, or negotiations on arms reduction or disarmament; in the U.S. and the U.S.S.R. this has hardly been a "growth industry" when compared to the military establishment. Other indicators come to mind, but for now we will leave this as a matter of judgment.

Thus, it seems evident that the peace forces in the world are not exactly having their way, and that "preparedness" programs serve not only to misallocate resources within nations, but also to generate tensions between nations. Further, they absorb energies and funds that might help break the log-jam of economic development in the third world. Perhaps most dangerous of all, in the longer run, is the extent to which they inhibit efforts to develop, articulate, or experiment with policies that might lead to certain essential modifications in the global environment.

All of this leads, in turn, to consideration of a menacing *non*trend: the lack of real movement toward the disarmament of the world's nations and a concomitant growth in the political efficacy of supranational institutions. Despite the occasional international agreement on arms control—usually intended to make the system less prone to accidental war—little has happened to reverse the trends in vertical and lateral proliferation of nuclear and conventional weapon systems. And for the reasons outlined earlier, as well as the destabilizing effects of much of the new weapons technology, this leaves us with a system that is fundamentally as war-prone as it has been since the Congress of Vienna. Whether it is with conventional or nuclear weapons (assuming the difference is not obliterated by the deployment of enhanced radiation warheads or their miniaturization), whether it involves major powers or minors, and whether the theater is central Europe or Africa, war remains all too likely.

For the United States, the options are several, and may be crudely classified as passive, provocative, or adaptive. The first, or passive, option is that which has been followed for most of the post-World War II era by the U.S. and more erratically by the U.S.S.R. It consists essentially of accepting the strategic and other characteristics of the international environment, paying lip service to the need for system transformation, maintaining a military arsenal that is too large for strategic deterrence and too small for a credible first strike threat, and generally responding to external opportunities and threats in accord with the current distribution of power and interests at home. Remaining with this option seems an effective way of preserving the century-and-a-half-long tradition of from five to nine international wars every decade (Table 1) until the final one in the series.

The second, or provocative, option is that which has been advocated by an important domestic coalition that has not been strong enough to have its way nor weak enough to be ignored. With a few breaks at home (such as continuing economic dislocation, renewed racial/religious conflict) or abroad (such as increased Soviet bellicosity, major U.S. setbacks in the Third World), this coalition could move into a dominant role. With that might well come an even more rapid arms buildup, more vigorous military intervention, a more intense ideological assault on the enemies of the moment, and a general propensity to exploit the contemporary international environment. Given the physical impossibility of regaining the strategic and industrial preponderance enjoyed by the U.S. in the late 1940s, this strategy could readily produce a sharp upward trend in both the frequency and the severity of international war in the years ahead.

The third basic option would reflect an awareness of the international system's fundamental flaws and set about modifying the environment in a vigorous but incremental fashion. Recognizing the extent to which major power policies can worsen or improve—as well as perpetuate—the system's structure and culture, the U.S. could take a variety of initiatives in several sectors. Most pressing would be, in our judgment, the military-security sector, with economic and cultural initiatives playing a supporting role.

To shift from the passive to the adaptive option, while foreclosing the provocative option, will require (as Holsti and Rosenau point out in this volume) a conscious political decision on the part of America's elites. But there is little evidence of even the mildest tendencies in that direction. Our diplomatic, economic, and military policies remain as conventional and opportunistic as they have been since the Spanish-American War. Despite occasional initiatives, the central tendency has been to follow in the footsteps of those other major powers whose ascendancy and decline we have witnessed with fatal regularity.

In sum, the legitimacy and the expectancy of war remains all too firmly embedded in the structure and culture of the system and its nations, despite the modestly encouraging economic, technological, and psychological trends that we have noted here. Unless and until war and the preparation for war—psychic as well as material—are consciously rejected, all of these countervailing tendencies remain vulnerable to quick reversal. Most of the more visible auguries were equally promising in June of 1914, only weeks before the guns of August shattered the fragile structure of peace. For American foreign policy then, building a new political and security order will be the crucial test, but the omens are far from encouraging.

NOTES

1. We deal here with only 100 of the 103 international wars. Because we do not examine the years from 1915 through 1918 and from 1940 through 1945, three qualifying wars are omitted from the analyses: the extra-systemic wars between Russia and her nationalities beginning in 1917; between France and her colony in Vietnam in 1945; and between Holland and her colony in Indonesia in the same year. Conversely, we include the following wars that were continuing as of December 31, 1977: the two seccessionist wars against Ethiopia; the Cambodian (Kampuchea)-Vietnamese border war; and the Moroccan-Mauritanian war against the Polisario Front in the Sahara.

2. The major powers and their years of tenure are: England (1816-present); France (1816-1940 and 1945-present); Germany/Prussia (1816-1918 and 1925-1945); Austria-Hungary (1816-1918); Italy (1860-1943); Russia (1816-1917 and 1922-present); China (1950-present); Japan (1895-1945); and the United States (1899-present).

3. Because we do not consider here the period during which the Two World Wars were being fought, the following qualifying civil wars are omitted from the analyses: Russia, 1918-1921, and Greece, 1944-1949. Further, we do include two civil wars that were continuing as of December 31, 1977: those in the Philippines and Angola. It is also worth noting that there were civil wars in some of the nations that did not qualify early as sovereign system members, and hence our 19th century figures are accordingly lower than some might expect.

4. Other compilations that should be compared are Woods and Baltzly, 1915; Wood, 1968; and Bloomfield and Leiss, 1969.

5. If we define periodicity in terms of peaks and valleys of approximate magnitude, occurring at more or less equal intervals, we find no evidence for such a claim. Even using spectral analysis methods, which are explicitly designed to *find*, no less confirm, any clear cyclical patterns, we turned up nothing of significance.

6. This theoretical and empirical work continues apace; much of it has already been reported in the scholarly literature, and many of those articles will be assembled in several anthologies scheduled to appear in 1978 and 1979.

REFERENCES

ARON, R. (1954). The century of total war. Garden City, N.Y.: Doubleday.

ASCH, S.E. (1952). Social psychology. Englewood Cliffs, N.J.: Prentice-Hall.

BLOOMFIELD, L., and LEISS, A. (1969). Controlling small wars. New York: Knopf.

BOUTHOUL, G., and CARRÉRE, R. (1976a). Le defi de la guerre. Paris: PUF.

——— (1976b). "La violence mondiale en 1975." Etudes Polemologiques, 20-21:49-74.

CHAMBERS, F.P., HARRIS, C.P., and BAYLEY, C.C. (1950). This age of conflict. New York: Harcourt Brace.

ELLIOT, J. (ed.) (1891). The debates in the several state conventions on the adoption of the Federal Constitution. 2nd ed. Philadelphia: Author.

HELMER, O. (1973). The systematic use of expert judgement in operations research. Santa Monica: Rand.

deJOUVENAL, B. (1967). The art of conjecture. New York: Basic Books.

KAHN, H., and WIENER, A. (1967). The year 2000. New York: Macmillan.

KENDE, I. (1971). "Twenty-five years of local wars." Journal of Peace Research, 8(1):5-22.

——— (1977). "Dynamics of war, arms trade, and of military expenditure." Paper presented at the Armament, Tension, and War Symposium, Helsinki, September.

KENNAN, G. (1957). Hearings, U.S. Senate Subcommittee on Control and Reduction of Armaments, Part II. Washington, D.C.: U.S. Government Printing Office.

MAY, E.R. (1973). "Lessons" of the past: Uses and misuses of history in American foreign policy. New York: Oxford University Press.

MORGENTHAU, H.J. (1948). Politics among nations. New York: Knopf.

MYDANS, C., and MYDANS, S. (1968). The violent peace. New York: Atheneum.

NICOLSON, H. (1961). The Congress of Vienna. New York: Viking.

RICHARDSON, J.D. (ed.) (1904). A compilation of the messages and papers of the Presidents, 1789-1902. Washington, D.C.: Washington Post Co.

RICHARDSON, L. (1960). Statistics of deadly quarrels. Chicago: Quadrangle.

ROSECRANCE, R. (1963). Action and reaction in world politics: International systems in perspective. Boston: Little Brown.

———, ALEXANDROFF, A., HEALY, B., and STEIN, A. (1974). Power, balance of power, and status in nineteenth century international relations. Beverly Hills, Cal. Sage.

SINGER, J.D. (1958). "Threat perception and the armament-tension dilemma." Journal of Conflict Resolution, 2 (March):90-105.

——— (1962). Deterrence, arms control, and disarmament. Columbus: Ohio State University Press.

——— (1970). "The outcome of arms races; a policy problem and a research approach." Proceedings of the International Peace Research Association, Third General Conference, 2:137-46.

——— (1973). "The peace researcher and foreign policy prediction." Peace Science Society (International) Papers, 21:1-4.

——— and SMALL, M. (1972). The wages of war, 1816-1965: A statistical handbook. New York: Wiley.

SIVARD, R.L. (1977). World military and social expenditures, 1977. Leesburg, Va.: WMSE.

WALLENSTEEN, P. (1973). Structure and war: On international relations, 1920-1968. Stockholm: Raben and Sjogren.

WILSON, J.H. (1977). "Foreign policy trends since 1920." Society for Historians of American Foreign Relations Newsletter, 8 (3):1-17.

WOOD, D. (1968). Conflict in the twentieth century. Adelphi Papers, 48. London: Institute for Strategic Studies.

WOODS, F.A., and BALTZLY, A. (1915). Is war diminishing? Boston: Houghton Mifflin.

Chapter 5

RESOURCE POLITICS AND U.S. FOREIGN POLICY

CHARLES F. DORAN
Rice University

1973 was a critical year for U.S. foreign policy not so much because it marked the effective beginning of cartel politics and resource pricing controlled by producer governments, but because it signaled the end for the United States of an era of comparative resource independence. In fact, cartel politics obtains its current great significance for foreign policy only in the context of larger U.S. resource dependence. Resource dependence delineates an entirely new environment in which various commercial issues impact significantly on U.S. foreign policy options and strategies. The importance of petroleum to the world economy and its low capacity for substitution (supply inelasticity) has undoubtedly influenced the dimensions of its price effects. But many observers (e.g., Bergsten, 1974) see petroleum as a precursor of shortages, price hikes, and similar if perhaps less severe politico-economic consequences in other resource areas as well. This chapter examines the emergence and inescapable implications of this new linkage between U.S. foreign policy and resource availability in the context of three interrelated questions.

First, will it be possible for the United States to continue to obtain one-quarter to one-third of the total resources consumed annually by the

EDITORS' NOTE: This paper was first submitted for review in January 1978. The version published here was received in April 1978.

world economy even though the United States possesses only a declining 6% of the world's population? Contained within this question are numerous issues both normative and empirical. For example, the issue must be considered whether such disparate magnitudes of consumption across countries are ethically justifiable (Tucker, 1971; Cohen, 1973). Likewise, is the new distribution of commercial and political power likely to support continued high levels of consumption occurring primarily in one sector of the world economy, and constrained production levels for certain commodities in another (Nordhaus, 1973)? The causal issue of how disparate patterns of consumption emerge and are sustained (Lewis, 1974) also warrants analytic and ideological debate. Thus, an answer to the principal question regarding the ability of the United States to sustain its standard of living based on high resource consumption requires the further examination of this series of subordinant issues (Garvey, 1972; Enthoven and Freeman, 1973).

Second, what is the appropriate mix for the United States of foreign and domestic resource supply? In other words, to what extent should the United States (whatever its relative level of consumption) attempt to rely on imports for the bulk of its natural resources? This question suggests that the society enjoys room for choice. It implies that government policy can and ought to affect the way in which the world marketplace allocates resources among nations. It suggests that should the U.S. Government attempt to rely more heavily on domestically produced resources, such reserves inside the territorial jurisdiction of the United States already exist or could be discovered at reasonable cost and within an adequate time-frame. Conversely, this question also implies that, if the United States were to rely more heavily on foreign sources of petroleum and nonfuel minerals, other governments would be willing to sell these commodities at acceptable prices. The logic of this question takes us directly to a third question relevant to foreign policy.

To what extent will the resource demands placed on Third World countries by advanced industrial nations (whatever the level of that demand and whatever the division between internal and external supply) lead to greater world tension (Kemp, 1978) and perhaps to resource wars? Is violent conflict a likely outcome of growing resource scarcity and the scramble to obtain access to dwindling reserves of precious materials? Appropriate perhaps is an analogy to the late 19th century in which Europeans rushed to colonize the remaining areas of Africa and Asia in hopes of expanding the domestic power base of the rising nation-state. Today conflict might stem from the competition to divide and annex portions of the seabed, or from imperialist rivalries among advanced industrial states intent upon "guaranteeing" access to mineral rights in semideveloped regions. Military intervention calculated to protect the trading rights of socialist states is a possibility, just as is intervention by capitalist democracies to defend the interests of private foreign investors (Rosenau, 1969). But how likely is it that the resource-scarcity problem per se will act as a catalyst for worldwide grievances, frustration, and ultimately violent conflict (Choucri, Laird and Meadows, 1972)?

American foreign policy is thus seen as both a dependent and independent variable in the assessment of resource politics. It is a dependent variable in the sense that the resource environment impacts on U.S. policies through increased commercial competition abroad by other industrial nations for energy; through rejection of free trade principles and adoption of cartel strategies by some Third World governments; through shifts in the role and outlook of multinational corporations; and through increased interventionist activity by the Soviet Union and other advanced industrial governments in parts of the world otherwise free of a foreign military presence. American foreign policy is also an independent variable, however, in that it helps shape the international resource environment: the United States is the single largest consumer of raw materials; it can apply or ignore domestic measures to conserve resources; it can expand or contract domestic production of various resources through tax policies and incentives; and it can act as a moderator or a stimulant to the international political rivalries possibly associated with resource usage. American foreign policy is thus both an actor and a target, a stimulus and a response (McGowan, 1975), in each of the senses addressed by our three resource questions. Hence, these questions lie at the core of the new foreign policy environment of resource dependence and are its inescapable challenge.

WHITHER U.S. RESOURCE CONSUMPTION?

In a relatively short span of history, the United States built the largest economy in the world, and achieved one of the highest standards of living of any nation in part because it was rich in natural resources and has consumed minerals and energy avariciously. Unlike the native Indian population, which in general respected "ecological limits," the new Americans took as quickly as possible what was available for the taking. While soil and timber were among the most important resources to the colonists of the 18th century, iron, coal, and water power soon replaced them as critical elements of the economy in the 19th century. Growth in the consumption of some of the standard metals and energy, as Figure 1 reveals, enabled the country to expand its power base and to twice defend its security in the first half of the 20th century, establishing American foreign policy at the center of the Western alliance system by 1950.

Figure 1: ANNUAL U.S. CONSUMPTION OF ENERGY, ALUMINUM AND
MAGNESIUM 1950-1974

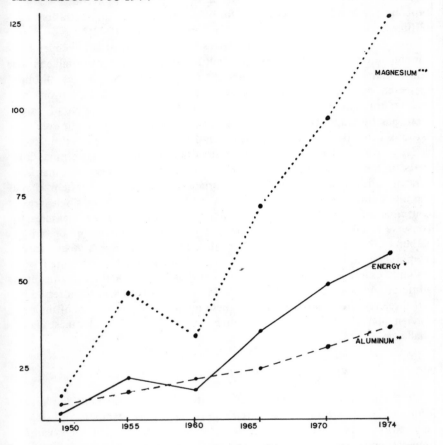

*in millions of barrels per day of oil equivalent. Source: Joint Congressional Com-
mittee on Atomic Energy Report (1973), "Understanding the National Energy Dilemma," Center for Strategic & International Studies.

** in 100,000s of short tons. Source: U.S. Fact Book, 1976.

***in thousands of short tons. Source: U.S. Fact Book, 1976.

High rates of resource consumption have been important to the American
people for at least two reasons. First, this level of consumption has under-
written the material prosperity enjoyed so broadly (but not universally) by
Americans. Second, national defense has absorbed large quantities of steel,

copper, aluminum, and nickel, which has provided security for the United States and its allies throughout the 20th century. Although international cost-sharing seldom reflects those benefits fully, much of the increase in energy and metals consumption has contributed to the defense of people living outside American borders.

As of 1973, American industry was processing 40% of the lead, 28% of the nickel, 32% of the tin, 18% of the tungsten, 42% of the aluminum, and one-third of the petroleum produced in that year worldwide. Consumption of these materials over the past 40 or so years has increased at similarly high percentage rates: steel (2.4), aluminum (4.3), and petroleum (4.5) (Committee on Resources and Man, 1969). Yet by the mid-1970s U.S. population growth actually fell beneath 1% per year—among the lowest growth rates in the world. Total U.S. population amounted to less than 6% of the people currently inhabiting the earth. Thus, when compared to the way in which the majority of the world's population lives, the disparity between relatively small population size and relatively large resource consumption is matched only by the disparity in wealth between the United States and the rest of the world.

Whether the disparity in consumption levels is ethically defensible is both a function of how these statistics are interpreted and which value preferences one brings to the argument. Perhaps because nationalism has been a stronger force in the 20th century than other political ideologies, socialism has not been practiced globally. Instead, all nations (communist as well as capitalist) have struggled to amass as large a fraction of the total global product as they are able. Revolutions fought on behalf of the elimination of internal inequalities of income and privilege seem ludicrous on the *international plane* where these same societies appear to reject such principles.

Liberal political thought, on the other hand, has sought to redistribute income incrementally, reforming the structure of the international system a step at a time. But the measure of redistribution which has occurred via this mechanism is modest since most advanced industrial governments (certainly the United States) have not even approached the 1% of GNP threshold posited as the UNCTAD assistance goal. Those governments like France, moreover, that have approached the goal have often tied the assistance to their own exports, thereby using aid as a kind of export subsidy rather than as a true redistributive instrument. Others have found the process of getting aid to the people who need it most inside the recipient countries an exercise in frustration. Thus, in the absence of other more effective income equalization, it is not surprising that enormous disparities in consumption levels across countries still remain.

But even when we consider the United States relative to other advanced industrial countries, we note a disparity in the proneness to consume. In Japan, the emphasis has been on growth in the export sector, savings, and investment rather than on consumption; and in the Soviet Union consumption has been overwhelmed by emphasis on growth in heavy industry and military spending. The American consumer is thus still the envy of the world's rich as well as its hungry. Just as they have often encouraged industrial growth instead of greater income equality, Western economists (who often have been reluctant to discuss values) have implicitly encouraged this sort of consumption.

Resource waste, for example, has frequently been treated as merely an ethical notion without economic content. Waste cannot be eliminated in the absence of a loss of efficiency according to this argument. Yet by defining the economic system broadly enough to include the true social costs and the "opportunity" costs of certain behavior, the elimination of waste may have a positive economic benefit without loss of efficiency. For example, the clear-cutting of timber in such a fashion that soil erosion occurs is wasteful in a sense that other equally efficient techniques of harvesting timber might not be. Carelessness and thoughtlessness may cause waste because of the imperfect transmission of information. But waste can also stem from what Veblen labeled "conspicuous consumption," a practice which is doubly open to challenge in a society which fails to meet the needs of all its citizens on the one hand and faces presumed resource limits on the other.

Possibly the greatest ethical issue underlying the consumption of nonrenewable resources, however, concerns intergenerational access (Pearce, 1976; Vousden, 1973). If Americans persist in driving cars that get 12 miles per gallon of gasoline instead of the 24 which is technically feasible without loss of efficiency or mobility, we must consider the social consequences for a future generation lacking equal access to the gasoline which has been so wantonly consumed. If one can demonstrate (as I think possible on theoretical grounds) that the use of gasoline today for the status associated with driving a large car deprives a future generation of petroleum which might be used, for example, to develop new pharmaceutical products (not yet envisioned perhaps by the innovation process) having major health value, Americans may regret having "wasted" a precious resource (Institute for Contemporary Studies, 1977; Vernon, 1976). The old economic norm that one exploits the most cost-efficient resource first and less efficient resources thereafter applies perfectly only in a universe which is technologically omniscient.

Such questions of resource ethics apply directly to U.S. foreign policy today in that of the 19 titular members of the International Energy Agency, the United States ranks last in terms of its ability to apply conservation techniques to energy consumption (deCarmoy, 1977), although the United States ranks highest in terms of per capita energy consumption and thus presumably in terms of the potential to find imaginative and fruitful applications of conservation measures. Lacking much of an energy conservation program, the United States has heretofore further undermined its credibility as a leader in terms of energy policy among the consumer nations. Policy makers must recognize that ethical questions of resource use can in fact have direct influence on aspects of the nation's foreign policy.

We must now move from the ethical examination of the high resource consumption question to the behavioral question of whether such levels of resource usage can in actuality be sustained. Because this issue is a function of the cost of resource extraction and refining, we must consider the possibility of long-term shifts in these costs. Rapidly declining stocks of high-grade minerals would be reflected in rapidly rising costs of extraction, for example, and hence in problems of maintaining a high U.S. standard of living (which is in part a function of the availability of cheap natural resources).

Table 1 shows the results of an analysis of the resource cost question for the United States in the period 1870-1957 (Barnett and Morse, 1963). The results do not all point in the same direction. Forestry products, for example, reveal rising costs as the index of productivity declines 15% over the period 1919-1957. In general, however, the index of productivity shows no decline in the extractive industries. What this must mean is that technological innovation has been sufficiently dynamic and economies of scale have been sufficiently prevalent so that despite the exhaustion of higher grade ore deposits, the cost of extraction has not increased. These cost considerations would tend to reinforce the current level of U.S. minerals consumption, although the U.S. percentage share may decline for reasons of a smaller relative population and increasing foreign bargaining power.

TABLE 1. EFFICENCY OF RESOURCE EXTRACTION –
LABOR-CAPITAL INPUT PER UNIT OF EXTRACTIVE
OUTPUT (1929=100)

	Total Extractive	Agriculture	Minerals	Forestry
1870–1900	134	132	210	59
1919	122	114	164	106
1957	60	61	47	90

SOURCE: Barnett and Morse, 1963:8.

Lest we accept these results as definitive, however, a number of qualifications must be borne in mind. First, the bulk of the improvement in productivity occurred in the early part of the period when breakthroughs in ore concentration, processing, and transfer were greatest. Furthermore, these were largely mechanical innovations and since machines have virtually replaced all human labor the limits to this form of enhanced efficiency have probably been reached. For this reason, costs could thus begin to rise abruptly. Second, the index itself is highly generalized and may include some minerals showing the same pattern as that of forestry. Concerning such commodities the United States may experience increasing cost pressures and constraints. Third, we need to know more regarding the relationship between resource use and the growth both of the *economy as a whole* and of *population:* If the GNP and the U.S. population continue to grow rapidly and

Figure 2: INDEX OF U.S. RESOURCE CONSUMPTION RELATIVE TO GNP (1950 = 100)

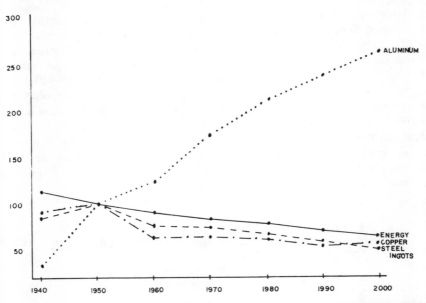

*Data in Figures 2 and 3 are based upon medium level projections of growth in GNP, man year productivity and consumption expenditures extrapolating beyond the 1930-1960 U.S. experience as published in Landsberg, Fischman, and Fisher, 1963:293-332, 508-515. Population projections are straight-line regression estimates using data drawn from *World Population (1975): Recent Demographic Estimates for the Countries and Regions of the World*, U.S. Department of Commerce, Bureau of the Census, 1976.

continue to use resources at the same rate as in the past, then the U.S. demand for resources will surely remain large. On the other hand, if the ratios of resource size to population size and to GNP become more favorable (that is, decline), while the growth rates in these primary variables themselves begin to fall off, the U.S. appetite for minerals and energy may shrink. Data in Figure 2 and 3 test this hypothesis.

Figures 2 and 3 reveal three important observations that impinge on the question of future U.S. resource consumption. First, for some resources the per dollar GNP usage (Figure 2) is actually projected to decline. This is true for energy, steel, and copper. Thus the rate of consumption of these materials is growing more slowly than the rate of increase of the GNP. Interpreted in the context of our question regarding the maintenance of U.S. consumption levels, we must conclude from this evidence that pressure on resources is likely to decline somewhat relative to the growth of the economy. If the economy itself grows more slowly, resource pressures will further decline. Stemming from a shift toward services and away from heavy goods production, this finding with respect to changing usage ratios should not be underestimated in its positive consequences for resource politics.

Figure 3: INDEX OF U.S. RESOURCE CONSUMPTION RELATIVE TO POPULATION

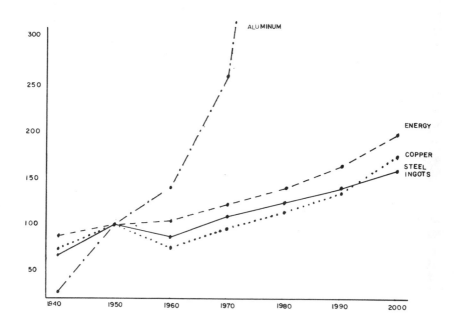

Second, and conversely, however, in none of the four cases that we have looked at has per capita resource use (Figure 3) dropped appreciably. While there was initial evidence for such a pattern in the 1950-1960 period in both steel and copper, the projected results suggest increasing usage thereafter. If a diminishing marginal returns effect is operative (as has been predicted for energy following the five-fold price increases), such an effect appears to be washed out in the longer-term projected results. One must conclude from these scattered per capital resource usage results that Americans are not likely to use fewer resources on an individual basis in the future; rather, they are likely to use greater amounts. As long as population continues to grow the combination of larger population size and greater per capita usage will have an even more serious impact. Hence the per capita resource consumption results tend to offset the brighter previous picture of falling ratios of resource usage per unit of GNP.

Third, some commodities may have to be treated as special cases. Aluminum appears to be one such anomaly. The index of aluminum consumption per dollar of GNP is projected to rise over two and one-half times between 1950 and the year 2000. This amounts to an increase in per capita terms for the same period of over eight times the 1950 base value. Such enormous increases in projected aluminum consumption indicate that the politics surrounding this commodity may be somewhat different than that for the other minerals. One would anticipate that with this kind of projected demand bauxite production would be quite susceptible to cartel pressures (Oppenheim and Moran, 1977). One would also assume that substitution away from aluminum, especially in a period of high energy costs (aluminum production is very energy intensive), would become more likely.

In a general sense these findings on resource consumption relative to GNP and population size give rise respectively to hope and concern. The findings are hopeful because of what they suggest with regard to the changing nature of an economy which uses resources less intensively. But the findings are of concern because Americans are predicted to use greater amounts of resources on an individual basis. Moreover, some commodities such as aluminum may create unique political problems because of the unusually high demand for this type of output.

Having established that greater amounts of future resources are likely to be needed, we must address the key question of the next section, namely, from where are these greater amounts of resources to come? If the United States is able to meet its needs principally from domestic stocks, the consequences for U.S. foreign policy are likely to be quite different than if it must obtain the bulk of its future resources from abroad.

WHOSE RESOURCES WILL THE UNITED STATES USE?

More than two decades ago, the famous Paley report (President's Materials Policy Commission, 1952) examined the relationship between resource use and U.S. foreign policy. It stressed several points.

With the exception of petroleum, it correctly forecast only moderate price increases for raw materials over the period 1952-1972. It also recommended that stockpiling and other techniques be used to ensure defense preparedness. Another important policy recommendation was that the United States should increasingly rely on foreign sources of raw materials. Part of the reasoning here was to create markets in which developing nations could sell raw materials, thereby expanding their own national incomes and growth opportunities. Reliance by the United States on external supply was looked upon perhaps ironically as a means of improving international relations.

The data in Table 2 on external raw materials supply reveals one overwhelming trend. Over the period 1930-1960 the United States has become far more foreign resource dependent. Judged by past behavior, the United States is likely to obtain the increasing amounts of minerals and energy it needs from regions which have been less developed industrially and less exploited in resource terms, namely regions outside the United States. In all instances cited including iron ore, bauxite, copper, lead, and zinc, reported levels of

TABLE 2. U.S. IMPORTS AS A PERCENTAGE OF APPARENT CONSUMPTION OF FIVE MAJOR METALS 1930–1960

	Iron Ore	Bauxite	Copper	Lead	Zinc
1930	5	64	64	9	4
1935	4	58	58	3	3
1940	3	65	49	35	23
1945	1	30	60	28	42
1950	8	76	48	43	40
1951	9	71	38	22	36
1952	10	82	46	56	46
1953	9	75	47	46	57
1954	17	78	48	40	56
1955	19	70	44	38	56
1956	24	73	44	40	58
1957	26	93	48	47	59
1958	30	111	43	58	60
1959	38	94	48	38	60
1960	32	98	46	35	60

SOURCE: Landsberg et al., 1963:427.

imports as a percentage of consumption are high. With the exception of copper and lead, this level of imports to consumption has increased over the same period. More and more the United States seems to be relying on foreign stocks of raw materials because they are cheaper.

In numerous cases, for reasons of declining domestic reserves of high-grade fuel and nonfuel minerals, the United States probably does not have much of a choice as to whether it relies on foreign imports. In other instances, however, where domestic reserves remain large or where domestic reserves could be increased through accelerated exploration and development (Patterson, 1976), the United States does have to make a decision regarding domestic versus foreign supply. Upon which grounds can such a judgment be made? Two alternative resource strategies with differing foreign policy effects describe the options.

Preservationist Strategy

According to this strategy, the United States seeks to preserve domestic stocks of raw materials for use by future generations while exploiting foreign reserves to whatever extent possible. Advantages of the strategy are that irrespective of possible future international political problems which could impede access to foreign reserves, domestic reserves will remain available. Moreover, if commodity prices enjoy a sharp upturn for reasons of either unanticipated upsurge of demand or weaknesses in the quality or quantity of the materials supplied, additional benefits would flow to the United States rather than to a foreign producer.

But the disadvantages of the strategy are at least as pronounced as the advantages. By stressing foreign resource production through foreign investment tax credits, various programs to ensure foreign investment against loss, guaranteed access to investment capital, and related subsidy techniques, the United States runs the risk of higher-cost resource production abroad.

The preservationist strategy also must contend with the possibility that the government may simply be denied access to foreign reserves either for political reasons or because of trade impediments or cartel actions. Overly dependent on foreign supply, the United States might not be able to expand domestic operations quickly enough to offset shortages should domestic supply suddenly have to be relied on. This strategy also may encourage intense competition among advanced industrial governments for limited foreign reserves, thus bidding raw material prices upward excessively. Such competition could occur among governments not having the same options for domestic production enjoyed by the United States.

A preservationist strategy cannot be pursued without risk. Indeed, too zealous pursuit of the strategy may induce precisely the risk the strategy is designed to avoid, namely loss of future security and welfare for the polity. Conservation-oriented in appearance, the preservationist strategy sacrifices global welfare and environmental benefits for domestic ones. By importing raw materials from abroad, it exports its own resource shortage problems to others. Preservationist or "drain them first" strategies are unlikely to provide satisfactory long-term solutions to the U.S. resource dilemma.

Developmentalist Strategy

A developmentalist strategy, which maximizes the exploitation of domestic stocks of raw materials, has several advantages. In the U.S. situation, since such a large fraction of the global production of resources is home based, a developmentalist strategy has the potential of either postponing the cartel behavior of foreign suppliers or undermining collusionist activity already underway. An important by-product of developmentalist strategy is that it facilitates an independent contemporary foreign policy. In contrast to the preservationist approach, which narrows the range of foreign policy options because of dependence on foreign resource supply, this strategy expands those options. The developmentalist strategy thus offers freedom from external constraint to the contemporary foreign policy maker.

On the other hand, the developmentalist strategy is also accompanied by a variety of costs and risks. In using one's own high-grade resource stocks first, one potentially sacrifices the welfare and security of a future generation of Americans who may regard the prior exhaustion of domestic reserves as a short-sighted act of their forefathers. The freedom from external constraints on foreign policy advertised by the developmentalists must be weighed against possible future foreclosure of options. The strategy may also tend to keep the international price of raw materials down, thus accelerating the *world consumption* of these materials and accelerating the *decline of world reserves*. A related consequence is that domestic resource emphasis in the United States may reduce the flow of American capital abroad that would otherwise be available to developing countries exporting raw materials. Whether Zaire, Venezuela, and Indonesia, for example, would genuinely like to see the United States aggressively expand its copper and petroleum production is questionable. Moreover, the impact on world trade as well as on international financial stability of a contraction of markets is not entirely without consequence. Hence a developmentalist strategy which is over-zealous could have markedly negative effects for the government initiating the policy and perhaps for the international system.

An alternative strategy which combines both preservationism and developmentalism is based on an assessment of the current price of raw materials and the rate of return on alternative investments. Insofar as the United States can use its own resources and invest the proceeds from the sale of these resources in education, infrastructure, or industrial plant at a rate of return that is far higher than the current inflation rate (the rate determining the increase in value of the resources left in the ground), the United States should use its resources as rapidly as possible. Future generations will benefit, for example, from the legacy of educational development (with its accompanying potential for accelerated innovation in all fields) far more under these circumstances than they will from a legacy of undeveloped resources.

At the same time prudent environmental safeguards to limit the effects of "waste" incurred in the extraction and production processes and conservation measures designed to discourage "excess" or extravagant personal consumption can extend the life of current high-grade resource stocks. A mark of the success of both environmental safeguards and conservation measures is that they should not depress the real growth rate of the economy upon which all schemes for income redistribution must depend. In the context of finite natural resources, the question of income distribution becomes even more important as a catalyst of political stability (Rosecrance, 1973; Russett, 1968) for both the individual nation-state and the international system as a whole.

A provisional answer to the question—where will the United States obtain its future resources—is that increasingly they are likely to come from outside the territorial boundaries of the country. Our evidence suggests that the United States will become increasingly dependent on foreign resource stocks in a period when other governments are themselves competing more vigorously for the same resources. Insofar as the United States has a choice in these matters (determined largely by the size of its potential domestic reserves), the government may opt for either a preservationist or a developmentalist resource strategy. In theory, the choice should be made in terms of whether the return on alternative social investments is higher than the rate of inflation, i.e., the return which mineral and nonmineral resources would obtain if left in the ground.

In a country like the United States where many opportunities for social investment exist, the best resource strategy is probably to develop domestic reserves as rapidly as market prices allow. Little sense can be made of a strategy which attempts to withhold domestic production in the context of increasing world resource scarcity while attempting to rely on foreign sources of supply. The distortionary consequences of such a resource ideology are explored in the next section.

RESOURCE SUPPLY AND CONFLICT—A FOREIGN POLICY PROBLEM?

Given that the trend of resource usage in the United States continues to move upward, and given that a larger fraction of these resources has come from abroad each year, is the political consequence likely to be greater foreign competition among governments, increased tension within the international system, and hence a growing threat of major war? Classical Marxist-Leninist argumentation would predict this result. Imperialism according to Lenin is the "monopoly stage of capitalism." At this stage foreign resources as well as markets are critical to the expansion and "concentration" of capitalist enterprise. Neo-Marxists have refined the interpretation of resource acquisition (Magdoff, 1972:158):

> The impetus to invest abroad arises out of this competitive struggle among the giants. . . . the ownership of raw material supplies is of strategic importance in the push for control over prices, to hold one's own against competitors who also control supplies, and to restrict the growth of competitors who do not have their own sources.

Radical Marxist thought has emphasized the conflict aspects of resource behavior. Referring to U.S. foreign policy commitments in Africa, Che Guevara (1971:363) for example has written that the United States "does not have great interests to defend there except its assumed right to intervene in every spot of the world where its monopolies detect the possibility of huge profits or the existence of large reserves of raw materials."

Yet, non-Marxists have also predicted the rise of violent conflict over resources, such as the possibility that the Soviet Union would intervene in the Middle East, first to prevent its own oil production from dwindling and second, to deny non-Communist industrial governments access to that oil (Laqueur, 1969; Ulam, 1974; Abir, 1974). Hence, the prospect of increasing tensions over resource questions is documented from a number of perspectives.

War Without Resource Scarcity

One of the problems with resource/conflict arguments, however, is that they often tend to exaggerate the role of economic calculation in politics (Connelly and Perlman, 1975). Changes in other factors of world politics such as border grievances, communal disputes, ideological differences, and alliance relations are de-emphasized yet not properly "controlled for" in the analysis. If one considers the foreign wars involving the United States since 1945 (Rummel, 1972), neither the Korean nor the Vietnam conflict had a resource justification and indeed the financial costs of each war could not possibly have been repaid by known raw materials obtained from either of the disputed areas. Nor have any of the four Arab-Israeli Wars begun because of the presence of oil within the region (Burrowes and Spector, 1973). Likewise the military interventions of the United States into Cuba and the Dominican Republic and those of the Soviet Union into Hungary, Czechoslovakia, and Angola may have had a commercial rationale as well as military and strategic significance, but scarcely any meaning in resource terms per se. For the wars which occurred throughout the 20th century (see Small and Singer, this volume) very little attention was given by statesmen to resource availability as a primary cause.

Resource Scarcity Without Violent Conflict

Resource scarcity is, after all, a very relative concept. Since resources were never free, they have always to some degree been scarce. Resource scarcity exists in periods of peace as well as war. Moreover, some of the easiest conflicts to resolve have been those relating directly to resource questions, e.g., the "cod war" between Iceland and Britain, the dispute over oil rights between Abu Dhabi and Saudi Arabia, and numerous confrontations over water rights between nations. The conflicts were solved easily because the terms of disagreement were precise. Resource *availability* perhaps was a key to conflict resolution.

No matter how much advanced industrial governments may deplore the loss of independence in having to import raw materials, and no matter how much developing countries may dislike having to import technology and manufactured goods, the exchange forms one basis of international trade which is disrupted only at a cost to both parties. Moreover, multinational corporations have begun to view their role as that of a buffer between the developing and the advanced industrial countries, leaning in some instances (e.g., oil and bauxite) more closely toward the former than the latter (Barnet and Mueller, 1974).

Elsewhere we have described this emerging phenomenon of balance between resource exporters and importers as *codependence* (Doran, 1977). It is perhaps epitomized by the association between the United States and Saudi Arabia. Unlike the relationship of interdependence where states are substantially equal in capability, with codependence the respective states are often highly unequal in size (Saudi Arabia has an indigenous population amounting at most to 7 million, while the U.S. population numbers in excess of 215 million), yet the smaller state because of its quasi-monopoly over a resource obtains substantial leverage. Unlike interdependence which emphasizes cooperation and an absence of power politics, codependence displays a capacity by both parties for punitive sanctions. But mutual benefits of cooperation also exist in codependence, further binding the parties to each other and reducing the risk of a violent disruption of commerce and alliance ties. Indeed one of the realities of codependent exchange is that resource sales have purchased access to security both directly and indirectly.

Finally, apart from codependent systemic relationships which may foster stability, resource scarcity is not a necessary precipitant of violent conflict because of the flexibility of resource supply and substitution. Loss of natural rubber during World War II led to the American production of an improved artificial substitute, just as the German loss of Balkan petroleum led to domestic reliance on the coal liquification process. Substitutes for almost all the major minerals currently imported by the United States are feasible under varying cost conditions. Scarcely a single raw material including phosphate is so localized in output that loss of a major foreign deposit would hamper industrial production. Increased use of recycling, stockpiling, and more careful patterns of consumption help safeguard access to raw materials. Under these circumstances it is difficult to envision how raw material supply inherently must become the focus of increased international tensions and war.

Resource Scarcity as a New Ideological Counterfeit

Yet outlining a rational basis for statecraft is one thing. Tracing the actual conduct of statecraft is quite possibly another. What the contemporary analyst of international politics has to fear is that resource scarcity will become a new code word for acts of belligerency. Resource scarcity is a convenient ideology which democratic governments could use to stir the ardor of mass participation for the hardships of war. Corporate elites anxious about continuity of supply for their own enterprises could be whipped into sympathy. Taking military countermeasures in response, an opponent such as the Soviet Union could easily imagine that the dangers of resource scarcity had driven the United States to contemplate military intervention to protect deposits of raw materials.

In this situation Third World countries would face a dual threat, albeit one that is based on a false understanding of resource reality (Jervis, 1968). First, the governments exporting raw materials might acquire a protectionist outlook in the wake of fears that a run on their resource endowments was occurring. Second, the raw material exporters might suffer a loss of political confidence in their associations with Western governments, fearing that they had become the targets of potential intervention. Thus aggravated suspicion concerning resource politics could hinder the maintenance of normal trade ties between Third World countries and the more industrialized nations.

Resource scarcity could thus emerge as a new counterfeit ideology (Mannheim, 1936) poisoning the relations between North and South and between East and West, particularly in situations where the industrial countries seem to be pursuing a preservationist strategy of using the stocks of others first. Regardless of whether artificial substitutes for embargoed commodities are available and regardless of whether large alternate deposits of a naturally occurring mineral are known to exist elsewhere, the specter of resource scarcity could begin to enter foreign policy calculations, narrowing the definitions of state interests.

Shifts away from domestic production for reasons of cost could also be seen as a threat to the security of the importing polity. In contrast to most increases in trade between nations which are looked upon as a positive measure of growing interdependence and therefore of peaceful relations, increases in commodity trade might be viewed as a measure of fading autonomy by some nations and therefore as a threat to the flexibility of their own foreign policy.

The interpretation offered here has suggested the existence of a large potential for misinterpretation of present trends in resource usage and distribution. A foreign policy ideology built on notions of resource scarcity is subject to distortions far more unsettling to the international system than the facts of increased raw material usage would warrant. U.S. foreign policy has less to fear from the changing realities of resource production and distribution than from false extrapolations of these trends into the political consciousness of the nation.

FORGING TECHNOLOGY-RESOURCE DYADS BETWEEN NATIONS

The conclusion seems warranted that resource scarcity is probably less a physical than a distributional problem, but shortages whether real or imagined can become a serious threat to the peace of the international system. Following the precepts of the developmentalist strategy, the Carter Administration might take the following steps to preclude shortages in critical minerals and commodities while at the same time advancing the interests of those governments which are poor and have too little investment capital but an abundance of natural resources.

(1) Identify those resources such as petroleum in which a current or anticipated global shortage may exist.

(2) Determine which countries have a potential untapped supply of these resources and would like to accelerate their development.

(3) Offer an exchange of technology for the right to import a given volume of these resources at the world price.

(4) Offer guarantees against expropriation to American companies who are willing to enter joint venture arrangements with companies of the host country (either national or privately owned) to accelerate discovery, extraction, and processing of the resources, thereby opening up an enlarged stream of tax revenue to the host government and greater resource availability to the United States.

In effect, by this procedure the United States could selectively create technology-resource dyads with other countries, hastening the transfer of needed technology to them and at the same time expanding the world production of natural resources in which short-falls may occur for reasons of market imperfections or sudden, perhaps irreversible down-turns (at current prices) in domestic U.S. production capacity.

Mexico is a clear but neglected example of a technology-resource dyad opportunity. During 1977 the Mexican GNP increased less than 2% in real terms while population grew by 3%. While it thus actually fell back in terms of economic growth, this extremely poor country nonetheless has estimated petroleum reserves in excess of 50 billion barrels. But without an infusion of outside capital and technology, Mexico will not be able to extract, transport, and market this resource at a time when the world price of energy is high.

In contrast, the United States has an enormous petroleum deficit in its balance-of-payments which threatens to worsen as energy prices climb. The United States also produces high-quality petroleum technology for export and possesses a huge import market for semi-manufactured goods, a market that would mean a great deal to Mexico in growth terms were Mexico given preferential trade treatment. The illegal alien situation moreover would perhaps be better solved by creating jobs in Mexico instead of having workers rely for employment, often unsuccessfully and with intense hardship, on an already over-strained U.S. economy. What better opportunity for the technology-resource mechanism to flourish than in relations between Mexico and the United States, creating positive side-effects such as an increase in trade between the partners and a resolution of immigration difficulties? But such a dyadic response to energy shortage, to faltering economic growth, and to political tension has not been tried. Indeed, because the Carter Administration did not want to embarrass its energy program by purchasing natural gas abroad for more than it was willing to offer domestic producers in the interstate market, the one large recent natural gas contract proposed between the United States and Mexico was cancelled.

Now is the time to reverse apparent resource scarcity through dyadic technology-resource arrangements. In the aftermath of the worst recession in 40 years, pessimism concerning economic growth and resource availability seems warranted by the energy experience. Yet we may discover in the medium-term at least that pessimism and lack of imagination concerning policy instruments are a far greater obstacle to Third World development and full employment among the industrial countries than any reliable evidence of physical resource constraints.

CONCLUSIONS

Our examination of contemporary resource politics and U.S. foreign policy has led to essentially three conclusions. First, while resource usage may in general be leveling off relative to GNP, that usage continues to climb in per capita terms. Second, the growing U.S. demand for resources has been accompanied by an increasing dependence (largely for cost reasons) on foreign imports of fuel and nonfuel minerals. Third, despite these resource usage trends, we conclude that no *necessary* relationship exists between apparently increasing resource scarcity and political conflict. Resource scarcity has always been prevalent in a relative sense yet has played a very small role as a cause of war in the 20th century. Resource substitution, alternative sources of supply, recycling, stockpiling, and the mutual benefits which flow from trade in natural resources all support the logical *rejection* of the resource/conflict hypothesis.

The hypothesis cannot totally be disregarded, however, because of the possible emergence of *nonrational* foreign policy ideologies that incorporate distorted notions of resource scarcity which themselves have unsettling consequences for international peace.

REFERENCES

ABIR, M. (1974). Oil, power and politics: Conflict in Arabia, the Red Sea and The Gulf. London: Frank Cass.
BARNET, R.J., and MÜLLER, R.E. (1974). Global reach: The power of the multinational corporations. New York: Simon and Schuster.
BARNETT, H.J., and MORSE, C. (1963). Scarcity and growth: The economics of natural resource availability. Baltimore: Johns Hopkins Press.
BERGSTEN, C.F. (1974). "The threat is real." Foreign Policy, 4 (Spring):94-90.
BURROWES, R., and SPECTOR, B. (1973). "The strength and direction of relationships between domestic and external conflict and cooperation: Syria, 1961-67." Pp. 294-324 in J. Wilkenfeld (ed.), Conflict behavior and linkage politics. New York: David McKay.

CHOUCRI, N., LAIRD, M., and MEADOWS, D. (1972). Resource scarcity and foreign policy: A simulation model of international conflict. Cambridge, Mass.: MIT, Center for International Studies.

COHEN, B.J. (1973). The question of imperialism: The political economy of dominance and dependence. New York: Basic Books.

Committee on Resources and Man, National Academy of Sciences (1969). Resources and man: A study and recommendations. San Francisco: W.H. Freeman.

CONNELLY, P., and PERLMAN, R. (1975). The politics of scarcity: Resource conflicts in international relations. London: Oxford University Press.

DE CARMOY, G. (1977). Energy for Europe: Economic and political implications. Washington, D.C.: American Enterprise Institute for Public Policy Research.

DORAN, C.F. (1977). Myth, oil and politics: Introduction to the political economy of petroleum. New York: Free Press.

ENTHOVEN, A.C., and FREEMAN, A.M., III (eds.) (1973). Pollution, resources, and the environment. New York: Norton.

GARVEY, G. (1972). Energy, ecology, economy: A framework for environmental policy. New York: Norton.

GUEVARA, C. (1971). In K.T. Fann and D.C. Hodges (eds.), Readings in U.S. imperialism. Boston: Porter Sargent.

Institute for Contemporary Studies (1977). Options for U.S. energy policy. San Francisco: Author.

JERVIS, R. (1968). "Hypotheses on misperception." World Politics, XX (April): 454-479.

KEMP, G. (1978). "Scarcity and strategy." Foreign Affairs, 56, 2 (January):396-414.

LANDSBERG, H.H., FISCHMAN, L.F., and FISHER, J.L. (1963). Resources in America's future: Patterns of requirements and availabilities, 1960-2000. Baltimore: Johns Hopkins Press.

LAQUEUR, W. (1969). The struggle for the Middle East: The Soviet Union in the Mediterranean, 1958-1968. New York: Macmillan.

LEWIS, J.P. (1974). "Oil, other scarcities, and the poor countries." World Politics, 27, 1 (October):63-86.

MAGDOFF, H. (1972). "Imperialism without colonies." Pp. 144-169 in R. Owen and B. Sutcliffe (eds.), Studies in the theory of imperialism. London: Langman.

MANNHEIM, K. (1936). Ideology and utopia. New York: Harcourt.

McGOWAN, P. (1975). "Meaningful comparisons in the study of foreign policy: A methodological discussion of objectives, techniques, and research designs." Pp. 52-90 in C. Kegley, Jr. et al. (eds.), International events and the comparative analysis of foreign policy. Columbia: U. of South Carolina Press.

NORDHAUS, W. (1973). "The allocation of energy resources." Brookings Papers on Economic Activity 3. Washington, D.C.: Brookings Institution.

OPPENHEIM, U.H., and MORAN, T.H. (1977). "Why oil prices go up." Foreign Policy, 25 (Winter):24-77.

PATTERSON, W.C. (1976). Nuclear power. New York: Penguin.

PEARCE, D.W. (1976). Environmental economics. London: Longman.

President's Materials Policy Commission (1952). "Foundations for growth and security." Resources for Freedom I. Washington, D.C.: U.S. Government Printing Office.

ROSECRANCE, R. (1973). International relations: Peace or war? New York: McGraw-Hill.

ROSENAU, J.N. (1969). "Intervention as a scientific concept." Journal of Conflict Resolution, 8:149-171.

RUMMEL, R.J. (1972). "U.S. foreign relations: Conflict, cooperation, and attribute distances." Pp. 71-113 in B.M. Russett (ed.), Peace, war and numbers. Beverly Hills, Cal.: Sage.

RUSSETT, B. (1968). "Is there a long-run trend toward concentration in the international system?" Comparative Political Studies, 1, 1 (April):101-122.

TUCKER, R. (1971). The radical left and American foreign policy. Baltimore: Johns Hopkins Press.

ULAM, A.B. (1974). Expansion and coexistence: Soviet foreign policy 1917-73. New York: Praeger.

VERNON, R. (ed.) (1976). The oil crisis. New York: Norton.

VOUSDEN, N. (1973). "Basic theoretical issues of resource depletion." Journal of Economic Theory, 6 (2):126-143.

Chapter 6

THE UNITED STATES IN AN INTERDEPENDENT WORLD: THE EMERGENCE OF ECONOMIC POWER

JAMES A. CAPORASO
University of Denver

MICHAEL D. WARD
Northwestern University

Foreign policy represents purposeful actions par excellence. In studying foreign policy, our eyes are drawn to attempts to conceptualize, formulate, and execute plans of action that deal with the threats and opportunities posed by the external environment. Our focus is on the activity and behavior of states taking place within foreign policy contexts that are themselves not the object of foreign policy manipulation. Typical dependent variables include the amount of conflict and cooperation in a nation's foreign policy actions, the level of commitment evidenced by these actions, and the proportion of foreign policy behaviors related to economic concerns (East, Salmore, and Hermann, 1978).

This focus on activities (events) follows closely the actor-oriented strategy of political analysis. According to this approach, foreign policy execution is

EDITORS' NOTE: This paper was first submitted for review in January 1978. The version published here was received in April 1978.

comprised of numerous attempts to bargain successfully with other actors in the international system. The behavior of these actors is visualized as transpiring within predefined settings, contexts that exist and which may affect behavior but which themselves are fixed and resistant to any planned change. This is not to say that the real world offers no examples of diplomatic attempts to condition global structures. The Nixon-Kissinger "pentagonal world" involved an ambitious attempt to foster the diffusion of responsibility (if not real power) to centers outside the Soviet Union and the United States, in particular Japan, Western Europe, and the People's Republic of China. Similarly, Germany's Third Reich developed the foreign economic policy of bilateralism, which involved an effort to shape dependence structures in such a way as to place other countries in an inferior position with respect to Germany. The purpose of these strategies was not to exert the will of one state over another, but rather to shape the matrix of human interaction in such a way as to "make the pursuit of power a relatively easy task" (Hirschman, 1945). There are also academic studies focusing on structure-creating foreign policies (Hirschman, 1945; Katzenstein, 1977; and Cotler and Fagen, 1974), but these are a distinct minority.

The focus of this chapter is not on any particular foreign policy activity, but on the emerging structure that conditions that activity and, more relevant for our purposes, on the ways in which foreign policy actors can shape this structure to suit political ends. More specifically, we are interested in the ways in which the emerging international economic structure can be shaped to further U.S. foreign policy objectives. Our basic argument is that while the use of military capabilities to pursue foreign policy goals has declined, there is at least an increased opportunity to exploit economic resources.

For a foreign policy to be effective, decision makers must have knowledge about the relationships and trends in the external environment. What we are adapting to (goals) and how we are to adapt (means) are the two most fundamental foreign policy issues. Yet the contemporary global system is very volatile and uncertain. As one observer pointed out (Hoffmann, 1975:184), modern power is so elusive that it is not clear whether statesmen from various countries would produce the same list of most powerful nations. There are so many different "power maps" that consensus is difficult. The bipolar world rests on a measure of nuclear capabilities; the tripolar world of the United States, the People's Republic of China, and the Soviet Union rests partly on military power (particularly the infantry) and partly on the sheer weight of numbers; the trilateral image of North America, Western Europe, and Japan reflects economic capabilities; while the Nixon-Kissinger "pentagonal world" of the United States, Soviet Union, People's Republic of China,

Western Europe, and Japan reflects an uncertain combination of military power, demographic weight, and economic might.

Furthermore, as Bundy (1977:1-2) has argued, uncertainty over the possession of power stems not so much from lack of information about the distribution of power on any one dimension as from uncertainty about which dimension is important. What counts in today's global system? Is it nuclear weapons, conventional capabilities, leadership resolve, or economic capabilities as reflected in gross national product (GNP), trade, or the supply of capital and technology? Despite the worldwide growth of military expenditures (Sivard, 1977), Bundy (1977) is probably correct when he argues that in terms of conventional measures of power military strength has probably become more concentrated in the United States and the Soviet Union. "Yet, real power—the ability to affect others—seems in fact more widely dispersed than perhaps at any time in the world's history" (Bundy, 1977:2). This uncertainty about both the components of power and its distribution makes the formulation of long-range foreign policy difficult.

Prior to the question "who has power?" is the question "what are the components or bases of power?" In answering this latter question many scholars (e.g., Hoffmann, 1975; Keohane and Nye, 1973, 1977; Morse, 1977) have argued that there has been a shift away from military capabilities toward economic capacity, trade and investment patterns, and monetary strength. Thus, the "declining utility of military power" and the "emerging utility of economic power" are, on hypothesis, two of the most important trends in the current international system. It is these two trends we wish to examine in this chapter. In both cases, our central focus is on the United States and its relationships with other European countries.

The central idea, that economic capabilities can be used as tools of foreign policy or more strongly, that economic resources may substitute for military ones, is not entirely new. Indeed, it has literally been around for centuries. Mercantilism, a doctrine that rested on a fusion of economic and political power, is often distinguished from "the outlook of classical political economy by its emphasis upon power rather than profit" (Semmel, 1970:29). Carrying the analysis one step further, there is no need to oppose "power" and "profit," nor to treat them as if an "either-or" choice were involved. Instead, the pursuit of profit along with prudent safeguards for critical industries, particularly defense-related ones, may make the acquisition of power relatively easy. We do not wish to overstate our case here, because we recognize many limitations of economic power. But we do want to open the possibility, in hypothesis form, that the shift from military to economic power is not unprecedented, that these two modes of influences are functionally related, and that the contemporary shift from the military to the economic, if it is occurring, involves a change of form rather than substance.

USE OF FORCE IN THE CURRENT INTERNATIONAL SYSTEM

Decline of Use of Force

The decline of the utility of military force is a theme touched on by many scholars (e.g., Keohane and Nye, 1973; Hoffmann, 1968; and Knorr, 1966). While the argument for such a decline may seem persuasive, we believe more careful analysis is required. An excellent starting point is with the formulation offered by Klaus Knorr (1966), who treats the utility of military power as a function of two separate factors: the value, or rewards achieved by the use of power; and the costs, or penalties associated with its use. Symbolically, this is represented by $U = V - C$, where U stands for utility, V for the value attached to achieving a particular goal, and C for the costs associated with pursuing this goal.

Changes Related to Cost

Though the above formula is quite simple and has an obvious air about it, we believe that a consistent analysis of the current international system in terms of these two central concepts is illuminating. To take an important example, the utility of military force may decline in value because the goals to which it is attached (e.g., territorial control) diminish in importance or because there is too great a cost involved in achieving these goals through military means.

Among the most important of the factors relating to the cost of military instruments of foreign policy is the transformation of warfare itself. It has become a commonplace to comment on the awesome nature of nuclear weapons; and the very existence of them, with a possibility of their use, is counted as a cost in the plans of statesmen.

Of course, the existence of nuclear weapons is not the only factor behind the destructiveness of modern warfare. There have also been major changes in the destructiveness of conventional weapons. Some of these changes are graphically portrayed by Keegan (1976:307):

> So abundant have these killing agents become (to say nothing of those fired from larger more distant weapons or launched from the air) that the underlying aim of weapon-training has now in many armies changed: for the traditional object, that of teaching a soldier to hit a selected target, has been substituted that of teaching a group to create an impenetrable zone. . . . "Wasting ammunition," for decades

the cardinal military sin, has in consequence become a military virtue; "hitting the target," for centuries the principal military skill, is henceforth to be left to the law of averages.

But these changes in the nature of warfare are not limited to the technological level. Perhaps of equal importance to these technological changes are those which have occurred in the social and political systems. The development of a centrally unified state, complete with a bureaucracy touching on many aspects of social life, the growth of the powers of taxation`and of the manipulation of credit and finances, and the ability to mobilize human and physical resources on an unprecedented scale all register their impacts. These increases in the ability of the state to wage war more "efficiently" and totally might be thought of as advantages. However, because many nations have developed these capabilities simultaneously, it has simply meant that each side must sustain more losses before the outcome of the conflict is decided.

Changes Related to Value

While the decline in the utility of warfare as an instrument of politics may be mostly due to the increased cost of warfare, there is some reason to suppose that the actual value attached to military means has diminished. For example, territorial conquest, certainly a prime expression of military force, is no longer esteemed as it once was. This in turn may be due to the perception on the part of leaders that *control* is what is important—not military conquest and territorial occupation. Control can be accomplished through the exploitation of subtler forces than military ones. Disraeli's complaint of "these wretched colonies [being] a millstone round our neck" (Semmel, 1970:2) was an indictment of the burdens of formal occupation and direct political control. It is important to remember that Disraeli's complaint took place at precisely the same time (1852) that the liberal free traders were laying the basis of a new international order, one tuned to British supremacy through nonmilitary means.

Military force has been valued traditionally because it was thought to lead to economic wealth; indeed, force was the ultimate bargaining tool in assuring open markets, cheap raw materials, and cheap or slave labor. But the present international system throws this linkage into question. To be sure the U.S. is a first-rate power in both economic and military terms. Yet, on economic grounds, so are Japan, Sweden, Switzerland, and the Federal Republic of Germany (Knorr, 1966:22). While Sweden and Switzerland maintain sizeable armies, contemporary usage of them is improbable. Nevertheless, such military readiness is the price paid for political neutrality. It is clear that all four of these countries have prospered immensely since World War II and that military force has played little or no role in this. Indeed, the absence of military spending may lie, in the cases of Japan and West Germany, at the center of their success.

The preceding argument downgrades warfare on instrumental grounds; it is simply not always effective, or even necessary, to achieve desired political ends. There is another argument, however, which attacks the value of war frontally—not as an inferior instrument of politics, but as an end in itself lacking in value. This school of thought takes its starting point with the theories of societal evolution put forward by Auguste Comte, Herbert Spencer, and Henry Sumner Maine, which posit an opposition between feudal society (based on heroic-military values), and industrial society (based on commercial-bourgeois values). Since the engines of history are moving further away from feudal to industrial organization, the deduction is that societal values will become increasingly less sympathetic to militarism. Industrialism spawns large middle classes whose interests are with economic advancement rather than military prowess or personal honor. To state this argument more strongly, in the end industrialism means the triumph of the material over the heroic, the rational over the romantic, and butter over guns.

If this theory were correct, it should have produced changes long ago, before World War I and World War II. Still, there are those who see fragments of this body of thought as relevant to changes currently going on in domestic society. While industrialization may not have resulted in the wholesale replacement of one form of society for another, there is taking place, so the argument goes, a series of structural changes that may alter society in important ways. Public opinion polls show a turning inward on the part of mass publics, a growing preoccupation with domestic as opposed to foreign issues, and economic as opposed to defense-security concerns. When a survey of a national cross-section was conducted in 1964 in the United States, the results showed that the five items of greatest public concern all related to foreign affairs, while in 1976 the top ten issues concerned domestic politics (Watts and Free, 1976:9).

To some observers (Geiger, 1973), this public opinion shift is seen as more than a transitory reversal in priorities, a mood change in electoral sociology; rather, it is seen as an integral part of basic structural changes in society. To these changes in attitudes we may add the fact that, in almost all advanced industrial societies, there is a definite raised expectation of people for greater governmental control of socio-economic issues. All of these demands—the emphasis on domestic concerns, the importance of economic goals, the expectation that governments will play a major role in managing economic affairs—work to produce what one observer calls the "new nationalism" (Geiger, 1973:49-53), a term intended to convey a benign, inward-looking phase of nationalism. Even if we are extremely skeptical that the attitude changes conveyed by the term "new nationalism" reflect any basic transformation in the psychology of men and women in the postindustrial period, in the short run the change signifies a lesser value for military force.

ALTERNATIVES TO FORCE:
ECONOMIC INSTRUMENTS OF POWER

According to the military strategist, Von Clausewitz (1976:7), "War is not an independent phenomenon, but the continuation of politics by different means." We are tempted to paraphrase Clausewitz' dictum by saying, "economics is not a sphere unto itself but the continuation of politics through non-coercive means." Before considering the attractions of pursuing goals with economic resources, let us take a brief digression into the analysis of power.

Power: Capabilities and Behavior

We can think of power, following closely Dahl's (1969) definition, as the ability of A to get B to do something that B would not otherwise do, at a relatively high cost to B and low cost to A. The components of a power relationship thus include: intentions (A's wishes), resistance (B's wishes), compliance (of B to A's wishes), the costs of power (of A's positive inducement and B's resistance attempts), and resources. This last component is important for our purposes. In extracting compliance, A must offer or threaten something. This threat (or promise) must be backed up by at least the capability of delivering to the threatened party a concrete punishment or reward (except in the case of pure bluff, i.e., threat without capability). Without this, there would be no incentive for the threatened party to comply.

Broadly speaking, there are two ways that we can think of power: as a capability or potential to influence others, and as the actual exercise of that influence. The first approach focuses on the resources available to various actors, both those which they inherently possess (military resources) and those which are derived from relations with others (e.g., allies, resource flows, capital flows), while the second focuses on the overt behavioral activity of one actor influencing another. Of course, there is a correlation between capabilities and behavioral power, but this relationship is far from perfect. Statements such as "the U.S. had the power to defeat the Communists in Vietnam but did not use it" reflect the basic tension between the two definitions of power. Many reasons may be suggested for this gap between capabilities and behavior, including the skill of individual bargainers, the will to resist the exercise of power, the level of stakes for the various actors, and the differential costs of losing to each party.

The preceding discussion should make it clear that, when we refer to economic and military power, we refer to capabilities and not to distinctive types of power behavior, i.e., not to outcomes of attempts to change behavior. Military power is power based on force or the threat of force while economic power is power based on economic rewards or threats of conferring or removing such rewards. The argument is sometimes made that military power has negative connotations, since it is based on coercion and a "hurt" principle embodied in the *threat,* while economic power has a more positive connotation, since it is based on rewards and a "help" principle embodied in the *offer.* We find the distinction specious and of little value. To be deprived, or to be threatened deprivation of vital materials or goods for which there is an inflexible demand is to be hurt.

Attractions of Economic Power

If politics is viewed in the manner suggested above, both military and economic capabilities can be seen as resources to achieve political goals. With the decline in the usability of military resources, it is natural to look to economic capabilities to take up the slack. As one scholar has noted (Nye, 1974:586):

> As the efficacy of force for the achievement of many states' positive goals has declined, the threats to state autonomy have also shifted, from the military area—in which the threat is defined largely in terms of territorial integrity—to the economic area. Thus the purpose of exercising power may be not so much to prevent another state taking military action as to prevent its shifting the costs of its own domestic policy actions on to one's own state—for instance, through trade restrictions, maintenance of an undervalued exchange rate, or non-tariff barriers of one kind or another.

There are definite attractions to the use of economic power. First, its use is expected to entail fewer costs than military power. It does not involve the same drain through taxation or the social and human costs associated with the military draft and wartime casualties. Second, economic power is divisible into smaller quantities than military power and this encourages its application in various quantities. The nuclear-tipped missile may be appropriate for the most extreme circumstances, such as national survival, but it is not useful for almost everything below that threshold. Statesmen during the 1950s felt uneasy because of the possession of weapons which threatened to "exterminate a termite with a cannon ball." In short, the military means were out of proportion to the scale of the political ends. Economic means, on the other hand, potentially allow a more variable and continuous set of initiatives and responses. They can be expressed in terms of currency units (e.g., dollars), commodities, and services. Third, excepting the use of some commodities such as food from the battery of economic resources, economic influence is not likely to incite the same reactions in public opinion as military means.

Sources of Economic Power

"What is economic power and who has it?" is the title of a recent article in international relations (Strange, 1975). Though the question is basic, the answers likely to be given are most certainly controversial. Some would say the United States, pointing to its gross productive capabilities as an index of economic power; while others might point to Saudia Arabia, which is relatively backward by GNP standards, but possesses control over a precious natural resource, oil. While the U.S. might be described as having attribute power, Saudia Arabia, through its oil and the Organization of Petroleum Exporting Countries (OPEC), might be said to possess market power, power flowing from the structure of economic exchanges.

Attribute Capabilities. There are other attributes of potential value to economic resources, such as the flexibility of the economy and its ability to adapt in response to changes in its environment (e.g., from the use of oil to coal, natural gas, solar, and nuclear energy). Similarly, the sophistication and efficiency of technology is a national possession that can potentially be used as a lever of international influence. The heated discussion over "technology transfer" among both advanced and less developed countries is a case in point.

Yet we speak of attribute capabilities as "potential levers" because by themselves they are of no use to one country bargaining with another. Country B will see no reason to be moved by consideration of A's GNP unless A is willing to utilize some of it in exchanges with B (or unless A uses some of it to back a military effort against B). It is therefore necessary to concentrate on relational capabilities, because these capabilities are tied up with interactions rather than possessions.

Relational Capabilities. A relational capability is a capability flowing from the structure of exchanges among countries. In contrast to attribute capabilities, which hinge on what nations possess, relational capabilities flow from what nations exchange among themselves.

An exchange is a transaction whereby something of value is surrendered by each party in return for something of value received by each. In permitting something of value to be supplied externally, each country creates a dependence. Of course, these dependencies may make very good economic sense, reflecting as they may the advantages of specialization. However, these economic benefits may come at the price of certain political costs, namely the increased vulnerabilities of the dependent countries.

Because all parties to an exchange are dependent, a feeling of security may be encouraged that is derived from the knowledge that "we are all in this together." The problem is that some may be in it more deeply than others; or in more academic prose, dependencies, though mutual, may not be balanced. It is these imbalanced dependencies that have greatest potential as levers of economic power (Keohane and Nye, 1973:121-126).

Saying that imbalanced dependencies are sources of power may be a useful starting point, but it tells us very little in terms of how to proceed to assess these dependencies. What are the basic ingredients of the exchange relationship? What are the basic conceptual components of the calculus of dependence? We see at least three things as important. First, there is the question of the size of A's dependence on B. What is the quantity of goods supplied by B to A and how does this quantity compare to A's total consumption of that good? Perhaps this can be phrased more simply in the question: what is the proportional quantity of A's consumption of a particular good supplied by B? As this sheer quantity goes up, A's dependence on B increases.

The size of the good supplied makes little difference, however, if either the good is unimportant or alternate routes of supply are open. If either of these two conditions exists, A's reliance on B is reduced dramatically. The second component of the calculus is the *importance* of the good considered, where importance is thought of in terms of the intensity of preferences of certain groups within society and the access of such groups to policy-making institutions. Exchangeable goods range in value from the trinkets and bric-a-brac of perfumed soap balls to industrial necessities such as oil and biological necessities such as food.

The third component of our calculus of dependence is the structure of available suppliers or substitutes. Given that A imports a large quantity of important goods from B, can A easily acquire these same goods elsewhere? More specifically, what is the cost of making this shift? Or, if an alternate source of supply is not available, perhaps some substitute service or commodity is. Similarly, we ask, what is the cost of invoking this substitution? Thus, the third component is the opportunity cost of foregoing the supply of a particular good from a particular supplier.

To summarize, three things are important in an exchange relationship: magnitude, importance, and availability of substitutes. A fourth condition should be added that is calculated from the basic information supplied in the mutual dependencies of A and B; that is, the balance of dependencies derived from a comparison of A's dependence on B and B's dependence on A. If the gap is large, it implies a capability for the superior actor to exploit, should it so desire, to its political advantage. Dependencies imply vulnerabilities and as such they entail the capacity to hurt and be hurt. To minimize one's capacity to be hurt and to maximize one's capacity to hurt others is to cultivate the sources of economic power.

Techniques of Economic Power

Neither national economic wealth nor international exchange inequalities is power per se. These resource advantages are translated into power when they are "used *deliberately* to modify the behavior or capabilities of states" (Knorr, 1973:9). The resource advantages or relational capabilities describe the basic anatomy of the economic power potential of actors in the global system. However, anatomy does not determine a unique physiology and in our case we would not expect a particular structure to be linked to a unique set of behavioral outcomes.

In using available economic resources, an actor draws on the reservoir of potential leverage implicit in its exchange capabilities and channels these resources into various tactics or techniques. Thus, embargoes, blacklisting, and the freezing of assets are what constitute the activity of behavioral economic power (as opposed to power potential). The ability of states to shut off valuable markets, deny important sources of supply, discourage loans and investments in other countries, and alter the value of a country's currency are important capabilities that hold great potential in pursuing nonstrategic foreign policy goals. These examples involve the exercise of power, which is more dramatic, visible, and newsworthy than the structural inequalities silently operating in the background.

The list of concrete activities falling under the label "techniques of economic power" is too long to allow an adequate treatment here. In addition, a full appreciation of these techniques, quite specific themselves, requires a detailed understanding of the contexts in which they will be applied and this is clearly beyond the scope of our chapter.

Commodity Controls. The techniques of foreign economic policy may be divided into commodity controls and financial controls. Commodity controls are roughly those techniques that attempt to increase a country's advantage by affecting the physical movement of goods (Wu, 1952:86). There are tariffs and quotas (used to close off markets, thereby possibly destroying jobs), embargoes (wholesale refusal to supply commodities to a country), blacklisting, foreign exchange controls, and the manipulation of transit facilities (Knorr, 1975:83).

There are more ingenious uses of economic capabilities. A country may attempt to reduce an enemy's exports to others, hence reducing its foreign exchange earnings and ergo its ability to import goods, by subsidizing its own exports and then dumping them onto the world market at a low price. Or a country may engage in preemptive buying, i.e., purchasing commodities not primarily for domestic consumption but rather to prevent them falling into the hands of an adversary. A classic example of the use of subsidies and dumping is provided by the common agricultural policy of the European Community (EC). Through the use of large subsidies, legitimated by the agricultural decisions, the EC built up huge surpluses in many products, including wheat, butter and sugarbeets. At different times, it dumped these products onto the world market, e.g., wheat to Japan and China at 50% of its price (Zeller, 1970:19) and sugar to many countries. The policy of dumping sugar works chiefly to the disadvantage of underdeveloped sugar-producing countries such as Thailand and Cuba as well as African countries which produce manioc, for which sugar has sometimes been substituted in the feeding of animals (Zeller, 1970:57-58). In the EC, sugarbeets are supported for up to 70% of their production costs.

The preemptive buying of goods is usually done for the purpose of denying an adversary nation these goods. Thus, there is no presumption that the importing country actually values the commodities; what it values is the prevention of their acquisition by another country. However, preemptive buying can take place for more complicated purposes. The policy of bilateralism, perfected by the Third Reich, involved the curious situation in which Germany bought up commodities of several Southeastern European countries and subsequently dumped them onto the world market at a price well below their original purchase cost. Such bizarre behavior had, of course, a very self-serving goal, namely, to reduce the diversity of market outlets for these countries and hence to enhance their dependence on Germany (Wu, 1952:73).

Financial Controls. Financial controls are defined as "measures of regulating the acquisition and dispersal of specified assets" (Wu, 1952:87). Thus, using credit and loan facilities, infusing or withholding capital to others, granting or denying access to banking facilities, and manipulating currency rates are all financial measures. One purpose of these financial controls may be to limit the foreign economic activity of another in one's own country. For example, the denial of exports to an adversary, whether one's own or those of a third country, would be relatively pointless in the absence of restrictions on foreign assets in one's country. If holders of foreign assets in one's country were capable of converting these assets into exportable goods and transferring them abroad, the export embargo per se would be less useful (Wu, 1952:90). Since foreign economic penetration, in both direct and portfolio investments, has increased dramatically in the last several decades, no doubt partly in reaction to restrictions on commodity flows, financial restrictions are likely to increase in importance.

Finally, controls on the use of transit facilities, while at one level relevant for the restrictions on the movement of commodities, are perhaps even more important from the standpoint of denying foreign exchange, tax revenue, and jobs to others and increasing all three for one's own country. That this is no hollow issue is demonstrated by the fact that just two months prior to our writing this article, the U.S. House of Representatives voted on a bill that would have required no less than 9.5% of all oil shipped to the U.S. to be carried by American flag ships (Chamberlain, 1977:1).

All of these techniques, whether commodity controls or financial controls, have as their object the attainment of some goal. These goals include a change in the behavior of another actor (e.g., softening of racial policies through embargoes) as well as changes in the capabilities of actors (as in Germany's use of bilateralism). Since use of these techniques is likely to incite retaliatory measures, the country resorting to them must be in a strong passive economic position, i.e., it must be able to absorb and withstand the countermeasures. Capabilities are therefore relational in two senses: they have to do with movements or exchanges among countries and they respect not unilateral advantages, but the balance or "net" advantages between countries.

Up to this point in the chapter we have relied on reasoned arguments to establish our two main themes. In the next part we examine more carefully the empirical evidence for the decline of military power and the rise of economic power.

EVIDENCE AND TRENDS: MILITARY POWER

Military power has long been a primary component of the foreign policies of most members of the international system. In the 19th century, exercise of this means of influence was typically viewed as a sovereign right of national political units. Often times it was also pursued as a goal of foreign policy behavior per se, as for example in the case of Napoleonic France. The emergence of the League of Nations and its more permanent successor, the United Nations, was in part based on the recognition by the major military powers that continuation of the unrestrained use of military force in international affairs would present an evermore dangerous situation. The alliance system, thought so stable prior to 1914, had been fundamentally destablized by the eruption of the first World War. It was no longer propitious to perceive the unlimited use of military power as legitimate.

The actions of neither the League nor the U.N., however, proscribed the use of military forces; rather, the efforts of both institutions sought to make the use of military might for nondefensive purposes an illegitimate form of international behavior. While one can debate whether either the League or the UN was successful in curbing warfare, it seems clear that the 19th-century perceptions and behaviors with respect to military means and goals in foreign policy were markedly different from those which were to follow.

Warfare had become increasingly dangerous at all levels. Not only was the stability of the international system more precarious, but also the destructive potential in any military confrontation was considerably amplified. First of all, new technologies were to introduce entirely unforeseen facets of fire-power: mechanized infantry, air power—first for reconnaissance, later with weaponry—in terms of airplanes and then missiles, and finally a transformation in weaponry itself vis-à-vis, among other things, the nuclear bomb. At the same time that the military services acquired the ability to destroy more effectively enemy populations and territories, they also incurred the higher costs of military hardware. Both of these ingredients seemed to dampen the public enthusiasm for war; the former through spreading the desire to preserve one's home population and economy, and the latter by fortifying a desire to control enormous drains on the public treasury.

Figure 1: INCIDENCE AND DESTRUCTIVENESS OF INTERNATIONAL WAR, 1825-1965

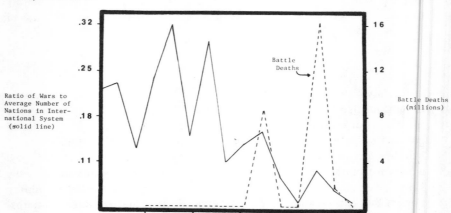

Source: Singer and Small, 1972:191-194.

Moreover, the number of nations in the international system had grown from around 20 in the early 1880s to over 100 by 1960 and around 160 in 1975. The bulk of these polities was not fundamentally aligned with any of the major powers which emerged from the two World Wars. Thus, the opportunity for war to erupt in the international system would, other things being equal, seem to have become more substantial.

Yet on average, the number of wars in the international system has not shown any marked increase, and in fact has declined from the high of 13 in the decade prior to 1865, which featured a host of intra-European as well as intra-Latin American hostilities, to an average of about five for each of the three decades subsequent to 1935 (Singer and Small, 1972:191-194). Considering the ratio of wars to the increasing number of nations in the international system, as shown in Figure 1, one is struck by the relative decline in the incidence of war in the growing international system. However, if one looks not at the trend of the number of wars over time, but at the destructiveness, in terms of deaths, of the wars fought, a very different picture emerges. In terms of battle deaths, the destructiveness of wars early in this period pales in comparison to the havoc brought about by the most recent international wars. The battle deaths of wars in the late 1880s, for example—including both the Ten Years War (1868-1878) and the Seven Weeks War (1866)—had battle death figures on the order of 100,000 or less (Singer and Small, 1972:62, 73). The corresponding figures for both the first and second World Wars are estimated at nine and fifteen million, respectively (Singer and Small, 1972:66, 67).

While the frequency of international wars has declined along with the increase in their destructiveness, the two major World Wars of the 20th century serve as reminders of the continued salience of warfare and military might. The picture after 1945 is quite different from that which preceded the Second World War. Historically, warfare and weaponry occupied the premier place on the agenda of national decision makers, with domestic and economic issues trailing far behind in importance. For example, the U.S. military budget typically comprised over 50% of the governmental outlays throughout the 1800s, and frequently went beyond the 60% mark (U.S. Bureau of the Census, 1975:1114-1115). Despite the fact that a period of intense, bipolar competition characterized United States and Soviet relations in the post-World War II era, the domination of the budget by the military has, to date, not approached the pre-1900 levels.

Even in the face of the armaments races between these two major superpowers, during the 1950s and 1960s the United States showed a more moderate role of the defense allocations in budgetary matters. For the most part, the military share of the budget ranged from a low of around 40% to a high of about 52% in 1955. Table 1 presents the general pattern of the relative increase in nonmilitary governmental expenditures within the U.S. budget. The welfare ratio gives the percent of the budget *not* devoted to military line items. As the data in Table 1 demonstrate, there is considerable fluctuation in the relative proportions of defense and nondefense spending

TABLE 1. NONMILITARY EXPENDITURES AS A PERCENT OF U.S.
TOTAL BUDGET AND TOTAL GOVERNMENT OUTLAYS
AS A PERCENT OF GROSS NATIONAL PRODUCT,
SELECTED YEARS, 1820−1975.

| | Pre−1945 | | | Post−1945 | |
Year	Welfare[a] Ratio	Budget[b] Ratio	Year	Welfare Ratio	Budget Ratio
1820	44	NA	1950	60	14
1830	38	NA	1955	41	18
1840	35	NA	1956	44	17
1850	52	NA	1957	45	18
1860	54	NA	1958	47	19
1870	70	4	1959	50	20
1880	59	2	1960	51	19
1890	44	2	1961	52	19
1900	36	3	1962	53	20
1910	32	2	1963	54	19
1920	60	7	1964	55	19
1930	68	4	1965	59	18
1940	74	9	1966	59	19
			1967	56	20
			1968	56	22
			1969	57	20
			1970	60	21
			1971	64	21
			1972	67	21
			1973	70	20
			1974	71	20
			1975	73	22

a. Welfare Ratio is defined as the percent of total U.S. governmental outlays not devoted to military spending. The pre−1945 series (and data for 1950) are from the U.S. Bureau of the Census, 1975:1114−1115. Prior to 1954, defense outlays are aggregated from the expenditures of the Departments of Army, Navy, and Air Force (after 1948). Post−1945 data were taken from the Office of Management and Budget, 1977:436.

b. Budget Ratio is defined as total U.S. governmental outlays as a percent of the Gross National Product. Data for 1870−1950 are taken from the U.S. Bureau of the Census, 1975:1114−1115. Data for years subsequent to 1950 are from the Office of Management and Budget, 1977:435.

from 1820 to 1940. However, within this fluctuation, the military's share of the budget has shown a general downward trend.

The years from 1940 to 1950 are somewhat aberrant, owing to the upheaval in the U.S. economy and budget brought about by the mobilization for the war effort. In the post-war years there is a clear, distinct, and almost continual increase in nonmilitary spending of about 2% or 3% per annum. In 1955, only some 41% of the U.S. budget was devoted to nonmilitary items, while in 1975, almost three-quarters of all federal spending was in the social-welfare category. The magnitude of these two related trends is even doubly underscored when the growth of both national product and the powers of taxation are considered. Not only has the ability to extract taxes from U.S. citizens and corporations accelerated considerably in the 20th century, but the sources of these revenues have also been augmented by a national product which has grown several orders of magnitude from its level of some 11 billion dollars in 1880 to a 1975 figure of about $1451 billion. In the late 1880s, the budget comprised only about 2 or 3% of the national product, while throughout the post-World War II era it has fluctuated only slightly from the 20% mark. This rapid deceleration in the prominence of military as opposed to social-welfare spending, evident throughout the last three decades, but particularly striking in the period from 1970 to the present, is further indication of the reduction of the role given to the military sector in the U.S. national agenda.

Figure 2: U.S. ARMS EXPENDITURES IN 1970 MILLION DOLLARS AND AS PERCENT OF GROSS DOMESTIC PRODUCT, 1948-1976.

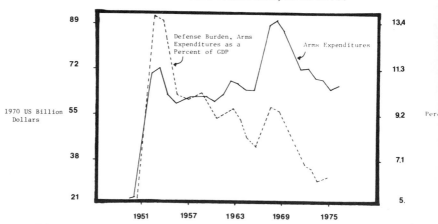

Sources: Stockholm International Peace Research Institute Yearbooks for 1974, 1976, and 1977.

Turning to an examination of the actual level of arms expenditures, and focusing upon the U.S. experience subsequent to 1950, one finds marked variation in the amounts spent by the United States on weapons and armies. Figure 2 depicts this trend. The early 1950s brought the rapid increase in arms levels shown by the first spike on the graph. A corresponding escalation in the Soviet arms levels is also evident, but is not presented. Much of this increase in spending is attributable to the Korean War effort. The intensification of the Cold War in the very early 1960s as evidenced, for example, in the construction of the Berlin Wall in August of 1962, and the changes in U.S. strategic posture from a counter-city to a counter-force doctrine, ushered in a new period in which armaments were acquired by each of the major powers. Subsequently, the Vietnamese War and the American involvement there account for the highest arms levels reached by the United States in the late 1960s.

Irrespective of the relative decline in military priorities in the U.S. budget, Figure 2 demonstrates that U.S. arms levels have grown, in constant dollar terms, considerably in the 1950-1976 period. When compared to the gross domestic product (also Figure 2) however, American arms expenditures have strikingly declined vis-à-vis the more purely economic aspects of U.S. productivity—from a high of some 14% in 1952 to a current level of about 6%. If the cost of the Vietnamese war is factored out of these trends in defense spending, a real decline of about 2% may be observed in the 1963-1976 years (Hoeber and Schneider, 1977:7). Undoubtedly, the demonstration of the eventual ineffectiveness of the overt military involvement of large with small powers has tempered the perceived utility of military force by the large powers.

While there does appear to be a lessening of the emphasis placed on the military aspects of American, and perhaps Soviet, foreign policy, there is no absence of military confrontation in the world. The almost constant military engagement of Arabs and Israelis in the Middle East is but one example. Somalian and Ethiopian hostilities, purportedly unresolved disputes between Iran and Iraq, and several "localized" wars currently underway in West and South Africa each underscore this point. Thus, for the bulk of nations comprising the international system, the means of conducting foreign policy via military policy have far outdistanced the nuclear bomb in terms of proliferation. This massive spread of access to military weaponry has meant that Armies, Navies, and Air Forces are all relatively easily obtained by small, nonindustrialized nations that may be involved in regional antagonisms.

The military supplies for such ventures are overwhelmingly provided by the U.S. (cumulatively some 46% since 1961) and the U.S.S.R., which jointly have accounted for over three-quarters of all arms sales in the past 15 years

(Sivard, 1977:9). The Americans and Soviets have not tended to explicitly involve themselves in these many localized conflicts. However, the (in)famous Pakistani "tilt" and the "encouragement" rendered by the Soviets for the Cubans regarding their Angolan involvement are examples which fall very closely to the boundary of active involvement. Nonetheless, United States and Soviet military *absence* from these conflicts is in large part what restrained their escalation beyond local and regional boundaries.

Digesting these trends in the role of military power in U.S. foreign policy is difficult. On the one hand, military force is more destructive and potentially decisive in actual confrontations today than ever before. Yet, contemporary international norms and practices seem to inhibit, if not curtail, its actual usage by the major military powers. The nuclear holocaust implied by superpower confrontation is simply too great a risk to bear. On the other hand, while the centrality of defense spending in the budget has declined considerably in the past 50 years, the current international system was largely born out of two global wars, each resolved by military power. It would seem that despite the decline in the salience of the use of military power in the foreign policy of major powers, military might in its actual usage, as in the Second World War, and in its implied form, as in the evolution of post-World War II bipolarity, has the ability to transform the international system.

EVIDENCE AND TRENDS: ECONOMIC POWER

As argued above, the changing status of the military power of the United States in particular, and other super powers as well, is not based solely on the fluctuations of attributes held by national political units. Rather, power generally is a relational characteristic of interaction among political actors. Thus, whatever declines that may be evident in the utility of military force as a component of U.S. foreign policy cannot be viewed in a vacuum. The heightened importance of the economic side of the foreign policy behavior of nations must also be addressed. This section will briefly examine U.S. involvement in the international economic system, and explore the relationship between the military and economic trends.

The etiology of the post-war supremacy of America in global politics is based on both its military and economic relationships with the rest of the international system, and with Europe in particular. If the Second World War left the United States as the major military power, it even more clearly established the dominance of the United States in the world economic system. Not only was the dollar established as the staple of financial intercourse at the international level by the 1944 Bretton Woods agreement, but also the gold standard, on which the dollar itself was valued, remained fixed until the early 1970s at the level of 35 dollars *per* ounce. In practice, the dollar, and thereby the U.S. economy, was confirmed as the cornerstone of both the stability and the growth of the world economy. Throughout the 1950s and the early 1960s, the dollar was to remain strong vis-à-vis other prominent currencies such as the mark, franc, pound, and yen. This meant that American economic policy, whether made with respect to domestic or foreign environments, had a profound and driving impact on the other industrialized economies of the world, particularly European economies.

While American-Soviet strategic competition was severe during this period, the Russian economy was largely unconnected to the international scene. National economic development plans for industrializing the impoverished Soviet economy, concentration on the establishment and solidification of economic and social ties to socialist partners in the Warsaw Treaty Organization (WTO) and the Council for Mutual Economic Assistance (COMECON), and a healthy apprehension of exploitation accompanying global economic involvement among nonsocialist economies were three strong reasons which curtailed Soviet involvement in the world economy. This very low profile was to continue for many years despite the military prominence held by the U.S.S.R. in world affairs. Thus, the United States faced, for a relatively long period, no major challenges to its desire to stabilize the international economy through the promotion of international financial and commodity structures.

Additionally during this period, while suffering several setbacks, the U.S. economy was still primarily in a growth period. Until the late 1950s, America was still self-sufficient in the commodity which was to provide the catalyst for the next major transformation of the international economic order: petroleum. Domestic agricultural markets were strong, and technology seemed to be advancing hand-in-hand with productivity. The U.S. economic goal of liberalized free trade in the international arena was not completely fulfilled, but there was a considerable "opening up" of trade particularly in the industrial world. Despite the growth of trade in general, the United States and the major economies in Europe showed a continued preference for each other's goods and services. As shown in Figure 3, the exports of the European Economic Community (EEC) and the United States to one another demonstrate marked increase in the years since 1945.

If the U.S. trade to European polities is overlaid with this trend, one notices that while the relative affinity for European products has until very recently been on the ascent, the converse is far from holding true. Figure 4 shows that the relative proportion of EEC imports which originate in the United States has shown a steady decline from the late 1940s to present. Ironically, the year in which U.S. imports from EEC nations began account-

Figure 3: TOTAL U.S. EXPORTS TO EEC AND OF EEC TO U.S., 1948-1975.

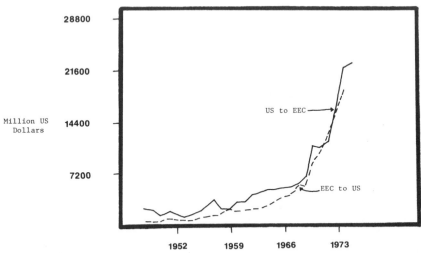

Sources: United Nations *Yearbook* for 1953, 1957, 1966, 1974, and 1975. International Monetary Fund and the International Bank for Reconstruction and Development *Annual* for 1962, 1966, 1970, and 1974.

Figure 4: RECIPROCAL IMPORTS OF THE U.S. AND EEC AS A PERCENTAGE OF THEIR TOTAL IMPORTS, 1948-1975.

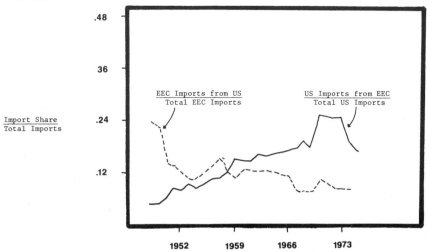

Source: Same as Figure 3.

ing for a greater percentage than the corresponding statistics for EEC imports from the U.S. is 1958, the year in which the European Economic Community was borne.

It should be emphasized, of course, that the EEC is not 'the same type of organized political unit as the United States. In addition to whatever common, coordinated economic policies may characterize the nine nations of the EEC, substantial diversity and competition still are reflected in their individual economic policies.

Despite the increase in regionalism in the post-1945 years, changes in trading patterns which may reflect the growth of regional economic and political interaction have typically been interpreted vis-à-vis their domestic implications. However, the international consequences have also been considerable, and deserve not to be ignored (Caporaso, 1976), particularly from the point of view of U.S. decision makers. Dependence, in terms of proportional reliance on suppliers of valued goods (Caporaso, 1976:349), is clearly one important variable greatly affected by structural change in, for example, regional trading patterns. The issue may be posed generally in terms of changes in the international environment of U.S. foreign policy behavior. More specifically, how have U.S. relations with Western Europe changed as a partial consequence of changing intra-European behavior patterns?

Irrespective of the domestic consequences, it may be that the growing gap shown in Figure 4 reflects a gap in the interdependence of these two economic forces on the contemporary world, the U.S. and the EEC. The post-World War II growth of the EEC nations was stimulated by the U.S. economic assistance embodied in the Marshall Plan. However, wherever possible, that growth itself has taken the path of declining dependence on U.S. products and increasing self-reliance. Thus, the economic environment of U.S. foreign policy has undergone considerable change as a consequence of not only the growth of European economic strength after World War II, but also the way in which that growth has promoted decreased interdependence between Europe and the United States.

The increased level of multilateral trade that was stimulated by a growing world economic order encouraging free trade among its members also fostered, in conjunction with *regional* free-trade schemes, concentration of trade. The European case presents considerable evidence for this trend. The EEC, the European Free Trade Association (EFTA), and COMECON represent such regional coordination of trade patterns. Almost in contradistinction to the growth of trade across expanding international horizons, trade patterns within Europe have become more compartmentalized. Since 1958 and until 1972, the concentration of intra-European trade has demonstrated almost continual increase. Most of this can be attributed to the growing vitality of the EEC itself, a point which directly ties in to the relative decline in the EEC reliance upon the United States.

This trend of growing involvement of the EEC, among other actors, as a powerful element in world politics is of considerable importance for U.S. foreign policy-making. The relative deterioration of the strong American position in European and world economic affairs is tied to the balance-of-payments and inflation problems faced by industrialized nations in the late 1960s. But, it was also sculpted by the emergence of new sources of economic power in the nonindustrialized "Third World" which would also become increasingly competitive in the global hierarchy of who gets what. These forces were also to have major consequences for the international political environment of U.S. foreign policy decision-making.

Though in existence since October 1960, the Organization of Petroleum Exporting Countries (OPEC) was of little importance in world affairs until the 1970s. The story of OPEC's ascent to a powerful position is relatively well known. Based on essentially singular efforts culminating in 1970 and 1971 respectively, Libya and Algeria were able to demonstrate to other oil exporters that the producers of petroleum held considerable economic power with respect to the oil consuming nations. This demonstration effect triggered the collectively negotiated Tehran accords of 1971 which obtained the first substantial industry-wide increase in petroleum prices in the history of the industry. The emergence of OPEC's unilateral behavior toward the oil consumers represented a complete reversal of the previous interaction patterns. The success of such strategies fueled the rising sense of nationalism and power held by the OPEC nations, and in December of 1973 the coup de grace occurred: the quadrupling of oil prices.

This came as a shock to the United States and the western oil consuming nations. Yet, the roots of such behavior were well embedded in the plans of oil exporting nations even in the early 1950s. Given the current "oil inspired" balance-of-payments, the trade problems faced by the United States in the late 1960s seem mild. More important than the economic dislocations in the American and European economies caused by the increased cost of energy supplies is the example provided by the successful exercise of economic influence by the small upon the large. The unsuccessful nationalization attempts by Iran in the early 1950s were essentially identical in structure to the successful OPEC programs of the 1970s. While the United States had used its military and economic influence to ensure the failure of Mossadeq's plan, this was no longer a feasible course of action in the 1970s.

The late 1960s provided a credible example of small versus large military confrontation: the victory of the North over the South Vietnamese and U.S. Armies. Yet in the military sphere the United States had been required to "pull its punches" in a sense, and the threat of nuclear power was never really a pertinent factor. In the economic sphere, though the Third World was still "undeveloped," it appeared that no holds were to be barred.

The example set by OPEC did not create a previously nonexistent set of economic concerns among both the industrial and nonindustrial nations. However, as the OPEC nations became the Wünderkinder of the developing world, they brought about a crystallization of a myriad of economic issues which were to rise to ascendency in global affairs. The umbrella-like coalition of the Third World Group of 77 exerted considerable influence in a host of international organizations, not the least of which was the United Nations. The North-South conference continued the separate organizational dialogue along a host of economic issues including financial and monetary matters, development planning and assistance, raw material trade, as well as energy. As the call went out for a New International Economic Order, so too did economic issues come to dominate the international agenda.

Thus, in addition to heightened economic "competition" among the United States, Europe, and the Soviet Union, each of these actors was to face new opportunities opened up by the North-South economic facet of international politics.

Stepping back for a moment from specific trade patterns in the Atlantic and Global arena, it is informative to look at the more general composition of trade in the European context. If bipolarization is "a process by which the members of a system . . . through their patterns of interaction group themselves into two subsystems" (Goldmann, 1974:109), then the economic bipolarization of European relations should reflect some of the changes in the international system brought about by the military and economic transformations discussed above. Using a modification of an index of bipolarization developed by Wall (1972), Goldmann (1974), and Goldmann and Lagerkranz (1977) have examined the extent to which European nations have oriented their trade toward one or the other of the super powers, the U.S. or the U.S.S.R. Basically, they found that from 1947 to 1951 there was a strong increase in trade with the U.S. and U.S.S.R. Since 1951 however, the extent of trade orientation toward the super powers has dramatically declined in an almost constant fashion. Currently, the bipolarization of economic interaction in this subsystem is considerably less polarized than it was even in the mid-1940s (Goldmann and Lagerkranz, 1977:260).

Goldmann (1974) also developed a procedure for charting the relative levels of tension perceived to exist across the East and West blocs. By content analyzing the public speeches of American, European, and Soviet decision makers and elites, an assessment of the collective perceptions of tension is developed. Figure 5 displays these data for NATO members. It should be

Figure 5: PERCEPTIONS OF NATO LEADERS TOWARD TENSION IN EUROPE, 1948-1975[a].

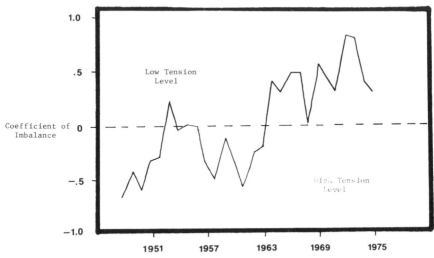

Source: Goldmann and Lagerkranz, 1977:256.

[a]Goldmann's Coefficient of Imbalance, Method R is used: $C=(f-u)/r$, where f= favorable units, u= unfavorable units, and r= relevant units in the content analysis of the speeches.

pointed out that Goldmann's coefficient of imbalance, the index used in his studies, has a high positive value when tension is perceived to be low; it has a high negative value when tension perceptions are high.

Note on the graph that the level of East-West tension shows two phases during the 1948-1960 period. A relatively steady decline in tension until about 1953 is followed by the escalation of the Cold War and the increased tensions which resulted until about 1962. Since that time, the general pattern has been one of continued, though variant, "relaxation" of tension between the two blocs between 1966 and the early 1970s. The high tension levels characteristic of the pre-1964 series are not matched by the low levels thereafter. In many ways, this corresponds to the more diplomatic and journalistic notions of "detente," which is believed to prevail in East-West relations since the late 1960s. Notice, however, that subsequent to 1971, the trend is for increased, rather than decreased, levels in East-West tensions, as they are perceived by leaders in the foreign policy sectors. This reflects, in part, the increased salience of economic issues in a world no longer totally dominated by the East-West military-security fissure.

The increased importance of economic over military aspects of global intercourse is matched by the renewed attention given by economic observers to politics (Bhagwati, 1972; Leontief et al., 1977; Herrera et al., 1976) and by political observers to economics (Morse, 1976; Keohane and Nye, 1973). The late 1940s ushered in an international system in which the United States held the dominant global role in military as well as economic affairs. Thus, while the security issues of the East-West split flavored global interaction, there was a concatenation of military and economic power in the hands of the United States.

As the 1950s and 1960s unfolded, the values and costs of these two primary arenas of the exercise of power and influence changed. The value of military power was seen to diminish as its relative ineffectiveness as a tool of U.S. foreign policy behavior was demonstrated. The intense destructive potential of the nuclear umbrella came, with experience, to imply also impotence in less than total military confrontations. Concomitantly, the cost of both maintaining the strategic deterrants and exercising them also inflated. On the other side, the value of economic power has been augmented not only by the increasing interdependence of the global system, but by its dramatic utilization by European and Third World coalitions as well. The costs of economic power are not so clear, but they are, in the short-run at least, substantially less ultimate than those associated with military confrontation on a global scale.

TRENDS, POLICY OPTIONS, AND RESPONSES

In this chapter we have explored the decline in the capability and use of military resources and the corresponding emergence of economic capabilities. Though we did not establish any of these trends with certainty, the evidence is strongly suggestive of important new ties among states. Nearly everyone is in agreement that international interdependence has increased in the last several decades, with commodity trade growing more rapidly than growth in world output, and with capital and technology playing an important global role. Increased dependence on foreign supplies of raw materials and the growing concentration of international trade, at least regionally (Caporaso, 1976; Preeg, 1974), have made countries more vulnerable to changes in international markets and threats of the disruption of supplies.

The emerging international interdependence of nation states brings with it new vulnerabilities and sensitivities to the actions of others, which in turn suggest a new foreign policy tool, the exploitation of these vulnerabilities toward one's political ends. For a country which can minimize its own vulnerabilities while maximizing those ties of other countries on itself, a new source of foreign policy leverage is open to it. Because the United States is the largest country in the world in economic terms, it is in a naturally favored position.

Despite the fact that many countries are highly dependent on the United States for commodities, capital, and technology, no coherent foreign policy response has yet taken place. There are scattered suggestions, some little more than cliches, that we "organize for interdependence," or create a new "interdependence council" composed of cabinet officers (Yost, 1976). Other suggestions have focused on the cultivation and exploitation of dependencies on the United States so that such dependencies can be used to pursue foreign policy goals. One observer (Schneider, 1976), taking his cue from the successful use of the oil weapon in the wake of the Yom Kippur War, has argued persuasively that the United States could use its food supplies as an effective international weapon. It is our opinion that such thinking is not an isolated instance, but only one of many studies we are likely to see in the coming decade.

If one allows that economic capabilities may be used to exercise political influence, and if further one concedes an earlier argument that economic capabilities flow from asymmetric interdependencies, a number of options emerge. The major question confronting states is not whether to choose isolation or involvement, but how to use involvement to create "situations of strength," in this case economic ones. Here a host of tactics suggest themselves: foster dependencies of others on oneself for important goods, discourage foreign supply of important goods to oneself but, if one must yield to such external supply, diversify reliance on outside sources, and finally, create counterdependencies as levers of economic retaliation. In a word, foster exclusive complementarities on oneself, but at the same time diversify reliance on others.

What might we expect in terms of the organizational response of the U.S. Government (and perhaps private actors too)? If new policies should flow out of emerging economic capabilities, is the present battery of foreign policy institutions, including Department of State, National Security Council, and the White House, equipped to respond to the challenge?

The organizational setting within which U.S. foreign policy is made is complex, and given the juxtaposition of that complexity and the relative simplicity of our argument, we shall limit our discussion to those few instances wherein there has been at least a stir of movement. The first thing to note is that it is difficult to locate the "center of gravity" for the formulation and execution of foreign economic policy. One observer (Malmgren, 1972:43) says that there are 60 agencies and departments which play some role in foreign economic policy. Another (Johnson, 1977:12) points out that power in Congress is even more dispersed, with 13 of the 19 standing committees in the U.S. Senate having some responsibility for foreign economic policy. Thus, the elusiveness of this "center" will continue, if not increase, in the years to come.

The overall picture is not a static one. On the contrary, there appears to be definite flux, with increasing responsibility gravitating toward some parts of the foreign affairs bureaucracy and away from others. These trends are convincingly argued by Hopkins (1976:413) who shows that several bureaucracies, including the Federal Energy Agency, and Departments of Agriculture, Treasury, and Interior, whose mandates are primarily "domestic," are increasingly responsible for a wide and expanding range of international activities.

Will not the emerging interdependence which ties countries to one another more closely than before, thus making it more and more difficult to fulfill domestic objectives without international complications, also lead to an increased role for international organizations? In general, the answer to this question seems to be "no," at least if we think of an international organization as a set of institutions which are organizationally distinct from the nation state. The chief reason for this expectation is that the organizational response to interdependence is taking place within our own domestic bureaucracies (Hopkins, 1976:11), in particular, the international role of the Departments of Energy, Agriculture, Commerce, and the Treasury is expanding and there are good reasons to suppose that these trends will continue. In comparison to international organizations, domestic organizations have "more secure budgets, long accepted legal authority for actions promoting domestic welfare (now increasingly linked with international activity), close working ties with domestic and international business officials, powerful, if latent, interest group support, and day-to-day operating command over the details of transnational flows of resources" (Hopkins, 1976:11).

The evidence examined makes plausible our argument about the decline of military power and the emergence of economic power. One should, of course, be wary of carrying this argument too far. Reality is fickle enough to pull the rug out from under many a plausible argument. There have been eras of military quiescence before which have erupted into militarism, notably the Second World War. Contemporary pressure to increase dramatically military expenditures, reflected in the "Team B" report (Pipes, 1977), suggests that social and economic concerns have not monopolized the attention of influential elites, and that defense interests have been building a head of steam even if they have not won the day.

The increased economic interdependence of advanced industrial countries would seem to be a solid trend, however, based on long-term forces, reversible perhaps, but only by a drastic shock such as the massive depression of the 1930s. This trend is important regardless of one's conclusion about military force. State power does not have to be either military or economic. It can be both.

REFERENCES

BHAGWATI, J.N. (ed.) (1972). Economics and world order: From the 1970's to the 1990's. New York: Free Press.

BUNDY, W.P. (1977). "Elements of national power." Foreign Affairs, 56(1):1-26.

CAPORASO, J.A. (1976). "The external consequences of regional integration for pan-European relations: Inequality, dependence, polarization, and symmetry." International Studies Quarterly, 20(3):341-392.

CHAMBERLAIN, W. (1977). "Flags of convenience and cargo preference legislation." Marine Policy Reports, 1(4):1-6.

COTLER, J., and FAGEN, R.R. (eds.) (1974). The United States and Latin America: The changing political realities. Stanford, Cal.: Stanford University Press.

DAHL, R.A. (1969). "The concept of power." Pp. 79-93 in R. Bell, D. Edwards, and R.H. Wagner (eds.), Political power: A reader in theory and research. New York: Free Press.

EAST, M.A., SALMORE, S.A., and HERMANN, C.F. (eds.) (1978). Why nations act. Beverly Hills, Cal.: Sage.

GEIGER, T. (1973). The fortunes of the West. Bloomington: Indiana University Press.

GOLDMANN, K. (1974). Tension and detente in bipolar Europe. Stockholm, Sweden: Esselte Studium.

——— and LAGERKRANZ, J. (1977). "Neither tension nor detente: East-West relations in Europe, 1971-1975." Conflict and Cooperation, 12(4):251-264.

HERRERA, A.O., SKOLNIK, H.D., et al. (1976). Catastrophe or new society? A Latin American world model. Ottawa, Canada: International Development Research Center.

HIRSCHMAN, A.O. (1945). National power and the structure of foreign trade. Berkeley, Cal.: University of California Press.

HOEBER, F.P., and SCHNEIDER, W. (1977). Arms, men, and military budgets: Issues for fiscal year 1978. New York: Crane, Russak.

HOFFMANN, S. (1968). Gulliver's troubles, or the setting of American foreign policy. New York: McGraw-Hill.

——— (1975). "Notes on the elusiveness of modern power." International Journal, 30(2):183-206.

HOPKINS, R.F. (1976). "The international role of 'domestic' bureaucracy." International Organization, 30(3):405-432.

International Monetary Fund. Direction of trade (annual). Volumes from 1958 to 1972. Washington, D.C.: Author.

International Monetary Fund and the International Bank for Reconstruction and Development. Direction of trade (annual). Volumes for 1962, 1966, 1970, and 1974. Washington, D.C.: Author.

JOHNSON, R.H. (1977). Managing interdependence: Restructuring the U.S. government. Development paper 23. Washington, D.C.: Overseas Development Council.

KATZENSTEIN, P.J. (1977). "Introduction: Domestic and international forces and strategies of foreign economic policy." International Organization, 31(4):587-606.

KEEGAN, J. (1976). The face of battle. New York: Viking.

KEOHANE, R.O., and NYE, J.S. (1973). "World politics and the international economic system." Pp. 115-180 in C.F. Bergsten (ed.), The future of the international economic order. Lexington, Mass.: D.C. Heath.

——— (1977). Power and interdependence: World politics. Boston, Mass.: Little, Brown.

KNORR, K. (1966). On the uses of military power in the nuclear age. Princeton, N.J.: Princeton University Press.

——— (1973). Power and wealth: The political economy of international power. New York: Basic Books.

——— (1975). The power of nations. New York: Basic Books.

LEONTIEF, W. et al. (1977). The future of the world economy: A United Nations study. New York: Oxford University Press.

MALMGREN, H.B. (1972). "Managing foreign economic policy." Foreign Policy, 6:42-68.

MORSE, E.L. (1976). Modernization and the transformation of international relations. New York: Free Press.

——— (1977). "The new nationalism and the coordination of economic policies." Paper delivered at the Annual Meetings of Committee on Atlantic Studies, Luxembourg.

NYE, J.S. (1974). "Collective economic security." International Affairs, 50(4):584-598.

Office of Management and Budget (1977). The budget of the United States government: Fiscal year 1978. Washington, D.C.: Author.

PIPES, R. (1977). "Why the Soviet Union thinks it could fight and win a nuclear war." Commentary, 64(1), reprinted by National Strategy Information Center, New York, 1-14.

PREEG, E.H. (1974). Economic blocs and U.S. foreign policy. Washington, D.C.: National Planning Association.

SCHNEIDER, W. (1976). Food, foreign policy, and raw materials cartels. New York: Crane, Russak.

SEMMEL, B. (1970). The rise of free trade imperialism, 1750-1850. Cambridge, England: Cambridge University Press.

SINGER, J.D., and SMALL, M. (1972). The wages of war 1816-1965: A statistical handbook. New York: John Wiley.

SIVARD, R.L. (1976). World military and social expenditures: 1976. Leesburg, Va.: WMSE.

——— (1977). World military and social expenditures: 1977. Leesburg, Va.: WMSE.

Stockholm International Peace Research Institute. World armaments and disarmament: SIPRI yearbook. Volumes for 1974, 1976, and 1977. Cambridge, Mass.: MIT Press.

STRANGE, S. (1975). "What is economic power, and who has it?" International Journal, 30(2):207-224.

United Nations. Yearbook of international trade statistics, Volumes for 1953, 1957, 1966, 1974, and 1975. Washington, D.C.: Author.

United States Bureau of the Census (1965). Foreign commerce and navigation of the U.S., 1946-1963. Washington, D.C.: Author.

——— (1975). Historical statistics of the United States: Colonial times to present, part 2. Washington, D.C.: Author.

VON CLAUSEWITZ, C. (1976). On war. Edited and translated by M. Howard and P. Paret. Princeton, N.J.: Princeton University Press.

cluding gold and SDRs, the EC is stronger than the U.S., and Japan shows up better than the Soviet Union. Only in terms of military power are the United States and the Soviet Union substantially ahead of the Nine and Japan.

The data presented in Table 1 suggest that major challenges to American foreign policy makers in the 1980s are likely to spring from economic issues including questions of competing economic and political influence in various parts of the world. However, security issues have also produced their share of frictions despite the clear community of strategic interests among the three parties and the contractual obligations flowing from NATO in Europe and the U.S.-Japanese Mutual Security Treaty. Overarching both economic and security problems is the crucial matter of adequate energy resources in which the policies of the United States play a central role. Indeed, there is much interdependence and interplay between all three categories of sensitive issues and this interconnection must be carefully considered when American policies are being formulated.

To make projections regarding the U.S. relations with the Community and Japan in the 1980s and perhaps offer pertinent policy suggestions, our trend analysis for each of the areas will be structured as follows. We will begin with an assessment of military-political developments because security considerations remain basic to U.S. relations with Western Europe and Japan. This will be followed by an examination of economic-political developments with particular emphasis on international trade patterns and direct foreign investment. Next, our attention will turn to energy developments. Here we will touch on the exhaustion of petroleum reserves, nuclear reactor technology and uranium supplies and the nonproliferation of nuclear weapons issue. Finally, some comments will be made about the effect on U.S. policy if the Community member states were to unify.

THE EUROPEAN COMMUNITY

In 1973 the European Community was expanded from the original six member states (France, Italy, West Germany, and the Benelux countries) to nine members by the addition of Great Britain, Ireland, and Denmark, and thereby assumed the position of an economic super power in the world as was demonstrated in Table 1.

When and if Greece, Portugal, and Spain join the Community in the 1980s (Greece perhaps before the next decade), the weight of the EC in world affairs will be strengthened further. Only in the security sector must the Nine continue to look to the United States as the chief defender of the Free World.

Defense expenditures of the United States are more than twice as large as those of the Nine, and the number of military forces is larger than that maintained by the Community countries.

Military-Political Developments

Past Behavioral Patterns. While we do not assume that the past is prologue, the recent history in transatlantic relations is instructive as we seek clues to the future. All EC member states except Ireland are members of NATO. However, while France has remained a party to the NATO Treaty, in March 1966 it withdrew French personnel from the NATO integrated military headquarters and terminated the assignment of French military forces to the NATO international commands. Greece and Portugal, likely candidates for joining the EC, are also members of NATO, but because of the dispute with Turkey over Cyprus, Greek involvement in NATO has changed from enthusiastic support to reduced participation. Spain, another possible candidate for EC membership, may well be invited to join NATO since the stigma of the Franco dictatorship has been removed with Spanish transition to democratic government.

Despite the clear, fundamental community of strategic security interests between the United States and Western Europe, the record of transatlantic cooperation has been marred during the 1960s and 1970s by misunderstandings, exaggerated expectations, and frictions of varying magnitude. In the purely military and strategic sphere the highly advertised, equal partnership model for Atlantic Alliance affairs based on a united Europe was misleading in terms of defense management and unrealistic in the anticipation of a rapid unification process within the EC. The U.S. government has always insisted on unified (i.e., U.S.-dominated) control of strategic and tactical nuclear weapons, and the various proposals for sharing nuclear responsibilities, such as the ill-fated Multilateral Force (MLF) in the early 1960s and the establishment of the Nuclear Defense Affairs Committee with its Nuclear Planning Group, did not in any way modify the principle of basically U.S. control of nuclear weapons employment.

A lingering doubt has persisted in Western Europe whether the United States would not be reluctant to accept extensive casualties and destruction in American cities to save Western Europe, especially if a Soviet attack were directed against secondary targets (minor cities) in Europe. Closely related to this concern is the dispute over the withdrawal of American forces from Germany. From the American side this was linked to U.S. balance-of-payments difficulties and American insistence for compensatory payments or purchases of American goods. Strong pressure in the U.S. Senate to reduce American forces exacerbated this problem.

Particular foreign policy interests in various parts of the world diverged at times and this divergence generated serious tensions. The U.S. adventure in Vietnam received little material assistance from the European NATO member governments despite strong appeals by Secretary of State Dean Rusk and Secretary of Defense Robert McNamara in 1965. U.S. positions in the 1956 Middle East war and our near-intervention in the 1973 hostilities also reflected divergent interests. The alert of American military forces in October 1973 to counter possible military action by the Soviet Union caused consternation in Western Europe and the U.S. government complained bitterly when NATO countries with the exception of Portugal declined assistance to American re-supply efforts for hard-pressed Israel and refused requested landing rights to American air force planes.

Intimately involved in the 1973 dispute was the perennial problem of consultation. The basis of any lasting alliance is the continued process of consultation so that every alliance member state knows what its partners are planning and concerted action can best be undertaken. However, the notion of consultation itself is complex and means more than simply informing the partners of action taken or contemplated. It seems that as a minimum the concept of consultation must include serious consideration of advice and counsel given by other alliance member governments.

Indicators for the Future. A hopeful omen for the future is the extensive political consultation which took place in advance of the Conference on Security and Cooperation in Europe (CSCE), concluded in 1975, and continued regarding the post-CSCE implementation phase and especially the Belgrade review meetings in 1977-1978. There are also continuing extensive and effective consultations within the Alliance on the subject of Mutual and Balanced Force Reductions (MBFR) on which negotiations are currently in progress in Vienna. In the case of the MBFR, NATO members have taken a major step beyond negotiations and have assigned NATO a management role. This trend suggests increased intra-Alliance closeness on major questions and may portend an expanded role of NATO in arms control and détente in the 1980s.

The problem of sharing the burden of the common defense is being eased by valuable contributions made by the Eurogroup that was formed in 1968 and consisting at present of all EC members and Turkey. The Eurogroup is a vehicle for member countries to contribute to overall Alliance security by coordinating their defense efforts and by making best use of the resources available for defense. In 1970 it launched the European Defense Improvement Program at a cost of $1 billion (1970 prices) over a five-year period and in 1977 another program was initiated that includes the introduction of over

1500 tanks and armored vehicles, over 350 anti-aircraft guided missile systems, and more than 30 new ships and submarines. While these programs augur well for further cooperation in the 1980s, U.S. policy makers must attempt to curb impulses of national egoism which are a recurring problem in the United States and elsewhere.[1]

A challenge to fruitful defense collaboration in the next decade and indeed for NATO's cohesion may be the phenomenon of Eurocommunism. The concepts of Eurocommunism include (1) respect for democratic methods including majority rule and acceptance of and compliance with the results of periodic free elections; (2) basic recognition of the need for a free market economy and no insistence on complete nationalization of private enterprise, even though extensive state planning is considered necessary; (3) strong support for the European Community which, however, is to be "democratized"; and (4) continued membership in NATO.

While it is always possible that Eurocommunism represents a departure from Soviet totalitarianism, at present this is an untested assumption. The important question is not how the Eurocommunists behave when they are outside the government striving to participate in its control, but what actions they will take after they have achieved this goal. When the latter happens, the old undemocratic, staunchly pro-Soviet face may reemerge. This is a true dilemma for the present leaders and people in Italy and France as well as for their EC and NATO partners (Prinsky, 1977:40). The specter of Communists in either the Italian or French government of the future, or perhaps in Portugal, troubles many American leaders and some of the public although the Carter Administration seems to be more relaxed about such a development than its predecessors. But whatever the U.S. attitude, in such an event, NATO secrets may be jeopardized and the cohesion of the Alliance undermined. Thus, Eurocommunism may well represent a major challenge to American foreign policy in the years to come. If this challenge were to materialize, it might be unwise to put too much pressure on the French and Italian governments and people, and indeed on the EC as a whole. It may be better to work through other EC member governments, consult with them, and listen to their counsel rather than to engage in strident rhetoric across the Atlantic on the matter.

Economic-Political Developments

International Trade Patterns. U.S. trade with the European Community since 1958 has, with the exception of 1972, always shown a surplus. In 1976 the favorable trade balance exceeded $7 billion. Exports of agricultural products, with which the U.S. has been especially concerned since the introduction of the Community's Common Agricultural Policy (CAP), declined from 1966 to 1969, but showed a general upward trend through 1976. Imports of EC goods into the United States also increased by 5% during 1976, but imports of steel, a sore subject in America at the present time, were nearly halved (Executive Office of the President, 1977:26-27).

U.S. exports to the EC more than quintupled since 1958 and the reverse flow of trade more than quadrupled. This spectacular growth is in part due to multilateral trade liberalization measures such as the Kennedy Round negotiations which were concluded in 1967. In these negotiations the key roles were played by the United States and the EC which, on many issues, but especially agricultural commodities and nontariff barriers, had very conflicting interests. Nevertheless, the negotiations were successful and resulted in tariff reductions exceeding 35% (Feld, 1976:170-192).

Currently a new round of negotiations on tariff reductions is underway, the "Tokyo Round," named for the city where preliminary talks took place. Again, the United States and the EC are the main actors in this vital bargaining game and the expectation is that the negotiations will be completed in 1978. The tentative target is a 40% reduction of tariff with 25% of an automatic nature to be implemented over a period of five years, while the second 15% would be subject to specific economic conditions and also spread over five years. But tariff reductions will be only one part of the package; other parts will be a new code for customs evaluation, a search for new compromises on agricultural issues, assured adherence to new non-tariff-barriers provisions, and the introduction of selective safeguard clauses (Agence Europe Bulletin, 1977a).

Assuming these negotiations will succeed by the end of 1978, although the results may be more modest than the original targets, the new system will most likely be the basis for trade between the United States and the EC in the 1980s. However, further expansion of this trade will depend on the health of the economies of the transatlantic partners and this will depend on the rate of inflation which will be strongly influenced by the rise in oil prices. If inflation and other factors continue to impede economic recovery, countries on both sides may feel obliged to resort to protectionist measures and a new wave of economic nationalism could do much to riddle with many holes the new trade opportunities created by the Tokyo Round. Contributing to such a scenario are the huge balance-of-payments deficits suffered by some Atlantic Alliance states as a result of large crude oil imports. The United States in 1977 had a $30 billion deficit that cannot be sustained for long. Economic malaise and especially galloping inflation may also produce economic inequities among the people which in turn might engender serious political instability intensifying the trends toward national egoism. U.S. foreign policy makers during the 1980s must do everything in their power to prevent such developments and this will demand a high level of leadership. Continuing transatlantic consultations will be necessary, but they will be fruitful only if they culminate in close policy cooperation on all international trade matters.

Economic Policies Toward Third World Areas. While the trade relationship between the United States and the EC in the final analysis reflects the accommodation of national interests, divergent interests may be more difficult to bridge when it comes to the pursuit of economic policies toward the Third World. Indeed, in the past, American foreign policy makers were irritated by certain aspects of the EC's association policies in Africa and the preferential arrangements made with countries rimming the Mediterranean basin for which the Community claimed to have an historical special responsibility (Feld, 1976:131-154).

The primary bone of contention regarding the Community's association policy has been the granting of "reverse preferences." This means that the associate country is granted not only reduction or elimination of tariffs for goods shipped to the Community, but that it offers certain tariff preferences for the import of Community products. The United States and other nonmember states considered reverse preferences by the associated countries to Community exports of manufactured goods as discriminatory against third country manufacturers. The Lomé Convention, tying nearly 50 developing countries in Africa (south of the Sahara), the Caribbean, and the Western Pacific to the Community in 1975, dispensed with the need of reciprocal preferences. It gives the associated countries the option to grant special trade concessions to the EC countries, but also allows them to make the preferences available to third countries. Thus, this source of friction between the United States and the EC has been eliminated.

The Community's Mediterranean policy has succeeded during the last few years to establish a network of preferential agreements or associations with all Mediterranean states except Libya and Albania. Yugoslavia also has a trade agreement with the Community, but it is nonpreferential. The economic importance of the Community-Mediterranean relationship is illustrated by the fact that, apart from Libyan oil deliveries, 36.5% of the exports of all Mediterranean countries go to the EC while 37.6% of their total imports come from the Community (Ehrhardt, 1971:21-22).

The United States always deplored any kind of preferential treatment by the EC outside Europe proper. It opposed the Community's Mediterranean policy because of concern about the adverse effects on American exports of citrus fruits and other goods to the area, although the amounts involved are relatively small. As a matter of principle, the United States has proclaimed again and again that the preferential agreements are violations of GATT, which only permits full-fledged customs unions and free trade areas to be exempted from the most-favored-nation clause. The Community has admitted a possible violation but continues to claim its special responsibility for the countries of the area.

Indicators for the Future. Although the Lomé affiliates have expressed occasional dissatisfaction with the functioning of the Convention, the $4 billion European Development Fund disbursements, including the novel Stabex system of providing some measure of price stability for certain export commodities of the affiliated countries, are appreciated.[2] Indeed, the Stabex system is at least a partial fulfillment of a longheld aspiration of all developing countries: establishment of a mechanism to counter the wide fluctuations of primary commodities. However, this system covers *only* exports to the Community members, not to third countries. Another feature of the Lomé Convention and the Mediterranean agreements of the Community is a strong emphasis on industrial and technological cooperation. This is supplemented by institutionalized and at times purposely expanded contacts between parliamentarian and civil servants from the EC member states and the Lomé affiliates (Feld, 1976:129). The consequence is the development of close relationships between the Community and the affiliated states which may have long-term implications for the distribution of international power and influences. The main beneficiary of this close relationship is likely to be the Community business world, but the institutionalized cooperation with the Lomé affiliates and Mediterranean countries might also be helpful for the pursuit of EC member states' foreign policies in various international forums and particularly the United Nations.

While at this time the U.S. government appears to be quite relaxed about the potential rise of Community influence in the Lomé territories, the Mediterranean, and perhaps in the Third World generally, pressures by American business interests may give rise to different attitudes among American foreign policy makers. The quest for critical raw materials in Africa and other Third World countries needed to keep domestic industries running smoothly may spur competitive action and perhaps preemption of such materials, for which the Community could be in a better position than the United States. Although there is a clear economic imperative for economic cooperation between America and the Community, the perceived priority for national solutions to remedy adverse economic and political situations may prevent the formation of rational cooperation policies and thereby constitute a major challenge to U.S. foreign policy.

Transnational Direct Investment Patterns. Although direct investments by American firms in Europe continued to expand during the last few years, the increases have become smaller and fell by about 10% from 1975 to 1976. Nevertheless, investments in Europe at the end of 1976 amounted to $56 billion (U.S. Department of Commerce, 1977a:32-64). Among the major reasons for this development were host country policies making dismissals of workers very expensive and plant closings almost impossible even if, through price controls on certain items, profits are cut to zero. Other reasons are more rapid escalation of production costs in Western Europe than in the United States, and volatile foreign exchange markets. These factors have also induced some American multinational corporations to sell their subsidiaries in Western Europe. However, despite this recent trend, Western Europe retains the lion's share of American direct investment abroad with over 37% of total investment.

The reverse flow of investments shows a different trend. Direct investments by European firms in the United States have accelerated during the last few years at an increasing pace. Their total has risen from $6.1 billion in 1965 to $19.9 billion in 1976 and have continued to increase at a fast pace in the first half of 1977 (Executive Office of the President, 1977:85; Wall Street Journal, 1977a).

U.S. foreign investment policy is basically liberal with minimum restraint on the entry and exit of foreign investment and equal treatment with national firms. Some limitations, however, do exist regarding investments in shipping, communications, domestic air transport, the development of hydroelectric power and atomic energy. Some state laws also impose a variety of restrictions.

Will the transatlantic investment pattern persist in the 1980s, and what, if any, might be the reactions of American foreign policy makers? Several reasons seem to support the assumption that the acceleration of West European investments in the United States and deceleration of American investment flows to Europe are likely to continue:

(1) The United States has been able to shake off the economic malaise of the mid-1970s;

(2) Labor costs in Europe probably will continue to rise more rapidly than in the United States;

(3) Many left-wing unions in France, Britain, and Italy push for societal and economic changes giving them a much more significant voice in the management of plants than at present; and

(4) In the background looms the spectre of Eurocommunism which is frightening to many business leaders in the United States and the EC.

For all these reasons the future pattern of investment flows will benefit the American balance-of-payments, offer new opportunities for American labor, and might add in fact to U.S. exports if European subsidiaries would consider servicing foreign markets from America as desirable. But despite these desirable aspects, some Americans may argue for restrictions on investments in selected business sectors on the ground that large-scale penetration of sensitive manufacturing and service industries might impair the pursuit of U.S. national interests. On balance, however, American foreign policy makers should welcome the growing web of cross-Atlantic investment ventures among countries that are military allies because it will tend to reinforce existing areas of cooperation.

Energy Developments

It is not necessary to belabor the disarray in the relationship between the United States and the EC which followed the oil embargo of October 1973 and the subsequent meteoric rise of the petroleum price. In February 1974 the United States succeeded in convening the Washington Energy Conference in which the EC member states participated after the Nine had allowed themselves to be divided by the oil producing countries into friendly and not-so-friendly countries vis-a-vis Israel and its Arab adversaries. The purpose of the conference was to work out a common program for easing the energy crisis. The result was the creation of an Energy Coordinating Group (ECG) which later was transformed into the International Energy Agency (IEA) operating under the auspices of the OECD.

Subsequent to the Washington Conference the IEA formulated and activiated the so-called International Energy Program (IEP) which constituted a scheme for sharing oil resources in the event of future oil supply crises and obligated IEA members to adopt energy-saving measures and cooperate in the field of research and development of new energy sources (Agence Europe Bulletin, 1974). Although the French government was urged repeatedly to join the IEA, it declined official participation because it wished to keep its freedom for dealing with the oil producers (Ehrhardt, 1975:6).

With a possible petroleum shortfall to meet Free World petroleum demand beginning in 1985 (see Figure 1) and nuclear energy a viable and needed alternative energy source, assured uranium supplies have become a crucial necessity, especially for the EC countries.

Since the United States has not always been the most reliable supplier of uranium and has embarked on a nonproliferation of nuclear weapons policy that may cause difficulties for the future supply of enriched uranium, the Community countries have cast about for alternative sources of supply

Figure 1: FREE WORLD PETROLEUM DEMAND BY AREA

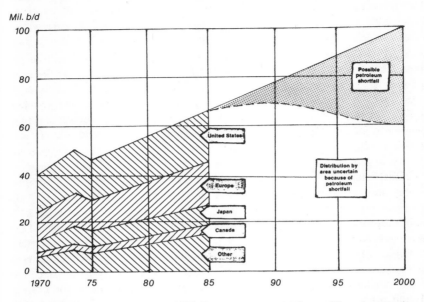

Source: *Oil and Gas Journal* (Vol. 75, No. 35, August 1977), special anniversary issue, "Petroleum 2000," p. 59.

including Canada and Australia which possess large uranium deposits. Meanwhile, other aspects of the U.S. nonproliferation policies have caused much consternation in West European governmental circles. American desires for halting the sales of reprocessing plants for nuclear waste and the transfer of appropriate technologies to countries not now possessing such facilities (Pierre and Moyne, 1976) have affected especially the Federal Republic of Germany and France. At least for the time being, the potential conflict with the United States has been largely defused by an agreement of 15 countries that have been major exporters of nuclear technology or on the threshold of joining this group. Under this agreement future sales of sensitive nuclear technology would be subject to tougher controls, and lax safeguards as found in the German and French contracts, possible a means of gaining a competitive advantage, would have to be avoided (International Herald Tribune, 1977).

For purposes of ensuring nonproliferation of nuclear weapons, the United States also has indicated the gradual suspension of shipments of highly enriched uranium and has strongly opposed the construction of fast breeder reactors. These positions have also given rise to serious concern in Western Europe although the American policies on fast breeders are only directed against the consequences for nuclear weapons construction. If fast breeders can be made proliferation resistant and are fully safeguardable, the U.S. government has no objection to this technology.[3] Nevertheless, the EC Commission seems to be determined to continue the present fast breeder pilot program which is close to reaching the industrial stage. It also persists in a policy of reprocessing nuclear waste. It points out that fast breeder reactors are 60 times more efficient than light-water reactors and reprocessing will save up to 20% a year in uranium costs.

What will the very complex energy situation hold for the 1980s in terms of American foreign policy? In view of the prospective short-fall of petroleum to meet especially the needs of the EC countries, competition for alternate energy sources and assured petroleum supplies may be stiff. The new U.S. nonproliferation policies, no matter how well meaning, may be rejected by the Europeans, who perceive fast breeders and enriched uranium as crucial for economic survival and who are irritated by the American stance of caution. American inability to evolve effective policies for reducing oil consumption and conserving energy will increase European resentment, especially since the EC countries have managed to reduce oil imports somewhat. While Great Britain may achieve oil sufficiency in 1980, this will not help much its EC partners.

American foreign policy is now prepared to create nonproliferation incentives through fuel assurances and assistance in the management of spent fuel for countries that forego a full fuel cycle. Moreover, joint studies on uranium enrichment and reprocessing of nuclear waste agreed upon at the London Summit in May 1977 are presently underway. Nevertheless, the already existing strong commercial competition regarding sales of nuclear facilities to third countries between the United States and major European countries[4] and the legitimate concern of Western Europe to ensure sufficient energy sources for its needs cannot but contribute to making transatlantic economic and political relations more difficult and create recurring tensions. The danger cannot be denied that instead of heeding the rational imperative of cooperation among the Atlantic alliance members, national egoism on both sides of the Atlantic will carry the day. This is a major challenge to America's top-level foreign policy makers and requires their careful consideration of the differential between the "cost" of divergent policies and the "cost" of closely coordinated policies in terms of international and domestic politics. The greater the cost of policy divergence, the more attractive will be close policy coordination, even if not all American objectives can be fully achieved.

Political Integration Effects

If political integration in the Community were to make progress and eventually a West European region state were to emerge during the 1980s, it would bring about a major redistribution of power in the international system. While the United States has continuously supported unification of Western Europe since the establishment of the European Coal and Steel Community in 1952, although the style and intensity of this support has varied, the actual achievement of unity would necessitate a major reorientation of all U.S. foreign policies. However, the realistic prospects for political integration in the 1980s are dim despite the likelihood of direct elections to the European Parliament before 1980. The reasons are that the economic benefits of the present stage of integration are basically satisfactory to member governments and that national political and bureaucratic elites see little pay-off in further political integration (Feld and Wildgen, 1977).

While the need for U.S. foreign policy to cope with a unified Europe may not have to be faced during the 1980s, intergovernmental coordination among the EC member governments in the foreign policy field *outside* the EC context has become institutionalized (Feld, 1976:Ch. 2), and has enabled the Nine member governments to speak "with one voice" on many foreign policy issues important to the American government. In addition, the external policy competences, which the Community institutions have by virtue of the constituent treaties, supplement and expand the range of foreign policy instruments available to the foreign ministries of EC member states.[5] In fact the intergovernmental coordination system which is likely to be intensified in the future and the EC institutional system reinforce each other and enhance the international power of the EC and its member states. Although these systems do not amount to a "truly common" foreign policy for EC member states, the U.S. government must take into account these complex arrangements whenever any kind of foreign policy is formulated and implemented.

Summary

The relationship between the United States and the EC has become more harmonious under the Carter Administration than during the period when Henry Kissinger guided American foreign policy. Within NATO the process of consultation has improved substantially and the procurement of arms and logistical materials is coordinated better and carried out in a more rationalized manner; trends American foreign policy should continue to support in the 1980s. Inroads made by Eurocommunism in Western Europe, however, may burden transatlantic military-political developments in the 1980s and pose serious challenges to U.S. policy makers. In the economic sphere the United States has enjoyed substantial surplusses in trade with the EC, but protectionist tendencies on both sides of the Atlantic and worldwide U.S. record balance-of-payments deficits may undermine the Tokyo Round efforts to liberalize international trade and produce various kinds of frictions in the 1980s. Problems may also arise from the continued endeavor by the EC and its member states to enhance Community-African solidarity as reflected in the present Lomé Convention. With preparations already under way for the renewal of this Convention when it expires in March 1981, the next decade may witness increased commercial and financial intercourse between the Community countries and the APC affiliates at the expense of export and investment activities by the American business community, resulting in lowered U.S. governmental influence in Africa. The security of raw materials supply for American industry may also be placed in jeopardy. Some of these economic developments may arouse Congress and will require carefully balanced, yet courageous, foreign policies by the Administration. As for transatlantic investments, the flow toward the United States has been accelerating while the reverse flow has been declining; this is a basically healthy trend for American interests. In the energy field, U.S. policies regarding the nonproliferation of nuclear weapons have generated serious apprehension on the part of the EC and its member governments because they could impair the nuclear energy sources upon which Western Europe is increasingly dependent for its electricity production. However, some misunderstandings about the U.S. policies that existed earlier are being cleared up and the basic principles underlying American policies may essentially be accepted. Although progress toward European political unification, a professed U.S. foreign policy goal, has been stagnant, intergovernmental foreign policy coordination by the Nine has progressed remarkably. This ability by the EC member governments to "speak with one voice" in the international arena is a significant factor likely to affect future American foreign policy.

JAPAN

One of the extraordinary features of Japan since World War II has been its rapid economic growth. From 1958 to 1973 Japan's growth of GNP averaged an astounding 10% in 1970 dollars; while the oil crisis of 1973 caused a decline in the growth rate, by mid-1976 it had accelerated again to 8.4% (Executive Office of the President, 1977:5-6). Data for Japan's share of world trade for 1976 set the figure at 7.3%, up from 2.2% in 1952. This percentage has been increasing even faster than the growth of GNP during the 1960s when exports rose at an average rate of 16.9% (Patrick and Rosovosky, 1976:4-5; Scalapino, 1972:25, 37). Large surplusses in the trade balance have given Japan substantial reserves in gold, SDRs, and foreign currencies. More will be said about this subject later.

In military terms Japan has retained a low profile. The number of its armed forces has remained fairly steady during the last few years; in 1977 it was 238,000. However, military expenditures have increased substantially from $4.3 billion in 1974 to $6.1 billion in 1976, but the percentage of GNP has remained steady during that period at 0.7%, much lower than that of the U.S. or NATO as a whole (International Institute for Strategic Studies, 1977:83, 85).

Strategic-Political Developments

The basic instrument for Japan's defense and security is the Treaty of Mutual Cooperation and Security with the United States, which came into effect in 1952. It was reaffirmed after certain revisions in 1960 despite strong opposition that manifested itself in the Japanese Diet and through extensive turmoil and violence in the streets. In 1970 the Security Treaty was renewed again but without much protest. Nevertheless, tensions have arisen from time to time between the United States and Japan regarding security issues, particularly as to the military role Japan is to play in the international arena and how far and with what weapons Japan should rearm itself. Beyond that, just as in Western Europe, the question has been raised by the public whether in the event of an emergency the United States would come to the defense of Japan and would be prepared to employ nuclear weapons incurring the risk of nuclear retaliation by potential adversaries such as the Soviet Union or the People's Republic of China. Public opinion polls during the early 1970s suggested considerable doubt that the United States would defend Japan and that perhaps the adoption of a neutral policy might be the best choice. On the other hand, a substantial increase of Japan's own military strength is frowned upon by many Japanese because of the cost involved (Scalapino, 1972:101-103). Nevertheless from 1958 to now the so-called Japanese Self-Defense Forces have been built up in order to fill the gap left by the 1957 withdrawal of all American ground combat forces (Muraoka, 1973:3-4).

Although Japan had always favored better relations with the People's Republic of China than the United States had during the 1950s and 1960s, and had successfully developed economic exchanges with Peking without straining relations with the United States, the sudden shift of American policy toward China in 1971 without advance consultation as required by the Security Treaty caused serious shocks. Public opinion polls taken during the latter half of 1971 in Japan suggested the likelihood of deterioration of U.S.-Japanese relations (Scalapino, 1972:65; Muraoka, 1973:38-39), but the surprise shift in American policy did not seem to have a long-run effect. On the other hand, this relationship benefitted from the return of Okinawa to Japan in 1972.

Indicators for the Future. The strategic American-Japanese relationship in the 1980s will depend to a large degree on Japan's policies toward and relations with China and the Soviet Union. Basically underlying U.S. foreign policy initiatives and responses will be the Nixon Doctrine, which, however, may be modified by the Carter Administration. Under this doctrine America's obligations toward the allies in Asia are maintained, but primary responsibility for supplying military manpower needs is placed on the allied country while the United States plays the major role in air and sea warfare (Crabb, 1972:381-383).

Although Japan's desire for improved relations with the PRC predated the U.S. efforts, it was only after the American shift of policy toward China that this objective could be fully realized. In September 1972 full diplomatic relations were assumed between the PRC and Japan, and because Taiwan was the main sticking point in the assumption of diplomatic relations, Japan's Treaty of Peace with Taiwan was terminated. This was done despite Taiwan's considerable strategic and economic importance to Japan, which has very large investments in and extensive trade with Taiwan. However, despite the break of diplomatic relations with Taiwan, economic, cultural, and other unofficial exchanges between Japan and Taiwan continue and a large Japanese staff remains in that country to handle what officially would be called consular duties.

The defusion of the Taiwan issue has made it possible for Japan to improve its relations with China and thereby to bolster her security. For this reason Japan may be inclined in future years to give assistance to the Chinese economy, partly in order to reduce any Chinese worries over Japan's rapid economic expansion (Muraoka, 1973:19).

The post-World War II history of the Soviet-Japanese relations has been marked by many frictions including a determined effort by the Soviet government to prevent the conclusion of the 1960 version of the Security Treaty with the United States. However, since March 1972 a decided turn for the better has taken place in Japan's relations with Moscow and economic exchanges have expanded. Nevertheless, the occupation of the islands of Kunashiri and Etorofu by the Russians at the end of World War II remains a continuing burden on the Soviet-Japanese relationship because these islands lie only 15 miles off the coast of Hokkaido and have always been under Japanese rule.

In the 1980s Japan, recognizing her inability to cope with the military strength of the Soviet Union, will seek to improve her political and economic relations with Moscow. She may well look to the Soviet Union as a source for important raw materials, including oil and natural gas, located in the eastern part of that country, but probably will be careful not to create too much of a dependency relationship. In view of the tremendous disparity in military power, a mutually beneficial balance in the Japanese-Soviet relationship can be achieved only if the Japanese remain assured of America's protective shield. This means that in the 1980s the United States must continue to provide nuclear protection as well as conventional forces in East Asia to counterbalance growing Soviet and Chinese military strength.

There seems to be little doubt that the U.S. government is willing to meet this challenge in the 1980s and base its Asian policies on the continuation of a vigorous alliance with Japan. But a number of factors may becloud the smooth and effective operations of this alliance:

(1) The existing, albeit somewhat uneasy, triangular balance-of-power relationship between the United States, the PRC, and the Soviet Union may be disturbed either by a Sino-Soviet rapprochement, which is not probable, but always possible, or by the eruption of the Sino-Soviet feud into a major military confrontation. Since in either event Japan may not want to upset its present policy of equidistant neutrality to either the Soviet Union and China, her anxiety would rise rapidly if either of these situations would occur, and only appropriate policy responses by the U.S. could mitigate such understandable anxieties and assure Japan's full confidence in the alliance.

(2) American foreign policy makers must realize that the normalization of Sino-American relations is important to Japan. The adoption by the United States of the Japanese formula for the break of diplomatic relations with Taiwan may prove to have broken the long impasse in U.S.-PRC relations.

(3) Korea will remain a difficult problem for U.S. policy toward Japan during the 1980s because the Japanese consider the security of the Republic of Korea essential to their own security (Wakaizumi, 1977:173-174). The Carter Administration's proposed gradual withdrawal of U.S. ground forces from South Korea has caused considerable apprehension in Japan because it may undermine not only military but also psychological stability (Wakaizumi, 1977:173-174). Nevertheless, many Japanese may be prepared to accept the principle of an eventual withdrawal of American ground forces if with the help of U.S. policy the defensive capabilities of South Korean military forces could be upgraded, giving greater self confidence to the Korean poeple, and a vigorous effort is made to reduce tensions between South and North Korea (Wakaizumi, 1977:173-174).

(4) Challenges to America's alliance policy with Japan in the 1980s may come from domestic politics in that country. Since its formation, the Liberal Democratic Party (LDP) has been the ruling force in Japan and it has consistently supported the Security Treaty. But the strength of the LDP has been declining and its present majority in both houses of the Japanese Diet is very narrow. Corruption, including the Lockheed scandal, and growing

arrogance of a party too long in power were the main reasons for the LDP's loss of popular support.

The leading opposition party, the Japanese Socialist Party (JSP), has constantly advocated the abrogation of the Security Treaty, but recently it has acknowledged that this would have to be done through diplomatic negotiations. A similar attitude is held by Komeito, the Buddhist party. Even the Japanese Communist Party (JCP), which used to urge immediate abrogation, seems to accept a more gradual approach. Nevertheless, a coalition government under JSP leadership may place the Security Treaty in jeopardy and Japan may assume a more neutralist stance, seeking to escape the strategic tutelage of the United States.

Economic-Political Developments

International Trade Patterns. One of the economic issues likely to produce more frictions between ·the United States and Japan in the 1980s than strategic and military problems is international trade. In 1976 Japanese exports to the United States amounted to $15.9 billion, or 23.7% of total

Figure 2: U.S. TRADE WITH JAPAN

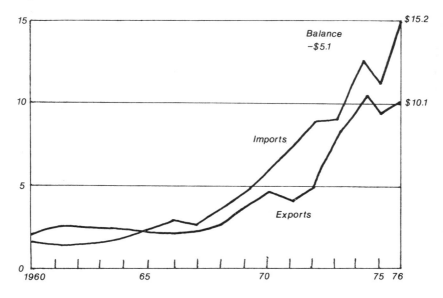

Source: *International Economic Report of the President* (January 1977), Figure 18, p. 26.

exports, compared with 20.2% in 1975. U.S. exports to Japan were $10.1 billion, representing 8.8% of all U.S. exports, about the same (8.9%) as in 1975. However, for Japan these American imports constituted 18.3% of total imports and the United States was thus the largest customer and supplier of goods and commodities for Japan. For the United States, imports from Japan were only 12.9% of total imports (Department of State, 1977). The expansion of trade between the two countries has been enormous since 1960, as can be seen in Figure 2. But Figure 2 also shows a widening gap in the trade balance with an estimated Japanese surplus of $8 billion for 1977 (Wall Street Journal, 1977c).

One of the reasons for the rapidly growing exports by Japan (expansion between 1955 and 1976 has been nearly 30 fold) is the high productivity of its workers, which compensates for rising wage levels during the last few years. In such industries as steel, automobiles, light electric products, chemical products, synthetic fibers, and sewing machines, Japanese productivity tops that of the United States, the United Kingdom, and Germany by a wide margin (Tsuru, 1976:26-27).

Another reason for the continuing increase in Japanese exports has been the fact that rising exports often are perceived by the Japanese government as an essential ingredient for the continuing expansion of Japan's economic growth in general (Tsuru, 1976:23). Thus, when the domestic economy shows signs of slack, greater emphasis is placed on Japanese exports. And indeed, during 1977, two important elements of overall growth, consumer demand and capital spending, have been sluggish, although with the support of export business Japan is likely to reach a respectable 6.7% GNP growth rate in 1977, a remarkable achievement.

But there are also other factors that have helped Japanese exports and created the wide trade gap vis-a-vis the United States and other countries. The Japanese government has on occasion provided promotional subsidies and from time to time has authorized dual pricing on various products, whereby export prices were set below domestic wholesale prices, if not below manufacturing cost. Examples are sewing machines, steel, and chemical fertilizers (Tsuru, 1976:18-22).

In some cases, the Japanese government seems to have resorted to clear and unjustified (in terms of GATT) protectionism. For example, U.S. computers enjoy a comparative advantage, but although Japan has removed quantitative restrictions, it levies tariffs on hardware and peripheral equipment at three times the rate charged by other advanced countries (Wall Street Journal, 1977c). It has also been accused of introducing hidden nontariff barriers to foreign consumer products, effectively impeding the importation of such goods. The upshot of all this is an enormous trade deficit for the United

States, which in view of an already large shortfall in the American balance-of-payments of about $28 billion in 1977, partly caused by oil imports, cannot be tolerated over a protracted period.

While the foregoing discussion has made it obvious that U.S.-Japanese trade carries with it the seeds for serious controversy, Japanese trade with Southeast Asia may also become a source of conflict. Beginning with the latter half of the 1960s, many developing countries, and especially Southeast Asia, have come to rely to a very large degree on goods imported from Japan. For example, all of Asia depended in 1971 on 70% of Japanese steel products and nearly 80% of plastics. The degree of dependence on Japan rose by about 50% from 1965 to 1971 (Tsuru, 1976:27-28). While the dependence on these and other products may not last because of indigenous industralization in some of the Asian countries, it provides Japan with enormous political leverage and influence.

The economic hegemony established by Japan in Southeast Asia and particularly over the member states of ASEAN—Indonesia, Malaysia, Philippines, Singapore, and Thailand—is illustrated by the trade figures for 1976. During that year Japanese exports to the area amounted to $6.1 billion, while the United States shipped only $3.7 billion and all of the EC less than $3.5 billion. Japan was also the best customer, purchasing nearly $9 billion in mostly raw materials including oil. U.S. imports from that area were somewhat less than $6 billion and those of the Community countries about $3.7 billion (OECD, Statistics of Foreign Trade, July 1977).

Indicators for the Future. We have pointed out in the section on the EC that the Tokyo Round multilateral negotiations are currently in process to reduce tariffs, perhaps by 40% below the level achieved by the Kennedy Round in 1967. Meanwhile, it has been estimated that the share of Japanese exports of total world exports will have risen in 1980 to 10.8% from 6.2% in 1970, while the U.S. share is likely to remain static at 13.7% (Muraoka, 1973:36; Scalapino, 1972:37). How will these projections be influenced by the protectionist pressures that have been generated by American firms and labor suffering from the flood of Japanese goods shipped to the U.S., especially steel, TV sets, and textiles? How will this affect American foreign policy during the 1980s?

Although the U.S. government claims it wants to avoid protectionist measures, it cannot ignore the layoff in such industries as steel and TV. In order to halt the sales of Japanese steel below production cost, the United States imposed antidumping duties which the Japanese are claiming to be unfair protectionism. Later it proposed to set up a system of reference prices for steel in the United States which would be used as a base for computing duties and which would stop sales below cost by Japanese firms (Wall Street Journal, 1977b, 1977c). The danger of this plan, which has been basically accepted by the steel companies, labor unions, and interested congressmen, may be that other industries affected by competitive imports will seek similar protection in the future. If these demands were accommodated, it would undermine the U.S. credibility regarding its commitment to trade liberalization in the Tokyo Round.

Other U.S. industries that have voiced major complaints about low-cost imports are the TV/CB producers. To curb Japanese shipments of TVs in the future, the Japanese government has accepted voluntary restrictions on such shipments by signing a so-called Orderly Marketing Agreement (OMA). OMAs have become a popular device for curbing imports into the United States that threaten particular American industries or firms and their employees. They avoid the disturbance of basic tariff systems and are less onerous than the unilateral imposition of quantitative restrictions or other NTBs (nontariff barriers).

As the Japanese trade surplus rose and Japan amassed foreign currency reserves, the U.S. government urged revaluation of the yen. Beginning with the devaluation of the U.S. dollar in 1971, the value of the yen has risen gradually from 360 to 190 yen to the dollar. But the revaluation of the yen has not perceptably narrowed the trade gap between Japan and the United States. Moreover, the Japanese government continues to resist pressures for upward change of the yen (Wall Street Journal, 1977d), although the stronger the yen, the lower the cost of imported raw materials and thus the production cost of industrial goods in Japan.

The Japanese government is fully aware of the hazards of the disequilibrium in trade with the United States and after strong urging did agree to unilateral tariff cuts on 318 items at an average of 23% and on the liberalization of NTBs effective April 1, 1978 (Wall Street Journal, 1977g). These reductions would be in advance of any world-wide tariff cuts negotiated in the Tokyo Round. However, while the Japanese proposal might avoid escalating retaliation against protectionist measures of the two countries, American government officials and Congressional leaders considered it short of what is needed because it would increase American exports by only $735 million (Wall Street Journal, 1977f). The U.S. ambassador to Japan, Mike Mansfield, former leader of the Senate and an experienced hand in U.S. political affairs, cautioned Japan that a real "buildup" in protectionist legislation with the labor unions in the forefront could come before next year's congressional elections if America's trade deficit with Japan is not narrowed. But American policy makers must realize that in the face of a domestic business slump and high unemployment in Japan powerful political forces operating in that country place limits on the options which the Japanese government can exercise. For this reason American policies must retain a measure of flexibility and take into account the particular vulnerabilities of the Japanese economic and political situation.

In Southeast Asia the Japanese trade activities may pose a different set of problems to American foreign policy makers. In this area memories still linger of Japan's crude, but determined attempts to establish the "Great Asia Coprosperity Sphere" during World War II. These memories were likely to be the partial cause of Japanese Prime Minister Tanaka's becoming the target of anti-Japanese demonstrations in Thailand, the Philippines, and in Indonesia in 1974. However, during Prime Minister Fukuda's participation in the ASEAN meeting of Heads of Government in 1977, the climate was friendly, perhaps partly because of the ASEAN expectation of financial support from Japan (Davis, 1977:18-23; Tasker, 1977:20-27).

An important development that eventually may emerge from the Fukuda visit is an agreement similar to the EC-Lomé Convention. Such an agreement may give the ASEAN countries preferred access to the Japanese market, although actual tariff preferences may have to overcome GATT objections. In addition, these countries may be offered a stabilization scheme for raw material prices and receive assistance for technology transfers and development aid in general. Other Third World countries may object to the special treatment for the ASEAN states by Japan. However, if the Japanese government were to double its currently rather low public foreign aid as it has announced (Agence Europe Bulletin, 1977b), it might mollify the Group of "77."

For Japan, a Lomé-type arrangement would not only bolster its markets for the exports of manufactured goods, but it would also offer greater supply security for needed raw materials. But for the United States, such a development would be the creation of another trading bloc that might well impair American exports to the ASEAN area. Moreover, similar to the Lomé Convention, Japanese intensified economic ties would engender greater political influence, perhaps at the expense of American foreign policy objectives. If the U.S. government were to give its blessing to such an arrangement, some ASEAN countries might see in it a signal that U.S. interests in Southeast Asia were waning and Japan was being given a surrogate role to ensure peace and stability in the region through its economic power and influence. For all these reasons, American foreign policy makers need to weigh carefully the strategic and political implications of Japanese moves in Southeast Asia.

Direct Foreign Investment Issues

Investment issues that might pose problems for American foreign policy in the 1980s are related either to flows between the United States and Japan or to Japanese investment activities in regions of economic hegemony by Japan such as Southeast Asia.

Following World War II Japan instituted strict controls on foreign investment which was permitted only when it helped to achieve Japanese self-sufficiency, and even then at most only 49% ownership of Japanese enterprises was authorized. However, over time controls were liberalized and beginning in 1973 foreigners could obtain 100% ownership, although some restrictions in a few industries continued.

The value of American investments has increased very gradually, amounting in 1976 to $3.8 billion. This is a small figure considering the large and growing size of the Japanese economy, represeting only 2.5% of total U.S. foreign investment (U.S. Department of Commerce, 1977a:45).

Foreign direct investments by Japanese firms were also controlled during the 1960s for balance-of-payments reasons. But beginning in 1971 the Japanese government was encouraging direct investment to develop natural resources of oil, coal, uranium, iron ore, and nonferrous metals. As a consequence, the amount of investments began to rise sharply and it was estimated to have reached between $8 and 9 billion in 1975. Again this is small compared to the foreign direct investments of the U.S. and U.K., but Japanese multinational enterprises have begun to expand rapidly (Yoshino, 1976:47-51). Nevertheless, by the end of 1976 Japanese direct investments in the United States amounted to only $900 million or 3% of total foreign investment in the United States (U.S. Department of Commerce, 1977b:26-27).

With the removal of restrictions on foreign investments Japan has eliminated a source of concern of U.S. foreign policy. Of course, screening of new investments will take place by both governments to monitor the inflow of capital. In the face of Japanese labor costs rising faster than those in the U.S. and despite the high productivity of their workers, Japan's multinational corporations are likely to increase their investments in the United States in future years for the construction of production facilities. The reasons are the protection of the market share of their products that had been imported so far and maybe even exports from the U.S. to other countries. Because this will create additional jobs, U.S. policy makers will generally welcome these investment initiatives.

A somewhat different American foreign policy stance may be taken toward the expansion of investments and establishment of subsidiaries by Japanese MNCs in Southeast Asia. It is noteworthy that direct investment by Japanese firms in Asia (excepting the Middle East) amounts to 25% of total foreign investment and that 76.2% of all manufacturing facilities are located in that region, with 36.8% of all resource-seeking subsidiaries also found there. Multinationals of other countries have a much smaller percentage of manufacturing facilities located in Asia; the United Kingdom has 27% and the United States, 15% (Tsurumi, 1976:118-147).

Most Japanese subsidiaries are concentrated in consumer and low technology goods. Their dominance in these industries is increasingly questioned by Asia and especially the ASEAN member states. During the 1977 ASEAN meeting of heads of government, Japan offered to finance a number of new industrial projects (Tasker, 1977:20) thereby deflecting some criticisms. Moreover, demands of ASEAN governments for gradual shifts of ownership of wholly owned subsidiaries of Japanese MNCs are likely to be accommodated. But it is doubtful that such developments will reduce Japan's economic power and political clout in Southeast Asia. Rather, the promise of new investment aid, public or private, and agreement to ownership transfer are likely to embellish the image of Japan in the region, and the investment pattern and the subsidiary network of Japanese MNCs tend to reinforce Japan's economic and political hegemony established through its trade relationship with the area. Again, U.S. policy makers must carefully evaluate the trend of these developments to assure that the United States will not suffer politically and strategically in this part of the world during the coming decade, or that U.S. access to raw material and energy sources will be jeopardized.

Energy Developments

The energy situation in Japan is very precarious. Some hydroelectric power sources are available and Japan has limited indigenous coal reserves. Thus, the dependency on foreign sources is very high, especially since oil makes up 75% of its total energy resources. In turn, 99% of its oil is imported and 85% comes from the Middle East and North Africa. In the future an increasing amount of crude oil may be shipped from the Tyumen oil fields in the Soviet Union (25 to 40 million tons per year), if the planned construction of a pipeline between Irkutsk and the port of Nakhodka on the Sea of Japan, to be financed by a substantial Japanese loan, is completed (Ebinger, 1977:15-16).

Meanwhile, Japan has been concentrating on the construction of nuclear power plants which are expected to produce one-sixth of Japan's electricity needs by 1980. The main supplier for enriched uranium is the United States and consequently Japan faces similar problems as the EC with respect to U.S. nonproliferation policies. Japan is anxious to install fast breeder reactors and experimental work is being done on a plutonium reactor for both the production of power and the plutonium needed for the initial input for the fast breeder reactor (Ebinger, 1977:25). Development work is also underway on a reprocessing plant. In order to assure meeting her energy needs, Japan has been casting about for suppliers of enriched uranium and advanced technologies from countries other than the United States, and France has offered to provide both.

Recognizing the nuclear energy dilemma of Japan, the U.S. government agreed to cooperate in the development of the Tokai reprocessing facility while Japan consented to a deferral of the plutonium conversion plans. This agreement is important not only for Japan, but also because it seems to lay the groundwork for U.S. policies regarding the peaceful use of nuclear energy and nonproliferation for the 1980s that may be applied to other countries.

As a consequence the Tokai facility will only reprocess a limited amount of U.S.-origin spent nuclear fuel and the United States promised to provide specified amounts of plutonium for Japanese advanced reactor research and development. Thus the United States assured Japan's progress in advanced research while retaining a strong position as supplier of uranium. Finally, Japan agreed to improve inspection opportunities by the International Atomic Energy Agency (IAEA) under its safeguards program and both countries will cooperate in strengthening the physical security of nuclear facilities and testing advanced safeguards instrumentation. The latter measures will aid the U.S. nonproliferation policies and hopefully will be accepted by the EC countries also in the 1980s.

Summary

The U.S.-Japanese relationship has been marked by recurring tensions in the strategic-political field, but the more serious problems have occurred recently, and during the next decade they will probably be in the international trade and perhaps investment sectors. The basis of the strategic relations is the Security Treaty which despite sometimes violent opposition has been renewed in 1960 and 1970, and is likely to continue as the foundation of American foreign policy toward Japan. The severe shock suffered by the Japanese when the United States announced its sudden policy shift toward China in 1971, as well as Carter's establishment of diplomatic relations with the PRC, have not altered this situation, because Japan's desire of maintaining an equidistant position toward the People's Republic of China and the Soviet Union can be achieved only with America's protective shield. Nevertheless, challenges to American military alliance policy vis-a-vis Japan may come from domestic politics, especially if the LDP, so far the dominant political party, should not be able to retain governmental control. In the economic sector the growing American trade deficit has stimulated U.S. government action pressuring Japan to curb her exports and to lower tariffs and nontariff barriers so that more American goods can be imported. Although the Japanese government has made some concessions to the American demands, a satisfactory equilibrium in the U.S.-Japan trade relationship is far from assured, and a controversy continuing into the 1980s must be anticipated by American foreign policy makers who will be caught between protectionist pressures at home and the goal of trade liberalization embodied in the "Tokyo Round" negotiations. An even more serious foreign policy challenge may arise in Southeast Asia where Japan's economic hegemony in trade, investments, and subsidiaries of Japanese MNCs could damage U.S. economic and political interests and credibility. The creation of a Japanese-East Asian economic bloc similar to the Lomé arrangement with Africa might jeopardize U.S. access to needed raw materials, impair American exports to the region, and undermine activities of U.S. multinationals. Finally, the difficult energy situation of Japan, depending heavily on external sources, requires the careful and sympathetic attention of American foreign policy officials who must seek to reconcile the legitimate needs of this U.S. ally with the overall goals of American nonproliferation policies. The complex inter-lacing of security, economic, and energy interests and concerns inherent in the U.S.-Japanese relationship are likely to severely tax U.S. policy makers in finding balanced solutions that are flexible enough to accommodate the interests and aspirations of both parties but also assure as a high priority item not only the security of the alliance partners, but of the Free World as a whole.

CONCLUSIONS

The challenges to U.S. foreign policy in the 1980s arising from the increasing international power of the European Community and Japan are more likely to stem from economic and energy rather than strategic-political developments and problems. However, these policy areas are interrelated and former President Nixon was correct when he stated on the occasion of the Washington Conference in 1974: "Security and economic considerations are inevitably linked, and energy cannot be separated from either" (Department of State Bulletin, 1974:230-234). Thus, when serious trade problems emerge, such as the enormous U.S. trade deficit with Japan or perceived discrimin-ation of American exports to countries or areas with which the EC has preferential arrangements, American foreign policy makers cannot loose sight of the "big picture."

It is interesting to note that the foreign policy problems encountered in the relations with the EC and Japan show similarities in the military-strategic field, the energy sector, and the changing distribution of economic and political influence in Africa and Southeast Asia, the latter tending to favor the EC and Japan respectively. On the other hand, there is a marked difference between the U.S.-EC and the U.S.-Japan trade relationship, with the former characterized by a substantial surplus for America and the latter by a severe trade deficit.

A significant aspect that cannot be ignored by U.S. policy formulators is the impact of political pressures applied by interest groups and the public in general in the EC countries and Japan to assure their economic welfare. The pressures impose powerful constraints at times on what can be done by the governments of these countries to accommodate American foreign policy objectives. Similar forces are, of course, also at work in the United States, making American foreign policy formulation sometimes a very difficult task. A combination of patience and persistence is needed to implement what has been considered *desirable and feasible* in the policies formulated to safeguard American interests and overall national goals.

The aim of U.S. foreign policy toward the EC and Japan must be the achievement of an optimal harmonious relationship which may require compromises when the interests of the United States and its allies significantly diverge. American policy makers should keep in mind that critical problems between allied nations usually do not appear suddenly or dramatically, but develop slowly from small misunderstandings or misjudgments. In this way they may be able to avert the sudden emergence of major conflicts that can spring from such dynamic situations as the expanding international power of the EC and Japan.

NOTES

1. An example of such egoism is the new model of the German Leopard tank which was proposed for uniform use by all NATO countries, but despite its many superior features was rejected by the Pentagon.

2. The commodities are ground nuts, coconuts, cocoa, coffee, cotton, palm and palm kernel products, hides and skins, wood products, bananas, tea, sisal, and iron ore.

3. See address by Joseph S. Nye, Jr., former Deputy to the Under Secretary for Security Assistance, Science, and Technology at Bonn, Germany, October 3, 1977.

4. France has succeeded recently in selling Iran two nuclear power plants worth $3 billion and has offered to reprocess nuclear fuel to Japan on a long-range basis.

5. The Convention of Lomé is an example of the association instruments.

REFERENCES

Agence Europe Bulletin (1974). July 11. Brussels: Agence Internationale d'Information pour la presse.

——— (1977a). October 19. Brussels: Agence Internationale d'Information pour la presse.
——— (1977b). October 28. Brussels: Agence Internationale d'Information pour la presse.
BLAKE, D.H., and WALTERS, R.S. (1976). The politics of global economic relations. Englewood Cliffs, N.J.: Prentice-Hall.
CRABB, C.V., Jr. (1972). American foreign policy in the nuclear age. New York: Harper and Row.
DAVIS, D. (1977). "A marriage is being arranged." Fareastern Economic Review, 97(30):18-23.
Department of State (1974). Bulletin. Volume 70, No. 1810, March 4.
——— (1977). Trade patterns of the West, 1976. Special Report #35, August.
EBINGER, C.K. (1977). Great power rivalry in the Far East: The geopolitics of energy. Washington, D.C.: Center for Strategic and International Studies.
EHRHARDT, C.A. (1971). "EEC and the Mediterranean." Aussenpolitik, 22(1):20-30.
——— (1975). "Europe and energy policy at top level." Aussenpolitik, 26(1):3-18.
Executive Office of the President (1977). International economic report of the President. Washington, D.C.: U.S. Government Printing Office.
FELD, W.J. (1976). The European community in world affairs. Port Washington, N.Y.: Alfred Publishing.
——— and WILDGEN, J.K. (1977). Domestic political realities and European unification. Boulder, Colo.: Westview.
International Herald Tribune (1977). September 23.
International Institute for Strategic Studies (1977). The Military Balance, 1977-78. London: Author.
MURAOKA, K. (1973). Japanese security and the United States. London: Institute for Strategic Studies.
OECD (1977). Statistics of foreign trade. Series A, Monthly Bulletin, July.
PATRICK, H., and ROSOVOSKY, H. (1976). Asia's new giant. Washington, D.C.: Brookings Institution.
PIERRE, A.J., and MOYNE, C.W. (1976). Nuclear proliferation: A strategy for control. New York: Foreign Policy Association.
PRINSKY, R. (1977). "Communist-Socialist discord in France confuses '78 elections and irks, or maybe pleases, Moscow." Wall Street Journal, October 25.
SCALAPINO, R. (1971). American-Japanese relations in a changing era. New York: Library Press.
SPERO, J.E. (1977). The politics of international economic relations. New York: St. Martin's.
TASKER, R. (1977). "Enter the Japanese." Fareastern Economic Review, 97(30), July 29.
TSURU, S. (1976). The mainsprings of Japanese growth: A turning point? Paris: Atlantic Institute for International Affairs.
TSURUMI, Y. (1976). "The multinational spread of Japanese firms and Asian neighbors reactions." Pp. 118-147 in D.E. Apter and L.W. Goodman (eds.), The multinational corporation and social change. New York: Praeger.
U.S. Department of Commerce (1977a). Survey of Current Business, 57, 8(August).
——— (1977b). Survey of Current Business, 57, 10(October).
WAKAIZUMI, K. (1977). "Consensus in Japan." Foreign Policy, 27(Summer):158-179.
Wall Street Journal (1977a). "Foreign investments in U.S. still ahead of year-ago pace." November 1, p. 4.

——— (1977b). "New approaches to protect steel industry from imports is weighed by Carter aides." November 9, p. 4.

——— (1977c). "New signs of slack in Japan's economy likely to induce further trade surplus." November 15, p. 48.

——— (1977d). "Japanese move to stem inflow of U.S. dollars." November 18, p. 20.

——— (1977e). "U.S.-Japan trade talks seen producing important results, but no final answers." December 12, p. 4.

——— (1977f). "Japan to try to turn its trade surplus with U.S." December 14, p. 4.

——— (1977g). "Japan's proposal to cut its tariffs covers 318 items." December 15, p. 5.

YOSHINO, M. (1976). "The developing role of Japanese multinationals." In A Changing Japan In A Changing World Economy, a Conference on the Japanese Economy sponsored by the U.S.-Japan Trade Council, New York, May 5-6.

Chapter 8

THE U.S. IMAGE UNDER STRESS: TRENDS AND STRUCTURE OF FOREIGN ATTITUDES TOWARD THE UNITED STATES

A L V I N   R I C H M A N
Bureau of Public Affairs, U.S. Department of State

The success of many U.S. foreign policies presupposes certain perceptions, attitudes, and behavior on the part of various individuals and groups in other countries. Sometimes the opinions of the general public, and fairly frequently the views of various elites, impose some pressures or limits on each government's area of foreign policy maneuver. These pressures or limitations may be sufficiently severe to restrict the effects of U.S. attempts to influence a government on particular issues, whether they involve trade policies, defense spending, diplomatic support, or other matters.

Some foreign policy objectives have direct "psychological requirements" and cannot succeed unless the attitudinal conditions they presuppose are met. The continued viability of West Berlin, for example, has depended on maintaining high morale in that city. The Bay of Pigs invasion in 1961, on the other hand, rested on the faulty assumption that the Cuban people were ready to overthrow Castro.[1]

EDITORS' NOTE: This paper was first submitted for review in December 1977. The version published here was received in April 1978.

AUTHOR'S NOTE: The views expressed are those of the writer and not necessarily those of the Department of State or the United States Information Agency.

More frequently, however, foreign attitudes are only one among a number of factors affecting the success or failure of U. S. policy. Although public attitudes in another country may limit the ability of its government to cooperate with the United States on a particular issue (e. g., sharing NATO defense costs, supporting U. S. policy in Vietnam), these limitations alone do not determine the outcome of U. S. policy. Pursuit of the policy may, nevertheless, involve some ancillary psychological costs (or gains) overseas, which should be considered in assessing the overall utility of a present policy direction. Objective information about foreign attitudes, together with other inputs, is essential for that type of assessment.

INTERPRETING PUBLIC OPINION DATA

Advising U. S. foreign-policy makers on the state of public opinion abroad and its implications for U. S. foreign policy has been one of the missions of the United States Information Agency (now International Communication Agency). In performing this psychological advisory role, USIA's Office of Research has conducted numerous surveys overseas covering basic attitudes and values and opinions on specific topics of current interest.[2]

During nearly three decades of public opinion surveying the Agency has accumulated what is probably the richest collection of data in existence on foreign opinions toward the United States and U. S. foreign policy. Starting in the early 1950s, many of USIA's projects have entailed simultaneous, coordinated multicountry surveys, utilizing a common core of basic attitude questions.

The survey data examined here come from two sources: (1) USIA trend data, involving mainly five general attitudinal questions about the United States repeated almost yearly between 1954-1976 in Japan and four countries of Western Europe (Great Britain, France, West Germany, and Italy);[3] and (2) an eight-country survey of general publics and elites in late 1974 directed by Lloyd Free.[4]

USIA's basic attitudinal questions are broad enough conceptually to apply as well today as they did in the 1950s. They have provided estimates of the overall psychological climate underlying views on numerous specific subjects and have measured major changes in the long-term direction of opinion since the mid-1950s.

In recent years, as we shall see later, favorable opinions of the United States have been in decline. We do not know the extent to which this is due to long-term factors, such as reduced allied dependency on the United States in an increasingly multipolar international system, or specific, shorter-term factors, such as the Vietnam war and events surrounding the U.S. presidency.

The trend data indicate that major differences persist in how foreigners view America and America's policies abroad. Opinions of U. S. society have generally been much more favorable and more stable than evaluations of U. S. foreign policy.

Dr. Free's survey and USIA's own "image surveys" provide concurring evidence about the features of U. S. society and foreign policy that are viewed most favorably and most unfavorably overseas. They indicate the conditions and policies which could most easily lead to further erosion of the U. S. image abroad, as well as policy approaches which could likely contribute to enhancing the U. S. image.

Two trend questions have been asked regularly about the Soviet Union,[5] permitting us to compare perceptions of the U. S. and the U.S.S.R. in the five surveyed countries. A finding having major implications is that the two major powers in the post-World War II international system have generally been perceived independently of one another—favorable attitudes toward one power usually have *not* implied unfavorable attitudes toward the other.

To facilitate comparisons between the different trend data, we use an index of "net favorableness" to represent the results for each survey item on a trend. This offers a convenient single figure for comparison which reflects the levels of both favorable and unfavorable opinion on the question rather than either alone. The index is obtained by subtracting the total percentage of unfavorable responses from the total percentage of favorable ones, with "no opinion" treated as neither favorable nor unfavorable. Thus, the index is positive when favorable views of the United States predominate, negative when unfavorable views prevail.

All in all, the survey evidence suggests that foreign opinions of the United States are especially attuned to three areas of U. S. behavior: (1) the degree of altruism/moralism in U. S. foreign policy, (2) the viability of U. S. socio-economic policies and institutions, and (3) the image projected by the top U. S. leadership.

CHANGES IN FOREIGN ATTITUDES TOWARD THE UNITED STATES

Periodicity of Attitudes

Employing the net favorableness measures as the basic units of analysis (percent favorable minus percent unfavorable responses), the serial data for the five general indicators of U. S. standing were first studied for evidence of changes in long-term upward and downward movement of opinion between 1954-1976. Examination of the five opinion series for all five countries reveals the following general periodicity in foreign attitudes toward the U. S.:

TABLE 1.   GENERAL OPINION OF THE UNITED STATES FOR FIVE
           COUNTRIES: NET FAVORABLE OPINION (PERCENT
           "GOOD" MINUS PERCENT "BAD") AVERAGED BY PERIODS

| | *"Do you have a very good, good, neither good nor bad, bad or very bad opinion of the United States?"* | | | | | | |
| | 1954–1960 | | 1961–1965 | | 1967–1968 | | 1969–1976 | |
Country	Mean[a]	N[b]	Mean[a]	N[b]	Mean[a]	N[b]	Mean[a]	N[b]
Great Britain	50%	13	55%	5			38%	6
France	16	13	37	5	Not		39	6
West Germany	59	13	74	5			53	7
Italy	59	13	64	5	Asked		49	4
Japan	44	7	46	5			23	2
Average:[c]	46%		55%				40%	

a. Average of "good" opinion minus "bad" opinion for each period (in percent).
b. Number of data points for the period.
c. Average means were obtained by taking the average for the five countries for each period.

TABLE 2.   PERCEIVED AGREEMENT OF BASIC INTERESTS WITH THE
           UNITED STATES FOR FIVE COUNTRIES: NET AGREE-
           MENT (PERCENT "IN AGREEMENT") MINUS PERCENT
           "DIFFERENT") AVERAGED BY PERIODS

| | *"In your opinion, are the basic interests of our country and those of the United States very much in agreement, fairly well in agreement, rather different, or very different?"* | | | | | | |
| | 1956–1960 | | 1961–1965 | | 1967–1968 | | 1969–1976 | |
Country	Mean[a]	N[b]	Mean[a]	N[b]	Mean[a]	N[b]	Mean[a]	N[b]
Great Britain	64%	5	62%	5	44%	6	59%	5
France	−2	5	15	5	−11	6	7	6
West Germany	49	4	71	5	6	6	68	5
Italy	33	5	47	5	16	6	26	5
Japan	4	4	25	4	22	1	26	6
Average:[c]	30%		44%		15%		37%	

a. Average of "very much" and "fairly well" in agreement minus "rather different" and "very different" (in percent).
b. Number of data points for the period.
c. Average means were obtained by taking the average for the five countries for each period.

(1) low U. S. net favorableness between the mid-1950s and 1960; (2) high between 1961 and 1965; (3) very low during 1967-1968, the height of U. S. involvement in Vietnam; and (4) mixed results (some items generally low, but others not) and high volatility between 1969-1976—including several very low results in 1976.[6]

Tables 1 and 2 contain the average net favorableness values for these periods for the trend items, general opinion of the United States, and agreement of basic interests with the United States. Table 1 shows that the general opinion of the United States has been much more favorable than unfavorable during each of the three periods it was asked, but has nevertheless declined appreciably since the early 1960s in each of the surveyed countries except France.

Table 2 shows that foreign perceptions of commonality of basic interests with the United States have generally been quite favorable on balance, but somewhat less favorable than their general opinions of the United States. In recent years, perceptions of agreement of basic interests with the United States have rebounded strongly from their 1967-1968 lows.

1976 Findings

The most recent multicountry surveys on general opinion and basic interests, conducted in July-August 1976, showed an erosion in America's image in Europe, especially in Italy and Great Britain (USIA, 1976). Record lows of general opinion were obtained in those two countries. Table 3 gives the 1972 and 1976 results for this question. The table shows favorable views exceeded adverse sentiment in all four European countries. But, for the first time, Italy and Great Britain joined France as countries in which less than half of the public held a "good" general opinion of the United States.

The declines in "good" opinion were *not* generally accompanied by increases in "bad" opinion, however. Those levels remained no greater than about 10%, except in Italy (16%), where there had been widely publicized charges of U. S. interference in Italian affairs. Rather, the shift was toward a neutral or mixed attitude ("neither good nor bad") or toward no opinion — perhaps indicating considerable uncertainty overseas regarding the U. S. presidential race and the post-Vietnam/post-Watergate American future in general.

There were marked differences in 1976 among the four European countries on perceived agreement of basic interests with the United States. Table 4 presents 1973/1974 and 1976 results for this question. It shows that the West German and British publics continued to see their national interests to be in accord with those of the United States. But in France opinions were about evenly divided on this issue. In Italy a plurality for the first time believed that their interests and those of the U. S. were "different."

TABLE 3.   GENERAL OPINION OF THE UNITED STATES: 1972 AND
1976

*"Please use this card to tell me your feelings about the U.S. (SHOW
CARD). Do you have a very good, good, neither good nor bad, bad
or very bad opinion of the U.S.?"*

	Great Britain		France	
	Mar–Apr 1972	*Jul–Aug 1976*	*Mar–Apr 1972*	*Jul–Aug 1976*
Very good	11%) 60%	8%) 34%	3%) 50%	5%) 38%
Good	49)	26)	47)	33)
Neither	28	49	37	42
Bad	10) 11	8) 10	10) 12	8) 10
Very bad	1)	2)	2)	2)
No opinion	1	7	1	10
	100%	100%	100%	100%
Net favorable:	+49	+24	+38	+28

	West Germany		Italy	
	Mar–Apr 1972	*July 1976*	*Mar–Apr 1972*	*Jul–Aug 1976*
Very good	6%) 57%	9%) 57%	18%) 68%	10%) 41%
Good	51)	48)	50)	31)
Neither	30	33	21	35
Bad	9) 11	6) 7	6) 8	9) 16
Very bad	2)	1)	2)	7)
No opinion	2	3	2	9
	100%	100%	99%	101%
Net favorable:	+46	+50	+60	+25

Presidential Image

Although general opinion and other attitudes toward the United States are
undoubtedly influenced by specific policies and events involving the United
States, there is evidence that they are also affected by the longer-term factor
of the presidential image projected by America. Two of the transition points
in the periodization of foreign attitudes toward the United States discussed
above correspond to transitions in the American presidency—those of
1960-1961 and 1968-1969.[7]

A Harris survey in France in late 1977, moreover, found that two-thirds of
the French public selected John F. Kennedy as the one U. S. President since
World War II for whom they felt the most affinity. Kennedy's presidency

TABLE 4. AGREEMENT OF BASIC INTERESTS WITH THE UNITED STATES: 1973/1974 AND 1976

"In your opinion, are the basic interests of our country and those of each of the following countries very much in agreement, fairly well in agreement, rather different, or very different? First, how about the U.S.?"

	Great Britain		France	
	June 1974	Jul–Aug 1976	June 1974	Jul–Aug 1976
Very much	11%) 66%	20%) 64%	4%) 37%	6%) 40%
Fairly well	55)	44)	33)	34)
Rather different	16) 23	17) 25	36) 44	27) 38
Very different	7)	8)	8)	11)
No opinion	10	11	18	22
	99%	100%	99%	100%
Net favorable:	+43	+39	−7	+2

	West Germany		Italy	
	June 1974	July 1976	April 1973	Jul–Aug 1976
Very much	21%) 75%	38%) 81%	12%) 53%	6%) 36%
Fairly well	54)	43)	41)	30)
Rather different	16) 20	11) 14	20) 31	25) 44
Very different	4)	3)	11)	19)
No opinion	5	5	15	20
	100%	100%	99%	100%
Net favorable:	+55	+67	+22	−8

coincided with a significant improvement in French opinion of the United States and was the most favorable period in overall foreign attitudes toward the United States between 1954-1976.

OPINIONS OF AMERICAN SOCIETY AND U. S. FOREIGN POLICY

Basic orientations regarding the United States (i. e., general opinion of the U. S. and perceived agreement of basic interests with the U. S.) have generally been much more favorable and less variable since 1954 than evaluations of U. S. foreign policy behavior and confidence in U. S. ability to handle foreign affairs. Table 5 presents the average levels and variabilities (average devia-

TABLE 5. AVERAGE LEVELS AND VARIABILITIES OF ITEMS RELATING TO NET FAVORABLENESS (U.S.): PERCENT POSITIVE MINUS PERCENT NEGATIVE

Item and Country	1954–1960			1961–1965			1967–1968			1969–1976			1954–1976[a]		
	Mean	Variab.	N[b]	Mean	Variab.	N[b]	Mean	Variab.	N[b]	Mean	Variab.	N[b]	Mean	Variab.	N[b]
General Opinion															
Great Britain	50	6.3	13	55	5.6	5				38	6.5	6	48	6.1	24
France	16	9.5	13	37	4.2	5				39	6.3	6	31	6.7	24
West Germany	59	3.9	13	74	4.2	5				53	6.1	7	62	4.7	25
Italy	59	4.9	13	64	6.0	5				49	11.5	4	57	7.5	22
Japan	44	4.4	7	46	7.8	5				23	3.0	2	38	5.1	14
Average[c]	46	5.8		55	5.6					40	6.7		47	6.0	
Agreement of Basic Interests															
Great Britain	64	3.2	5	62	7.2	5	44	12.3	6	59	16.2	5	62	8.9	15
France	-2	7.6	5	15	5.8	5	-11	6.7	6	7	20.0	6	7	11.1	16
West Germany	49	8.0	4	71	3.6	5	6	11.7	6	68	6.0	5	56	5.9	14
Italy	33	6.8	5	47	7.2	5	16	4.5	6	26	17.2	5	35	10.4	15
Japan	4	2.5	4	25	4.5	4	22	–	1	26	8.0	6	18	5.0	14
Average[c]	30	5.6		44	5.7		15	8.8		37	13.5		36	8.3	
General Evaluation of Foreign Policy															
Great Britain	-6	13.5	4	31	9.2	5				38	4.0	2	21	8.9	11
France	-20	13.8	4	6	11.4	5				24	15.5	2	3	13.6	11
West Germany	36	13.5	4	46	11.4	5				38	13.0	2	40	12.6	11

TABLE 5. AVERAGE LEVELS AND VARIABILITIES OF ITEMS RELATING TO NET FAVORABLENESS (U.S.): PERCENT POSITIVE MINUS PERCENT NEGATIVE (Cont.)

	Mean	Var.	n[b]	Mean	Var.	n[b]	Mean	Var.	n[b]	Mean	Var.	n[b]	Mean	Var.	n[b]
Italy	32	11.0	4	39	6.4	5				33	16.3	3	35	11.2	12
Japan	−2	6.0	2	6	16.0	5				4	6.0	2	3	9.3	9
Average[c]	8	11.6		26	10.9					27	11.0		20	11.1	
Peace Standing															
Great Britain	6	8.3	13	23	9.8	5	20	18.0	2	14	10.9	3	14	9.7	21
France	−15	9.3	12	5	8.8	5	−13	9.0	2	−26	6.4	3	−12	8.2	20
West Germany	15	10.5	13	45	13.2	5	12	17.0	2	−6	4.6	3	18	9.4	21
Italy	40	10.3	12	52	12.0	5	24	—	1	16	6.0	2	36	9.4	19
Japan	30	10.8	5	37	10.0	5	−9	—	1	18	22.0	2	28	14.3	12
Average[c]	15	9.8		32	10.8		7	14.7		3	10.0		17	10.2	
Confidence in Foreign Affairs															
Great Britain	−16	—	1	18	9.8	4	20	18.0	2	22	15.0	7	8	12.4	12
France	4	—	1	−4	9.0	4	−13	9.0	2	0	18.8	8	0	13.9	13
West Germany	23	—	1	56	11.0	4	12	17.0	2	24	27.9	7	34	19.5	12
Italy	17	—	1	41	6.8	4	24	—	1	35	11.6	5	31	9.2	10
Japan	—	—	—	10	9.5	4	−9	—	1	−16	12.3	6	−3	10.9	10
Average[c]	7			24	9.2		7	14.7		13	17.1		14	13.2	

a. Calculations of means and variabilities for the overall 1954–1976 period were obtained by averaging the respective values for the 1954–1960, 1961–1965, and 1969–1976 subperiods.

b. Number of data points for the period.

c. Average means and variabilities were obtained by taking the average for the five countries for each period and subperiod.

tions) for each trend question and country studied for the four subperiods between 1954-1976.

Opinion Levels

People in the five surveyed countries generally have held a predominately favorable opinion of America as a whole and perceived considerable community of basic interests between their country and the United States (+47 net and +36 net five-country averages, respectively, between 1954-1976). However, they have been much less positive about our actual conduct in foreign affairs (general evaluation of U. S. foreign policy, +20, and U. S. peace standing, +17), and less confident in our ability to deal wisely with foreign policy problems (confidence in U. S. in foreign affairs, +14). These and other findings noted below indicate that the United States possesses a substantial and relatively stable base of goodwill overseas toward our society and basic purposes, despite considerable dissatisfaction with some of our foreign policies.

Opinion Variability

The variabilities of these five items on the United States display an inverse relationship to their average levels.[8] That is, whereas general opinion (+47) and basic interests (+36) rate first and second among the items in net favorableness, they stand lowest (6.0% average deviation) and next to lowest (8.3%), respectively, in average variability over the 1954-1976 period. The other items, which are conceptually closer to the ongoing conduct of American foreign relations, display relatively low average levels, but relatively high average variability (confidence, 13.2%; general evaluation, 11.1%; peace standing, 10.2%)—that is, they have tended to be much lower and more unstable than general opinion and basic interests.

The higher variability of the items on confidence, general evaluation, and peace standing may be due to opinions on foreign policy being relatively sensitive to the vicissitudes of current events and media reportage. The nature of America as a country and the basic interests which link nations are comparatively broad and long-range concepts, and are probably described less prominently and dramatically in the foreign media than events related to current U. S. foreign relations.

Although attitudes toward American society have been more favorable and less variable than attitudes toward U. S. foreign policy, the two sets of views have been associated in the sense of varying together over the 1954-1976 period. Time-series correlations among the five trends on the United States show that general opinion and basic interests have correlated as strongly with the three foreign policy items as the latter have correlated with each other.[9]

IMAGES OF THE BEST AND WORST ASPECTS
OF THE UNITED STATES

Numerous surveys between 1969-1975 have indicated that the economic-technological features of American society have been the ones generally most admired abroad, whereas U. S. social issues (particularly racial discrimination) have been viewed as the worst apsects of the United States. The most comprehensive foreign survey of public and elite images of the United States in recent years was directed by Lloyd Free in eight countries in late 1974.

Respondents in Dr. Free's (1976:25-29) surveys were asked what they most admired and disliked about the "United States, its policies and actions."[10] Tables 6 and 7 present the results for the "best" and "worst" aspects of the United States as perceived by the foreign publics. They show that U. S. foreign relations were cited about two-thirds as often as U. S. domestic features within the eight countries as a whole.

Among the general publics, both U. S. foreign relations and U. S. domestic affairs received a rough balance of positive and negative comments. American altruism-idealism (11%, eight-country average) and peacekeeping activities (7%) were the foreign relations themes most frequently cited as positive aspects of the United States. American exercise of power/foreign interventions (21%) was by far the most salient negative aspect of U. S. foreign affairs.

Among domestic themes, U. S. economic-technological aspects (economic-technological strength, 12%, and high living standards, 9%) were most admired. Political institutions and rights (12%) also were frequently mentioned in the positive sense. Social aspects of America—racial problems (17%) and crime/permissiveness (6%)—had the highest frequency of negative mentions on the domestic side, but adverse comment regarding the American political system (10%) was also fairly widespread on this survey taken only a few months after President Nixon's resignation.

Opinions of the socio-economic elites in the eight countries (top 10% of the socio-economic pyramid in each country) generally paralleled those of the publics, except that negative comments led positive ones overall on U. S. foreign relations (56% negative to 40% positive), while the opposite was true on U. S. domestic issues (72% positive to 59% negative). Positive aspects of the U. S. political system (20%), in particular, were cited about as frequently by the elites as the admired economic-technological features of American society (22%). Negative comments on U. S. political and economic features averaged 11% and 6%, respectively, among the elites.

TABLE 6. BEST ASPECTS OF THE UNITED STATES AND ITS POLICIES: L. FREE SURVEY, LATE 1974

"Every country has its good points and its bad points. Taking its good points first, what do you admire most about the United States, its policies and actions?"

	Great Britain	France	West Germany	Italy	Canada	Mexico	Brazil	Japan	8-Country Average
International									
Altruism, idealistic policies	19%	3%	8%	11%	20%	7%	9%	10%	11%
Tension-reduction policies, working for peace	9	8	20	8	6	1	3	1	7
World leadership, responsibilities	2	1	4	–	2	1	3	3	2
International security policies, commitments	5	3	5	1	3	1	2	1	3
Strength: Political, economic, military	4	4	9	5	6	1	1	1	4
Other International	6	2	11	3	6	3	3	1	4
	45%	21%	57%	28%	43%	14%	21%	17%	31%
Domestic									
Domestic systems (Gen.), handling of domestic problems	11%	12%	5%	6%	18%	11%	10%	9%	11%
Political institutions, rights; Democracy	3	13	11	20	6	16	17	11	12
Economic-technological strength	17	20	7	9	13	15	9	4	12
High living standard	12	20	2	17	6	8	5	1	9
Characteristics of American people	4	4	2	6	7	7	3	2	4
American culture, civilization	4	6	2	1	1	3	5	–	3
Other Domestic	2	1	–	3	7	19	5	–	4
	53%	76%	29%	62%	58%	79%	54%	27%	55%
Total Favorable Aspects	98%	97%	86%	90%	101%	93%	75%	44%	86%
Don't admire anything about U.S.	14	19	11	4	17	9	13	11	11
Don't know	17	17	17	32	15	17	21	59	24
	129%	133%	114%	126%	133%	119%	109%	107%	121%

TABLE 7. WORST ASPECTS OF THE UNITED STATES AND ITS POLICIES: L. FREE SURVEY, LATE 1974

"And what do you dislike most about the United States, its policies and actions?"

	Great Britain	France	West Germany	Italy	Canada	Mexico	Brazil	Japan	8-Country Average
International									
Political-military agressiveness, arrogance, interventions	14%	27%	24%	16%	35%	12%	10%	29%	21%
Economic imperialism, exploitation	3	18	4	5	14	13	10	6	9
Failures, inability to handle foreign relations, internat. leadership	3	3	2	1	12	—	1	4	3
Other international	3	3	4	5	7	8	7	2	5
	23%	51%	34%	27%	68%	33%	28%	41%	38%
Domestic									
Domestic systems (Gen.), inability to deal with domestic problems	8%	6%	16%	4%	26%	2%	3%	2%	8%
Corrupt political systems (e.g., Watergate)	16	10	21	5	22	2	4	2	10
Economic system, materialism	4	13	3	2	4	1	—	2	4
Social aspects: racial and ethnic problems	18	18	16	18	13	30	18	5	17
Social aspects: crime, permissiveness	11	10	7	8	3	7	3	2	6
Characteristics of American people	8	8	1	3	6	3	2	—	4
Other Domestic	4	1	—	3	3	5	4	—	3
	69%	66%	64%	43%	77%	50%	34%	13%	52%
Total Unfavorable Aspects	92%	117%	98%	70%	145%	83%	62%	54%	90%
Don't dislike anything about U.S.	14	7	5	4	7	9	17	4	8
Don't know	19	19	20	45	11	17	23	53	26
	125%	143%	123%	119%	163%	109%	102%	111%	124%

ATTITUDES TOWARD THE U.S. AND THE U.S.S.R.

Opinion Levels and Variability

With only two long-term opinion series available concerning the U.S.S.R., general opinion and peace standing, it is not possible to say as much about the longitudinal patterns of attitudes toward the Soviet Union as it is for the United States. Nevertheless, at least two findings stand out: (1) The much lower average levels of opinion toward the U.S.S.R. compared to the U. S. (general opinion −24 net and peace standing −24 net for the U.S.S.R. between 1954-1973 compared to +47 net and +17 net, respectively, for the U. S. between 1954-1976); and (2) the relatively high volatility of U.S.S.R. peace standing compared to the general opinion of the U.S.S.R. (10.8% versus 6.8% average deviation), which corresponds to the findings obtained for the United States.

Table 8 gives the average levels and variabilities for general opinion (U.S.S.R.) and U.S.S.R. peace standing for three subperiods between 1954-1973. The table shows general opinion (U.S.S.R.) improved on the whole after 1965, but the U.S.S.R. peace standing declined sharply in all five countries. These declines paralleled the sharp drop in the U. S. peace standing in each country after 1964, coinciding with increased U. S. involvement in the Vietnam war.

Independent, Nonpolarized Attitudes Toward the U. S. and U.S.S.R.

Correlational analyses show that responses to questions about the U. S. and the U.S.S.R. have tended to fall into two distinct opinion clusters, favorableness (U. S.) and favorableness (U.S.S.R.).[11] This indicates that the U. S. and the U.S.S.R. have been evaluated essentially independently along the positive-negative dimension within the surveyed countries, so that favorable opinions of one power generally implied neither favorable nor unfavorable opinions toward the other.

There was evidence of some commonality among certain of the items representing favorableness (U. S.) and favorableness (U.S.S.R.) as we shall see below. But no findings emerged to support the hypothesis that attitudes toward the U. S. and the U.S.S.R. are negatively related or "polarized"—that is, those favorable to the United States being unfavorable to the U.S.S.R. or vice versa. Thus, over the 1954-1972 period as a whole, the surveyed populations have not perceived the two super powers in simple bipolar terms in which a gain for one was necessarily construed as a loss for the other.

TABLE 8. AVERAGE LEVELS AND VARIABILITIES OF ITEMS RELATING TO NET FAVORABLENESS (U.S.S.R.): PERCENT POSITIVE MINUS PERCENT NEGATIVE

Item and Country	1954–1958			1959–1965			1969–1973			1954–1973[a]		
	Mean	Ave. Dev.	N[b]	Mean	Ave. Dev.	N[b]	Mean	Ave. Dev.	N[b]	Mean	Ave. Dev.	N[b]
General Opinion												
Great Britain	−36	12.9	10	−18	9.0	8	−15	3.8	5	−23	8.6	23
France	−30	9.4	10	−9	9.0	8	7	1.8	5	−11	6.7	23
West Germany	−61	6.6	10	−57	6.8	8	−24	10.8	6	−47	8.1	24
Italy	−34	9.1	10	−12	7.0	8	−6	3.3	3	−17	6.5	21
Japan	−28	4.4	7	−20	6.6	5	−24	1.5	2	−24	4.2	14
Average[c]	−38	8.5		−23	7.7		−12	4.2		−24	6.8	
Peace Standing												
Great Britain	−36	16.4	10	−20	16.9	8	−43	7.0	3	−33	13.4	21
France	−31	14.4	10	−11	19.4	7	−28	2.7	3	−23	12.2	20
West Germany	−54	9.9	10	−48	12.0	8	−57	2.0	3	−53	8.0	21
Italy	−12	10.9	10	4	11.0	7	−40	5.0	2	−16	9.0	19
Japan	6	8.4	5	20	10.6	5	−14	16.5	2	4	11.8	12
Average[c]	−25	12.0		−11	14.0		−36	6.6		−24	10.8	

a. Calculations of means and variabilities for the overall 1954–1973 period were obtained by averaging the respective values for the 1954–1958, 1959–1965 and 1969–1973 subperiods.

b. Number of data points for the period.

c. Average means and variabilities were obtained by taking the average for the five countries for each period and subperiod.

Commonality of Attitudes Toward U. S.
and Soviet "Peace Efforts"

Correlational analyses indicate that on the issue of peace standing, the U. S. and U.S.S.R. have been perceived quite similarly—that is, viewed either favorably or unfavorably together. For example, analyses of time series relationships show that U. S. and U.S.S.R. peace standings have generally been more closely related to each other in the five countries than each has been to other indicators of favorableness toward the U. S. or U.S.S.R., respectively.[12] In France and Japan, moreover, the U. S. peace standing has been more closely related to the U.S.S.R. peace standing than to *any* of the other four favorableness (U. S.) items.

These results suggest that in many countries the promotion of international peace and stability are widely perceived by the general publics as the joint responsibility of both super powers. The effects of U. S.-Soviet relations on the general international political climate have been so pervasive that at times when this climate has become more (or less) tense, both powers have been given some of the blame (or credit). Moreover, the public's attribution of mutual U. S.-Soviet responsibility for maintaining international peace, which includes the absence of wide domestic bases of support for disruptive international actions by either power, may itself contribute somewhat to international stability. As in a "variable-sum game," both powers can suffer losses in public esteem with a rise in tension stemming from either source.

IMPLICATIONS FOR FUTURE U. S. POLICIES

Despite the declines in favorable attitudes toward the United States during the past decade, a potentially large reservoir of good feeling remains. Favorable general opinions of the United States exceeded negative views in each of the four West European countries surveyed in mid-1976; the decline in favorable opinions was accompanied by an increase in neutral and undecided views, rather than a rise in negative opinion. The level of negative opinion remained about 10-15%, while the proportion of neutral and undecided views rose from about one-third in 1972 to close to one-half in 1976 (four-country averages).

This large increase in the proportion of noncommitted attitudes may have reflected concern about the post-Vietnam/post-Watergate American future, as Europeans awaited the outcome of the 1976 U. S. presidential race. That most of the West Europeans surveyed who did not express a good opinion of the U. S. were uncertain or noncommittal, rather than definitely adverse, indicates that there is a considerable potential for raising foreign opinions of the United States to previous levels.

Our survey findings suggest that realizing this potential depends largely on three factors: (1) U. S. foreign policies that project a clear sense of altruism/ moralism and concern for maintaining peace; (2) U. S. socio-economic policies that indicate America is managing its economic activities successfully and its social relations fairly; and (3) a presidential image that stimulates confidence in U. S. ability to perform a leadership role.

U. S. Foreign Policies

Past survey data show that a foreign policy which stresses altruistic-moralistic principles and the promotion of peace has greater appeal than a policy in which U. S. self-interest, military power, and foreign intervention are highly salient (USIA, 1972; Free, 1976). Human rights advocacy by the United States seems to have struck a responsive chord among the more informed publics overseas. USIA surveys taken last summer in four countries of Western Europe found about two-fifths of the respondents on the average were familiar with U. S. statements criticizing human rights violations in other countries and that about two-thirds of these approved such criticisms (USIA, 1977).

Whether support for U. S. human rights advocacy has already been translated into a more favorable general image of America and greater approval of U. S. foreign policy as a whole are questions that cannot yet be confidently answered. However, a recent Gallup poll in Great Britain found that confidence in the "ability of the U. S. to deal wisely with present world problems" rose substantially between November 1976 and May 1977 (from 33% expressing considerable confidence and 55% little or no confidence in November 1976, to 54%-38% in May 1977).

U. S. Domestic Policies

The trend survey data indicate that foreign opinions of American society have been considerably more favorable and more stable than their views of U. S. foreign policy. Attitudes toward American society and U. S. foreign policy are not unrelated, however. Attitudes toward American society provide a relatively high and stable base of goodwill which may inhibit prolonged negative swings in attitudes toward U. S. foreign policy itself.

The most respected features of American society have been its economic-technological characteristics; the least respected features have been its social policies and characteristics. The U. S. societal image would be seriously hurt by clear evidence that the United States could not manage its economy successfully or maintain its technological leadership. On the other hand, our societal image would benefit considerably from showing others that our problems of racial discrimination, economic inequality, social indifference, and violence were being seriously tackled and often resolved.

U. S. Presidential Image

The fact that two major transition points in the foreign attitude trend data coincide with U. S. presidential transitions suggests that the U. S. presidential image may have a substantial influence (i. e., "halo effect") on attitudes toward American society and foreign policy as a whole. For many people overseas the President probably represents the clearest embodiment of American purposes and policies. For them, our nation's image is closely intertwined with the President's. As his image rises or falls, so does the nation's. To the extent that the President can generate confidence in his leadership and touch the aspirations of people in other countries, his rising stock abroad will parallel the nation's.

NOTES

1. A survey conducted in Cuba in 1960 reportedly showed Castro was actually popular with the Cuban people at that time (Free, 1971:63-64).

2. Survey research projects overseas have been contracted with indigenous organizations, principally commercial or market survey firms, that work under Agency specifications regarding questionnaires, basic sample design, and interviewing guidelines. Typically, the Agency receives simply raw data from these contractors and uses its own analysts to interpret and report the findings to appropriate foreign policy officers.

3. General opinion of the United States, perceived agreement of basic interests of one's own country with the United States, confidence in the U. S. ability to handle foreign affairs, general evaluation of recent U. S. foreign policies, and evaluation of U. S. efforts to promote peace (U. S. peace standing). The exact wording of the questions is contained in the Appendix to this chapter.

4. The countries surveyed were Great Britain, France, West Germany, Italy, Japan, Canada, Mexico, and Brazil (Free, 1976).

5. General opinion of the U.S.S.R. and U.S.S.R. peace standing. See Appendix to this chapter for exact wording of the questions.

6. Determining periodicity was aided by charting the highest quartile and lowest quartile results for each country and item over the 1954-1976 period, as well as by visual examination of the graphs. The complete survey-by-survey net favorableness results for the five general indicators of U. S. standing and the two indicators of U.S.S.R. standing are presented in the Appendix to this chapter.

7. Two presidential transitions between 1954-1976 did not show marked effects on foreign attitudes toward the United States: (1) America maintained a high standing overseas in 1964 and 1965 after John F. Kennedy's death, which might be explained by President Lyndon Johnson's emphasis on continuity with his predecessor; and (2) the trend data available between 1973-1975 are insufficient to determine whether the Nixon-Ford transition was associated with a major change of attitudes abroad toward the United States.

8. The variability of each series was measured by its average deviation—the average size of the absolute deviations of the series' net values from the series' mean values.

9. Rank-order correlation coefficients (Spearman's Rho) averaged .51 for general opinion with the three foreign policy questions in the five surveyed countries, .33 for basic interests with the three foreign policy items, and .33 for the three foreign policy items among themselves.

10. I am grateful to Dr. Free for the use of his original tables to report some results in more detail in Tables 6 and 7 than appear in his book.

11. Two types of analyses support this finding: (1) time series correlations between general opinion (U. S.) and general opinion (U.S.S.R.), which averaged a weak .13 (Spearman's Rho) for the five countries between 1954-1972; and (2) factor analyses of the British and French 1969 surveys, which contained a number of questions on the U. S. and the U.S.S.R. not included in our trend analyses. The two types of analyses employ different types of data and can yield different results. The factor analyses represent "cross-sectional" examinations of the interrelationships existing in late 1969 among a number of opinion items. The basic units of analysis here are the opinions of individual respondents. The time series correlations, on the other hand, represent "longitudinal" analyses of the relationships between different pairs of items. Their basic units of analysis are the aggregate results (i. e., net favorableness) obtained on particular survey questions for an entire sample.

12. The average Spearman's Rho of .52 between U. S. and U.S.S.R. peace standings is considerably greater than the overall .31 average Rho between the U. S. peace standing and the four other basic indicators of favorableness toward the United States within the five surveyed countries.

REFERENCES

FREE, L. (1971). "The role of public opinion." Forum, Spring:55-66.
——— (1976). How others see us: Critical choices for Americans (Vol. 3). Lexington, Mass.: Lexington Books.
United States Information Agency, Office of Research (1972). "Foreign evaluation of U. S. policies following the President's visit to China." Report No. R-39-72.
——— (1976). "European views of the United States in mid-1976." Report No. R-20-76.
——— (1977). "West European opinion on U. S. human rights advocacy." Report No. R-24-77.

APPENDIX: TABLES OF NET
FAVORABLENESS FOR U. S. AND U.S.S.R.

TABLE A1. GENERAL OPINION OF THE U.S.: NET FAVORABLE[a]

"Do you have a very good, good, neither good nor bad, bad or very bad opinion of the United States?"

	Oct. '54	Feb. '55	June '55	Aug. '55	Dec. '55	Jan. '56	Apr. '56	June '56	Nov. '56	May '57	June '57	Aug. '57	Nov. '57	Feb. '58	Oct. '58	Dec. '58	Nov. '59	Feb. '60	May '60	Oct. '60
Great Britain	+40	+50	+52	+58	+57		+54		+47	+41			+40		+52		+55	+60	+38	
France	0	+15	+4	+22	+25		+4		+8	+11			−3		+23		+31	+35	+27	
West Germany	+57	+59	+57	+55	+54		+49		+60	+54			+60		+65		+65	+68	+61	
Italy	+49	+53	+55	+61	+57		+63		+67	+63			+61		+53		+66	+61	+52	
Japan						+52		+42			+38	+41	+41	+50		+41				+60

	June '61	June '62	July '62	Feb. '63	Dec. '64	June '65	July '69	Aug. '69	Sept. '69	Oct. '69	July '71	Mar. '72	Apr. '73	July–Aug. '76
Great Britain	+56	+52		+44	+66	+57	+33	+43		+41	+37	+49		+24
France	+42	+36		+36	+41	+28	+41	+55		+38	+32	+38		+28
West Germany	+71	+68		+75	+84	+73	+59	+60		+63	+51	+46	+45	+50
Italy	+53	+61		+68	+74	+62				+52		+60	+57	+25
Japan			+51	+44	+42	+32			+26			+20		

a. "Very good" and "Good" minus "Bad" and "Very bad."

TABLE A2. PERCEIVED AGREEMENT OF BASIC INTERESTS WITH THE U.S.: NET FAVORABLE[a]

"In your opinion, are the basic interests of our country and those of the United States very much in agreement, fairly well in agreement, rather different, or very different?"

	Nov. '56	May '57	June '57	Aug. '57	Nov. '57	Feb. '58	Oct. '58	Dec. '58	Feb. '60	Oct. '60	June '61	June '62	July '62	Feb. '63	Feb. '64	June '65
Great Britain	+64	+56	+41	+55	+64		+68		+68		+66	+56		+50	+65	+73
France	−7	+5	−15	−20	−15		−4		+9		+26	+17		+6	+17	+10
West Germany	+38	+43	+35	+11	+49				+64		+69	+64		+71	+74	+77
Italy	+40	+31	+17	+17	+43				+27		+34	+42		+51	+51	+57
Japan			+1	+2		+7	+24	+6		+27			+29	+28		+16

	Feb. '67	May '67	June '67	Sept. '67	Dec. '67	Apr. '68	Dec. '68	Sept. '69	Oct. '69	Jan. '72	Mar. '72	Apr.–May '73	July '73	Mar. '74	July '74	June–July–August '76
Great Britain	+59	+54	+41	+55		+32	+21		+54	+78	+80			+43		+39
France	−11	−18	−15	−20		−6	+4		+3	+25	+49	−30		−7		+2
West Germany	+4	−9	+35	+11		−9	+2		+72	+75	+73			+55		+67
Italy	+16	+24	+17	+17		+3	+20		+21	+39	+56	+22		+56		−8
Japan					+22			+38		+21	+27	+27	+8	+24		+36

a. "Very much" and "Fairly well" in agreement minus "Rather different" and "Very different."

TABLE A3. CONFIDENCE IN U.S. ABILITY TO HANDLE FOREIGN AFFAIRS: NET FAVORABLE[a]

"How much confidence do you have in the ability of the United States to deal wisely with present world problems — very great, considerable, little, or very little?" (1960–1973)

	May '60	Oct. '60	June '61	June '62	July '62	Feb. '63	June '65	Apr. '68	Dec. '68	Sept. '69	Oct. '69	June '70	July '71	Jan. '72	Mar. '72	June '72
Great Britain	−16		+21	−1		+18	+35	+38	+2		+34	−14	+26	+32	+50	+20
France	+4		+11	−10		−16	−1	−22	−4		+30	−13	+28	−18	+14	−22
West Germany	+35		+68	+50		+66	+40	+29	−5		+65	0	+51	−3	+53	+4
Italy	+17		+35	+33	+12	+46	+49		+24		+41			+28	+48	+14
Japan		+23				+13	−10	−9		0		−36		−7	−5	−24

"How much confidence do you have in the ability of the United States to provide wise leadership in dealing with present world problems — a great deal, fair amount, not very much or none at all?" (1975)

	Apr.–May '73	May–June '75
Great Britain		+9
France	+3	−22
West Germany		−3
Italy	+46	
Japan		−26

a. "Very great" and "Considerable" confidence minus "Little" and "Very Little" (1960–1973).
"Great deal" and "Fair amount" of confidence minus "Not very much" and "None at all" (1975).

TABLE A4. GENERAL EVALUATION OF RECENT U.S. FOREIGN POLICIES[a]

"Have you a favorable or unfavorable impression of what the United States government has been doing in international affairs recently? (PAUSE) Very or only somewhat?"

	Nov. '56	May '57	June '57	Oct. '58	Dec. '58	Feb. '60	Oct. '60	June '61	June '62	July '62	Feb. '63	Feb. '64	June '65	Mar. '72	June '72	Apr. '73
Great Britain	−19	−20		−5		+20		+25	+15		+39	+46	+32	+42	+34	
France	−38	−29		−17		+5		+15	0		+25	+10	−19	+39	+8	
West Germany	+59	+37		+8		+38		+44	+54		+60	+52	+19	+51	+25	
Italy	+49	+36		+10		+31		+31	+36		+42	+53	+35	+58	+24	+18
Japan			−8		+4		+29			+18	−3	+10	−26	+10	−2	

a. "Very" and "Somewhat" favorable minus "Very" and "Somewhat" unfavorable.

TABLE A5. U.S. PEACE STANDING: NET FAVORABLE[a]

"Is the United States doing all it should to promote peace throughout the world?"[b]

	Oct. '54	Feb. '55	June '55	Aug. '55	Dec. '55	Jan. '56	Apr. '56	June '56	Nov. '56	May '57	June '57	Nov. '57	Feb. '58	Oct. '58	Dec. '58	Nov. '59	Feb. '60	May '60	Oct. '60
Great Britain	+9	−3	+5	+33	+21		+1		+9	+4		0		−3		0	+18	−15	
France	−8	−19	−15	+5	−25		−27		−9	−21		−34		−16			+7	−20	
West Germany	+21	+5	+7	+22	+12		−3		+45	+22		−1		+2		+21	+25	+13	
Italy	+26	+22	+31	+48	+38		+38		+64	+42		+45		+24		+57	+47		
Japan						+24		+12			+36		+50		+26				+35

	June '61	June '62	July '62	Feb. '63	Feb. '64	June '65	Sept. '69	Oct. '69	July '71	Mar. '72
Great Britain	+24	−1		+27	+40	+26		+19	−2	+26
France	+5	−5		+13	+25	−11		−24	−36	−19
West Germany	+33	+35		+59	+63	+33		−2	−4	−13
Italy	+35	+42		+63	+70	+48		+10		+22
Japan			+25	+44	+56	+27	+40			−5

a. "Yes" minus "No."

b. Question wording before 1969 was "Is the United States doing all it should to prevent a new world war?"

226

TABLE A6. GENERAL OPINION OF THE U.S.S.R.: NET FAVORABLE[a]

"Do you have a very good, good, neither good nor bad, bad or very bad opinion of the USSR?"

	Oct. '54	Feb. '55	June '55	Aug. '55	Dec. '55	Jan. '56	Apr. '56	June '56	Nov. '56	May '57	June '57	Aug. '57	Nov. '57	Feb. '58	Oct. '58	Dec. '58	Nov. '59	Feb. '60	May '60	Oct. '60
Great Britain	−38	−33	−26	−9	−35		−19		−76	−60			−31		−36		−9	−14	−34	
France	−32	−25	−20	−18	−23		−21		−60	−40			−28		−37		−6	−7	−22	
West Germany	−63	−57	−48	−46	−63		−61		−76	−70			−66		−62		−39	−57	−58	
Italy	−30	−38	−32	−22	−29		−30		−60	−48			−34		−14		+3	−4	−19	
Japan						−30		−32			−24	−34	−23	−22		−32				−24

	June '61	Feb. '62	June '62	July '62	Feb. '63	Feb. '64	June '65	July '69	Aug. '69	Sept. '69	Oct. '69	July '71	Mar. '72	Apr. '73
Great Britain	−11	−33		−22	−13	−6	−16	−12	−22		−16	−8	−2	
France	−19	−21		−7	−1	+13	+6	+9	+4		+9	+6	−1	
West Germany	−64	−62		−60	−68	−48	−28	−34	−34		−31		−12	−2
Italy	−7	−20		−15	−15	−19					−9	−8	−8	−1
Japan			−33		−15	−17	−12			−25			−22	

a. "Very good" and "Good" minus "Bad" and "Very bad."

TABLE A7. U.S.S.R. PEACE STANDING: NET FAVORABLE[a]

"Is the Soviet Union doing all it should to promote peace throughout the world?"[b]

	Oct. '54	Feb. '55	June '55	Aug. '55	Dec. '55	Jan. '56	Apr. '56	June '56	Nov. '56	May '57	June '57	Nov. '57	Feb. '58	Oct. '58	Dec. '58	Nov. '59	Feb. '60	May '60	Oct. '60	June '61
Great Britain	−35	−27	−23	+2	−45		−13		−73	−53		−43		−46		−22	−17	−49		−24
France	−20	−22	−11	−6	−33		−22		−61	−46		−42		−43			−8	−41		−28
West Germany	−52	−50	−36	−36	−57		−47		−71	−62		−66		−64		−45	−55	−61		−65
Italy	−7	−10	−8	+9	−8		+6		−45	−21		−24		−13		+21	0			−12
Japan						+2		−4			+16		+17		−1				+13	

	June '62	July '62	Feb. '63	Feb. '64	June '65	Sept. '69	Oct. '69	July '71	Mar. '72
Great Britain	−53	−12	+9	+7			−49	−33	−48
France	−33	−1	+14	+18			−30		−24
West Germany	−57	−36	−29	−32			−60	−56	−55
Italy	−15	+7	+26	+4			−35		−45
Japan		+1	+25	+40	+22	+3			−30

a. "Yes" minus "No."

b. Question wording before 1969 was "is the USSR doing all it should to prevent a new world war?"

PART III:

SOME SOURCES OF AMERICAN FOREIGN

POLICY ADAPTATION

Chapter 9

AMERICA'S FOREIGN POLICY AGENDA:
THE POST-VIETNAM BELIEFS OF AMERICAN LEADERS

O L E   R.   H O L S T I
Duke University

J A M E S   N.   R O S E N A U
University of Southern California

The two decades following World War II can appropriately be called the "age of the super powers." In its conduct of foreign policy during this period the United States could draw upon impressive resources: military capabilities second to none, a dynamic economy capable of expanding with only moderate inflation, a stable currency buttressed by favorable balances of payments, and important allies whose diagnoses of the international situation and prescriptions for a manageable world order more often than not coincided

EDITORS' NOTE: This paper was first received for review in September 1977. The version published here was received in January 1978. The authors state that the data reported on in this paper shall subsequently be made available to other researchers through the Inter-University Consortium for Political and Social Research at the University of Michigan.

AUTHORS' NOTE: We gratefully acknowledge support from the Duke University Research Council, the Duke Computation Center, and the Institute for Transnational Studies of the University of Southern California.

with those in Washington. And no less important as a resource was the prevalence of a widespread consensus among both governmental and non-governmental leaders about the nature of the international system, America's proper role within it, and the appropriate strategies to achieve major foreign policy goals. These widely shared beliefs were often grounded in "lessons of history" learned by those who had witnessed the American failure to join the League of Nations, the great depression, the emergence of militaristic dictatorships in Europe and Asia, and the failures of both appeasement and isolationism as policies to avert another global war (May, 1973).

Barring an unlimited nuclear war, the ability of the super powers to shape the course of international events may have crested in recent years. Other chapters describe global trends, strategic balances, economic resources, trade patterns, and the like that may limit or expand the repertoire of roles and choices for the United States during the coming decade. This chapter begins with the premise that American foreign policy will also continue to be shaped and constrained by the ways in which leaders articulate the nation's goals and aspirations, identify and define international issues, and establish agendas and priorities for policy. The manner in which they diagnose international problems and prescribe goals, strategies, and tactics may, in turn be affected by the experience of the Vietnam war. Just as many persons who witnessed the international relations of the 1930s came to learn—and perhaps overlearn—how most effectively to deal with expansionist dictatorships, those who have lived through the Vietnam experience may well have had their worldviews shaped by that experience.

Because the Vietnam war may prove to be such a watershed event, perhaps analogous to what students of domestic politics have called "critical elections," we have undertaken a survey of American leaders with a view to understanding how the conflict has been defined not only by those presently in leadership positions, but also by persons who are likely to occupy such roles in the future.[1] The 4,290 leaders who received our questionnaire included Foreign Service Officers, military officers, business executives, labor officials, political leaders, clergy, academics, leaders in the printed and electronic media, as well as a sample of persons listed in *Who's Who in America*. Responses were received for 2,282 persons, amounting to a return rate exceeding 53%.

UNDERLYING PROPOSITIONS AND SPECIFIC HYPOTHESES

This study, the fifth in a series relating to the Vietnam experience, will examine in detail some beliefs about foreign policy held by American leaders in the aftermath of that conflict. As was the case in the immediately preceding study (Holsti and Rosenau, 1977b), much of the analysis that follows will be organized around three foci: *consensus, Vietnam,* and *belief systems.* Specific hypotheses and analyses will be guided by three central ideas, the first two of which are:

(1) The broad consensus among American leaders that marked much of the period since World War II has been shattered.

(2) The Vietnam war was a watershed event in the sense that it has given rise to sharply divergent views on the nature of the international system and America's appropriate international role.

Observations about deep cleavages among American leaders on foreign policy issues have not been in short supply during the past decade. Nor has it escaped notice that the American intervention in Vietnam was a divisive rather than a unifying experience. If this is the case, why undertake an extensive survey of American leaders merely to document the obvious? There are several reasons for doing so. One is that our propositions posit cleavages that go far deeper than disagreements over specific policy issues. We have in mind differences that reach into such basic questions as the dynamics of the contemporary international system, the proper role for the United States within it, and the aspirations and strategies that should constitute the core of the nation's external relations.[2]

Secondly, the impact of experiences such as Vietnam may well persist far beyond the temporal boundaries of the event itself. To acknowledge that this issue divided American society is not to answer all the significant questions that can be raised about the impact of that conflict. Most Americans would probably agree with the assertion, "No more Vietnams!," but not necessarily about the specific policy implications of that slogan, or about the ways in which they would avoid repeating that disastrous experience.

Finally, if in fact American leaders disagree about the continuing meaning of the Vietnam experience, are these views merely isolated and, therefore, probably evanescent ideas in the cognitive maps of American leaders? The next hypothesis offers a negative answer to the question:

(3) The divergent beliefs about foreign policy can appropriately be described as competing *belief systems.*

This proposition extends the first two by predicting that deep, Vietnam-related cleavages among American leaders are rooted in and sustained by clusters of foreign policy beliefs that reinforce each other. In this we are adopting Converse's familiar definition of a belief system as "a configuration of ideas and attitudes in which the elements are bound together by some form of constraint or functional interdependence" (Converse, 1964:207).

In a previous study we found rather persuasive evidence that four clusters of beliefs are "bound together" in the way suggested by the Converse definition: *policy preferences* on the war in Vietnam, *diagnoses of the sources of American failure, prognoses of the likely consequences of the war,* and *prescriptions of the "lessons" that should be derived from the conflict* (Holsti and Rosenau, 1977b). This chapter extends that analysis by examining responses to three additional clusters of items: 18 questions about American foreign policy goals, using items that appeared in a Harris poll undertaken for the Chicago Council on Foreign Relations; seven questions about America's role in the world that also appeared in the Harvard-*Washington Post* survey of American leaders; and a seven-item question developed by Russett and Hanson on appropriate objectives for the United States in underdeveloped countries (Reilly, 1975; Sussman, 1976; Russett and Hanson, 1975).

A plausible test of these propositions requires not only a demonstration of cleavages on basic foreign policy questions and of the existence of coherent, internally consistent belief systems; it is also necessary to document the central role of the Vietnam issue. We have therefore used the respondents' policy preferences on the Vietnam war as the sole criterion for classifying them. In doing so we set aside until future analyses such interesting questions as: What are the generational, occupational, political, ideological, educational, and other attributes of respondents that are associated with persistent preference for withdrawal from Vietnam? With persistent support for the goal of military victory? With shifts in one direction or the other during the course of the war?

During the Vietnam war our respondents' policy positions underwent a dramatic change. When the war first became an issue, 51% preferred "a complete military victory," whereas only 22% wanted the United States to undertake "a complete withdrawal." The remainder either favored an option between these two (22%), or they were unsure of their positions (5%). Toward the end of the American involvement in Vietnam, supporters of a complete withdrawal outnumbered those favoring pursuit of victory by 57% to 22%.

These figures do not, however, reveal how many respondents maintained their positions throughout the course of the war and how many changed their views. Moreover, although it is clear that changes were predominantly in the direction of favoring withdrawal from Vietnam, the exact pattern of changes cannot be determined precisely from the figures. This deficiency is remedied in Table 1. Revealing all combinations of policy preferences during the two periods, it provides us with a way of classifying our respondents. Although

TABLE 1. THE 2,282 RESPONDENTS CLASSIFIED INTO SEVEN GROUPS BY POSITIONS ON VIETNAM DURING EARLY AND LATE STAGES OF THE WAR*

Some people felt that we should have done everything possible to gain a complete military victory in Vietnam. Others felt that we should have withdrawn as soon as possible. Still others had opinions in between these two. Please indicate which position came closest to your own feelings – both when the war first became an issue and later toward the end of U.S. involvement.

	TOWARD THE END OF U.S. INVOLVEMENT			
WHEN THE WAR FIRST BECAME AN ISSUE	*I tended to favor a complete military victory*	*I tended to feel in between these two*	*Not sure*	*I tended to favor a complete withdrawal*
I tended to favor a complete military victory	SUPPORTERS (n=363)	AMBIVALENT SUPPORTERS (n=346)		CONVERTED CRITICS (n=867)
I tended to feel in between these two	CONVERTED SUPPORTERS (n=128)	AMBIVALENTS (n=128)		
Not sure				
I tended to favor a complete withdrawal		AMBIVALENT CRITICS (n=63)		CRITICS (n=378)

*Nine respondents did not indicate their position on Vietnam in either the early or late stages of the war.

there are 16 combinations of responses, several of these are grouped together. Of the resulting seven groups, three represent respondents whose views on the appropriate American policy remained consistent throughout the period of the war: the *Supporters,* the *Ambivalents,* and the *Critics.* The remaining four groups consist of persons who underwent a change of position during the course of the war: the *Converted Supporters,* the *Ambivalent Supporters,* the *Ambivalent Critics,* and the *Converted Critics.*

Having identified seven groups of respondents on the basis of their policy preferences during the Vietnam war, we are now able to outline a series of hypotheses linking the groups to belief about American foreign policy goals, the appropriate international role for the United States, and American policy objectives in the underdeveloped nations:

A. *Goals for American Foreign Policy*
1. Compared to the Critics, the Supporters will, in assessing the importance of various foreign policy goals for the United States, attach greater importance to: (a) American responsibilities for global security (Table 3); (b) promoting the economic interests of the United States (Table 4); (c) promoting and defending the security of the United States (Table 7); (d) promoting the development of capitalism abroad (Table 7); and (e) helping to bring a democratic form of government to other nations (Table 7).
2. Compared to the Supporters, the Critics will, in assessing the importance of various foreign policy goals for the United States, attach greater importance to: (a) promoting international cooperation on nonmilitary issues (Table 5); and (b) promoting international cooperation on security issues (Table 6).
3. Compared to the Supporters and Critics, respondents in the other five groups (the Converted Supporters, Ambivalent Supporters, Ambivalents, Ambivalent Critics, and Converted Critics) will take intermediate positions in assessing the importance of various foreign policy goals for the United States. More precisely, the responses of these five groups will be arrayed in the order given.

B. *America's Role in the World*
1. Compared to the Critics, the Supporters will, in defining an appropriate international role for the United States, place greater emphasis on: (a) the role of the United States in opposing communism internationally (Table 10); and (b) the role of the United States in guaranteeing the security of Israel (Table 12).
2. Compared to the Supporters, the Critics will, in defining an appropriate role for the United States, place greater emphasis on:

(a) the role of the United States in providing international economic assistance (Table 11); and (b) a reduced international role for the United States (Table 12).
3. Compared to the Supporters and Critics, respondents in the other five groups, will take intermediate positions in defining an appropriate role for the United States.
C. *Policy Objectives in Underdeveloped Countries*
   1. Compared to the Critics, the Supporters will, in defining goals for American foreign policy in underdeveloped nations, attach greater importance to achieving (Table 14): (a) a stable government capable of preserving internal order; (b) a government which is neutral or pro-American in its foreign policy; (c) a government which retains the free enterprise system; and (d) a government which allows broad opportunities for American business investment.
   2. Compared to the Supporters, the Critics will, in defining goals for American foreign policy in underdeveloped nations, attach greater importance to achieving (Table 14): (a) rapid economic development; (b) a government which maintains civil liberties; and (c) a government which will not engage in unprovoked aggression against other nations.
   3. Compared to the Supporters and Critics, respondents in the other five groups will take intermediate positions in defining goals for American foreign policy in underdeveloped nations.

DATA ANALYSIS

Guided by these hypotheses, the remainder of the chapter is devoted to describing and analyzing the respondents' beliefs on a number of foreign policy issues. The data are presented in two types of tables. The first table in each section describes the distribution of answers for the entire sample of 2,282 respondents, as well as the results from other surveys that used the same questions. A set of subsequent tables presents the mean scores on each item for the seven groups identified in Table 1, indicating whether the pattern of responses is consistent with the hypotheses.

U.S. FOREIGN POLICY GOALS

Responsibilities for Global Security

The essential premise of the "revolution in American foreign policy" after World War II was a belief that only if the United States took an active part in

TABLE 2. U.S. FOREIGN POLICY GOALS: THE RESPONSES OF THREE SAMPLES

Here is a list of possible foreign policy goals that the United States might have. Please indicate how much importance you think should be attached to each goal.	1976 Survey of Leadership Attitudes Toward Vietnam [responses, in percentages, of 2,282 leaders]						1974 Chicago Survey of 328 Leaders and 1,573 Members of the Public	
	Very Important	Somewhat Important	Not Important at all	Not Sure	Uncodable and No Answer	Total	Public*	Leaders*
Maintaining a balance of power among nations	43.2	40.3	8.7	6.4	1.4	100.0	48	56
Defending our allies' security	36.2	54.2	4.4	3.9	1.3	100.0	33	47
Containing communism	38.4	41.7	13.4	5.3	1.2	100.0	54	34
Strengthening countries who are friendly toward us	22.3	63.0	8.6	4.7	1.4	100.0	37	28
Protecting weaker nations against foreign aggression	18.2	59.6	11.9	8.9	1.4	100.0	28	26
Securing adequate supplies of energy	71.1	24.7	2.3	0.9	1.1	100.1	75	77
Protecting the jobs of American workers	30.2	50.9	14.0	3.8	1.2	100.1	74	34
Protecting the interests of American business abroad	13.9	55.2	24.9	5.0	1.0	100.0	39	17
Fostering international cooperation to solve common problems, such as food, inflation and energy	69.7	25.6	2.4	1.2	1.1	100.0	67	86

TABLE 2. U.S. FOREIGN POLICY GOALS: THE RESPONSES OF THREE SAMPLES (Cont.)

Here is a list of possible foreign policy goals that the United States might have. Please indicate how much importance you think should be attached to each goal.	1976 Survey of Leadership Attitudes Toward Vietnam [responses, in percentages, of 2,282 leaders]						1974 Chicago Survey of 328 Leaders and 1,573 Members of the Public	
	Very Important	Somewhat Important	Not Important at all	Not Sure	Uncodable and No Answer	Total	Public*	Leaders*
Combatting world hunger	50.2	39.4	7.1	2.5	0.8	100.0	61	76
Helping solve world inflation	49.1	41.5	5.7	2.7	1.0	100.0	64	81
Helping to improve the standard of living in less developed countries	37.5	50.1	8.7	2.7	1.1	100.1	39	62
Strengthening the United Nations	24.5	36.5	29.6	8.3	1.1	100.0	46	31
Keeping peace in the world	69.8	24.3	2.4	2.5	1.1	100.1	85	95
Worldwide arms control	65.9	25.6	4.6	3.1	0.8	100.0	64	86
Promoting and defending our own security	84.0	12.7	1.4	0.8	1.1	100.0	83	91
Helping to bring a democratic form of government to other nations	7.4	43.8	38.4	9.2	1.1	99.9	28	13
Promoting the development of capitalism abroad	5.8	33.1	52.7	7.4	1.1	100.1	16	9

*Percentage of respondents answering "Very Important"

239

world affairs would it be possible to avoid another major war. Franklin D. Roosevelt's "Grand Design" for the postwar world included American membership in the United Nations and cooperation by the "Big Four" to ensure peace. With the deterioration of relations between the Soviet Union on the one hand, and the United States and Great Britain on the other, an active American role in the world came to include a policy of containing Soviet expansion, the first peacetime alliance in American history, and economic and military assistance to allies in Europe and elsewhere. For at least two decades thereafter the premises of the Truman doctrine, the Marshall Plan, and NATO served as the foundations of American external relations.

The first five items in Table 2 asked the respondents to rate the importance of the kinds of global responsibilities that the United States took on after 1945. The most striking result is that not one of these goals was rated as "very important" by as many as 50% of the respondents. Somewhat over a third of them did indicate that containing communism, defending allies, and maintaining a balance of power were "very important," but there was significantly less urgency attached to strengthening our friends abroad and protecting weaker nations from aggression. A plausible explanation is that many respondents attributed importance to maintaining certain global responsibilities (balance of power, containing communism), but they were not especially impressed with the importance of commitments that bear some resemblance to those undertaken in Vietnam (strengthening friends, protecting weaker nations from aggression).

Although there are some well known hazards in trying to compare results of different surveys (Mueller, 1973, 1977), we can compare ours with those of the Chicago Council on Foreign Relations with somewhat less trepidation because the questions were worded identically. Our respondents were, on balance, somewhat less inclined to attribute importance to American responsibilities for global security than were either the public or leadership samples of the Chicago survey (see the last two columns of Table 2). The 15 months between the two surveys were marked by a number of major events, perhaps the most dramatic of which was the sudden collapse of the Saigon regime in the face of an all-out attack by Communist forces. It is at least plausible that this event, ensuring failure of the American goal of preserving an independent government in Saigon, contributed to the differences between the two survey sets of results.[3]

When the findings for our survey are disaggregated into the seven groups defined in Table 1, we find striking and consistent differences among them (Table 3). Although the data have been subjected to various statistical tests, we shall avoid burdening the reader with more than the minimum discussion of them. To determine whether differences among the seven groups identified

241

TABLE 3. RESPONSIBILITIES FOR GLOBAL SECURITY [MEAN SCORES FOR SEVEN GROUPS OF RESPONDENTS CLASSIFIED BY THEIR POSITIONS ON VIETNAM DURING THE EARLY AND LATE STAGES OF THE WAR]*

Here is a list of possible foreign policy goals that the United States might have. Please indicate how much importance you think should be attached to each goal.	All Respondents [N=2,282]**	Supporters [N=363]	Converted Supporters [N=128]	Ambivalent Supporters [N=346]	Ambivalents [N=128]	Ambivalent Critics [N=63]	Converted Critics [N=867]	Critics [N=378]
***Maintaining a balance of power among nations (F=11.47)	1.37	1.49	1.41	1.49	1.48	1.24	1.36	1.13
***Defending our allies' security (F=28.81)	1.34	1.60	1.39	1.41	1.50	1.20	1.28	1.07
***Containing communism (F=101.45)	1.27	1.76	1.51	1.53	1.40	1.02	1.15	0.65
***Strengthening countries who are friendly towards us (F=22.10)	1.15	1.37	1.19	1.28	1.20	0.98	1.07	0.94
***Protecting weaker nations against foreign aggression (F=21.49)	1.07	1.32	1.11	1.15	1.19	0.96	0.99	0.86

*The mean scores were computed by scoring a response of "Very Important" as 2.00, "Somewhat Important" as 1.00, "Not Important at all" as 0.00.

**Includes nine respondents who failed to state their positions on Vietnam and thus could not be classified among the seven groups.

***Differences among groups significant at the .001 level, whether computed according to parametric (analysis of variance) or nonparametric (chi-square) statistics. F ratios (given in parentheses immediately following each item) exceeding 3.47 are significant at the .001 level.

in Table 3 are statistically significant, we have undertaken analyses of variance (ANOVA). The choice of a criterion of significance is always an arbitrary one; we selected the .001 level—that is, we accept differences among the groups as significant if such results could have occurred by chance less than once in a thousand times—mainly because any less demanding level has been found to be inappropriate to samples of the size of ours. The .001 level corresponds to an F ratio of 3.47. Because the use of parametric statistics on these data will not evoke universal approval, we have also done the same analyses using a nonparametric test (*chi* square). Both the analysis of variance and the *chi* square tests only indicate whether the differences between groups are sufficiently great to meet a specific significance level (.001 in this case). Since our hypotheses also specify a *direction* of difference among the groups, they are rejected unless they meet *both* the statistical and directional criteria (Table 15).

The range of responses is especially noteworthy on the question of containing communism: on a two-point scale (0.0 to 2.0), the difference between the Supporters and Critics is well over one point. Stated somewhat differently, 77% of the Supporters responded that containing communism was "very important," whereas only 7% of the Critics did so. Equally striking are the percentages of those in the two groups who responded "not important at all": 2 and 37%, respectively. The range of group scores on the other four items is somewhat smaller, but in all cases the differences among them are significant and, more importantly, they are generally in the predicted direction.

Promoting American Economic Interests

Since at least 1971, when President Nixon attempted to deal with a burgeoning balance of payments problem and the outflow of American gold by devaluing the dollar and rendering it no longer convertible into gold, the economic component of American foreign policy has become increasingly visible. The oil embargo, dubious payoffs abroad by some major corporations, and protectionist pressures against imports ranging from Japanese steel and television sets to textiles from Korea and shoes from Italy have also become controversial issues in American foreign policy.

Our questionnaire asked respondents to assess the importance of three such economic issues (Table 2, rows 6, 7 and 8). Not surprisingly, almost three respondents in four rated securing adequate supplies of energy as "very important." Substantially less importance was attributed to the other two issues—protecting the jobs of American workers, and protecting the interests of American business abroad. Indeed, one-fourth of the leaders rated the protection of business interests as "not important at all."

TABLE 4. PROMOTING AMERICAN ECONOMIC INTERESTS [MEAN SCORES FOR SEVEN GROUPS OF RESPONDENTS CLASSIFIED BY THEIR POSITIONS ON VIETNAM DURING THE EARLY AND LATE STAGES OF THE WAR]*

Here is a list of possible foreign policy goals that the United States might have. Please indicate how much importance you think should be attached to each goal.	All Respondents [N=2,282]**	Supporters [N=363]	Converted Supporters [N=128]	Ambivalent Supporters [N=346]	Ambivalents [N=128]	Ambivalent Critics [N=63]	Converted Critics [N=867]	Critics [N=378]
***Securing adequate supplies of energy (F=8.75)	1.70	1.78	1.72	1.79	1.65	1.73	1.71	1.54
Protecting the jobs of American workers (F=1.87)	1.17	1.27	1.18	1.17	1.10	1.22	1.16	1.10
***Protecting the interests of American business abroad (F=27.37)	0.88	1.16	0.93	1.03	0.85	0.76	0.84	0.58

*The mean scores were computed by scoring a response of "Very Important" as 2.00, "Somewhat Important" as 1.00, "Not Important at all" as 0.00.

**Includes nine respondents who failed to state their positions on Vietnam and thus could not be classified among the seven groups.

***Differences among groups significant at the .001 level, whether computed according to parametric (analysis of variance) or nonparametric (chi-square) statistics. F ratios (given in parentheses immediately following each item) exceeding 3.47 are significant at the .001 level.

Compared to the Chicago survey, the respondents to our questionnaire were somewhat less inclined to attribute importance to any of the three economic goals. The differences between our sample of leaders and those in the Chicago survey are relatively small, but there are notable differences between the views of the general public and those of leaders, especially with respect to protecting jobs and business interests.

Hypothesis A.1(b) predicted that those at the Supporter end of the scale would be more inclined than the Critics to attribute importance to promoting American economic interests. In all cases the differences between the seven groups are in the predicted direction, and they are significant on two of the three issues, the exception being on the importance of protecting the jobs of American workers (Table 4). The importance of protecting business interests engendered the greatest range of views, with the Supporters attributing substantially greater significance to that goal than did the Critics.

International Cooperation on Nonmilitary Issues

During and immediately after World War II the United States played a leading role in establishing a number of international institutions to cope with problems that seemed beyond the reach of effective unilateral action. In more recent years the agenda of problems that require international cooperation has grown. But there are also countervailing pressures, arising in part out of a sense of disillusionment with some international organizations, in part out of domestic pressures to cope with such problems as balances of payments or unemployment by means of policies that may run counter to commitments for international cooperation.

Five items on international nonmilitary cooperation appear in Table 2. Perhaps the most striking finding is the wide range of responses to the five items. International cooperation to solve common problems, combatting hunger and coping with inflation were accorded substantial importance, but improving the living standard in less developed countries was rated of somewhat less significance. On the other hand, only a quarter of the respondents considered strengthening the United Nations to be very important, whereas 30% of them considered that goal to be of no importance.

Although the American leaders in our sample generally attributed substantial significance to international cooperation on a wide range of issues, they consistently did so in smaller proportions than either the public or leadership respondents in the Chicago survey. The differences are most striking on the issues of inflation and hunger, perhaps reflecting lower rates of inflation in the United States by early 1976, as well as the bumper crops of the previous year that reduced immediate fears of global famine.

TABLE 5. INTERNATIONAL COOPERATION: NONMILITARY ISSUES [MEAN SCORES FOR SEVEN GROUPS OF RESPONDENTS CLASSIFIED BY THEIR POSITIONS ON VIETNAM DURING THE EARLY AND LATE STAGES OF THE WAR]*

Here is a list of possible foreign policy goals that the United States might have. Please indicate how much importance you think should be attached to each goal.	All Respondents [N=2,282]**	Supporters [N=363]	Converted Supporters [N=128]	Ambivalent Supporters [N=346]	Ambivalents [N=128]	Ambivalent Critics [N=63]	Converted Critics [N=867]	Critics [N=378]
***Fostering international cooperation to solve common problems, such as food, inflation and energy (F=18.40)	1.69	1.49	1.52	1.65	1.69	1.75	1.73	1.87
***Combatting world hunger (F=25.31)	1.45	1.19	1.15	1.37	1.56	1.43	1.50	1.71
***Helping to solve world inflation (F=5.06)	1.45	1.33	1.37	1.38	1.49	1.49	1.48	1.56
***Helping to improve the standard of living in less developed countries (F=24.94)	1.30	1.02	1.04	1.24	1.44	1.34	1.34	1.55
***Stengthening the United Nations (F=30.46)	0.94	0.56	0.79	0.84	1.04	1.15	0.96	1.34

*The mean scores were computed by scoring a response of "Very Important" as 2.00, "Somewhat Important" as 1.00, "Not Important at all" as 0.00.

**Includes nine respondents who failed to state their positions on Vietnam and thus could not be classified among the seven groups.

***Differences among groups significant at the .001 level, whether computed according to parametric (analysis of variance) or nonparametric (chi-square) statistics. F ratios (given in parentheses immediately following each item) exceeding 3.47 are significant at the .001 level.

245

The data in Table 5 bear out the expectation that, compared to the Supporters, the Critics would ascribe greater importance to international cooperation on nonmilitary issues. For each of the items the highest scores among the seven groups are those of the Critics and, with a single exception, those of the Supporters are the lowest. Differences among the groups are statistically significant for all five issues. Divisions on the importance of strengthening the United Nations are especially notable. Whereas nearly half of the Critics regarded strengthening of that international organization as an important foreign policy goal, less than 10% of Supporters did so, and over half of the latter believed that this objective was "not important at all."

International Cooperation on Security Issues

The Chicago survey also asked respondents to rate the importance of keeping peace and world wide arms control. Both of these goals were regarded as very important by a substantial majority of our respondents, although in neither case do the figures match those of the Chicago leadership sample (Table 2).

The expected differences among the seven groups of respondents materialized only on the question of arms control, with substantially greater importance accorded to the issue by the Critics than by any of the others (Table 6). The scores for the other six groups are arrayed in the predicted pattern with but a single exception, and the differences between them are statistically significant.

Promoting American Security and Institutions

The three remaining items on the Chicago survey involve protecting and promoting American security and institutions (Table 2). Not surprisingly, our respondents ascribed great importance to protecting the security of the United States, but promotion of neither democratic institutions nor capitalism abroad was similarly regarded. These results parallel those of both the public and leadership samples of the Chicago survey, although at a somewhat lower level.

Our hypothesis predicted that those at the Supporter end of the scale would tend to attribute greater urgency to each of these foreign policy goals than would the Critics. The figures in Table 7 sustain these expectations, except with respect to helping to bring democratic institutions to other countries, an undertaking that was not, on balance, even appraised as "somewhat important" by any of the seven groups. On the issues of protecting American security and promoting capitalism abroad, the differences between the seven groups are statistically significant and in the predicted direction.

TABLE 6. INTERNATIONAL COOPERATION: SECURITY ISSUES [MEAN SCORES FOR SEVEN GROUPS OF RESPONDENTS CLASSIFIED BY THEIR POSITIONS ON VIETNAM DURING THE EARLY AND LATE STAGES OF THE WAR]*

Here is a list of possible foreign policy goals that the United States might have. Please indicate how much importance you think should be attached to each goal.	All Respondents [N=2,282]**	Supporters [N=363]	Converted Supporters [N=128]	Ambivalent Supporters [N=346]	Ambivalents [N=128]	Ambivalent Critics [N=63]	Converted Critics [N=867]	Critics [N=378]
Keeping peace in the world (F=2.40)	1.70	1.66	1.56	1.72	1.73	1.63	1.71	1.75
***Worldwide arms control (F=18.42)	1.64	1.46	1.43	1.52	1.60	1.67	1.70	1.84

*The mean scores were computed by scoring a response of "Very Important" as 2.00, "Somewhat Important" as 1.00, "Not Important at all" as 0.00.

**Includes nine respondents who failed to state their positions on Vietnam and thus could not be classified among the seven groups.

***Differences among groups significant at the .001 level, whether computed according to parametric (analysis of variance) or nonparametric (chi-square) statistics. F ratios (given in parentheses immediately following each item) exceeding 3.47 are significant at the .001 level.

TABLE 7. PROMOTING AMERICAN SECURITY AND INSTITUTIONS [MEAN SCORES FOR SEVEN GROUPS OF RESPONDENTS CLASSIFIED BY THEIR POSITIONS ON VIETNAM DURING THE EARLY AND LATE STAGES OF THE WAR]*

Here is a list of possible foreign policy goals that the United States might have. Please indicate how much importance you think should be attached to each goal.	All Respondents [N=2,282]**	Supporters [N=363]	Converted Supporters [N=128]	Ambivalent Supporters [N=346]	Ambivalents [N=128]	Ambivalent Critics [N=63]	Converted Critics [N=867]	Critics [N=378]
***Promoting and defending our own security (F=31.62)	1.84	1.98	1.87	1.96	1.84	1.67	1.85	1.61
Helping to bring a democratic form of government to other nations (F=2.37)	0.65	0.72	0.57	0.70	0.77	0.53	0.62	0.62
***Promoting the development of capitalism abroad (F=26.33)	0.49	0.74	0.56	0.69	0.56	0.34	0.40	0.25

*The mean scores were computed by scoring a response of "Very Important" as 2.00, "Somewhat Important" as 1.00, "Not Important at all" as 0.00.

**Includes nine respondents who failed to state their positions on Vietnam and thus could not be classified among the seven groups.

***Differences among groups significant at the .001 level, whether computed according to parametric (analysis of variance) or nonparametric (chi-square) statistics. F ratios (given in parentheses immediately following each item) exceeding 3.47 are significant at the .001 level.

Conclusion

Data on 18 foreign policy goals for the United States generally provide substantial support for the hypotheses, as differences among the seven groups are significant and in the predicted direction in all cases except three. Another perspective on the data may be achieved by comparing the rankings accorded by each of the seven groups to the entire set of foreign policy goals (Table 8). Differences among the groups clearly emerge once again. In some cases goals that were appraised as very important by groups at one end of the scale—for example, containing communism—received a very low ranking at the other end. Indeed, despite the presence of such seemingly uncontroversial issues as peace and American security among the 18 goals, it is striking that not one of them was ranked among the four most important by respondents in all seven groups!

THE UNITED STATES' ROLE IN THE WORLD

Seven items on the international role of the United States that also appeared in the Harvard-*Washington Post* survey of American leaders have been grouped into three clusters: anticommunist leader, provider of economic assistance, and other.

Anti-Communist Leader

On any list of international roles played by the United States during the postwar decades, that of the global leader of anticommunist forces was at or close to the top.[4] A thorough exploration of that role clearly cannot be undertaken with a very limited number of questions, but the first three propositions listed in Table 9 probe some aspects of the issue. With respect to covert operations against hostile governments, our respondents were almost evenly divided between those who expressed approval and disapproval of the work of the Central Intelligence Agency. But their views were much more pronounced on the question of taking all steps, including the use of force, to contain communism; by a margin of roughly two-to-one they opposed such a policy stance by the United States. And, on a related question dealing more specifically with the desirability of better Soviet-American relations, less than 30% expressed disapproval. Owing to slightly different wording, it is not possible to make valid comparisons on the C.I.A. question with those of the Harvard-*Washington Post* leadership survey, but on the other two issues the results are fairly similar.

Table 9 conceals some rather dramatic differences among the seven groups of respondents. The data in Table 10 provide very strong support for the hypothesis that those at the Supporter end of the scale would provide

TABLE 8. U.S. FOREIGN POLICY GOALS AS RANKED BY SEVEN GROUPS*

	Supporters [N=363]	Converted Supporters [N=128]	Ambivalent Supporters [N=346]	Ambivalents [N=128]	Ambivalent Critics [N=63]	Converted Critics [N=867]	Critics [N=378]
Promoting and defending our own security	1	1	1	1	3**	1	5
Securing adequate supplies of energy	2	2	2	4**	2	3**	8
Containing communism	3	5	5	11	–	–	–
Keeping peace in the world	4	3	3	2	5	3**	3
Defending our allies' security	5	8	8	7	11	10	–
Maintaining a balance of power among nations	6**	7	7	9	9	8	–
Fostering international cooperation to solve common problems, such as food, inflation and energy	6**	4	4	3	1	2	1
Worldwide arms control	8	6	6	6	3**	5	2
Strengthening countries who are friendly to us	9	–	11	12	–	–	–
Helping solve world inflation	10	9	9	8	6	7	6
Protecting weaker nations from foreign aggression	11	–	–	–	–	–	–
Protecting the jobs of American workers	12	–	–	–	10	–	–
Combatting world hunger	–	–	10	4**	7	6	4
Helping to improve the standard of living in less developed countries	–	–	12	10	8	9	7
Strengthening the United Nations	–	–	–	–	–	–	9

*This table includes all items that received a rating of at least 1.20 on a scale of 2.00 (Very Important) to 0.00 (Not Important at all).

**Tied ranks

250

TABLE 9. AMERICA'S ROLE IN THE WORLD: THE RESPONSES OF TWO SAMPLES

Please indicate how strongly you agree or disagree with each of the following statements concerning America's role in the world.	1976 Survey of Leadership Attitudes Toward Vietnam [responses, in percentages, of 2,282 leaders]							1976 Harvard-Washington Post Survey* [responses of 2,469 leaders]
	Agree Strongly	Agree Somewhat	Disagree Somewhat	Disagree Strongly	No Opinion	Uncodable and No Answer	Total	
There is nothing wrong with using the C.I.A. to try to under-mine hostile governments**	20.9	29.6	19.5	27.9	1.1	1.1	100.1	46
The U.S. should take all steps including the use of force to pre-vent the spread of Communism	8.9	24.0	30.1	34.8	1.1	1.2	100.1	31
It is not in our interest to have better relations with the Soviet Union because we are getting less than we are giving to them	8.9	19.9	34.0	33.8	1.8	1.6	100.0	37

TABLE 9. AMERICA'S ROLE IN THE WORLD: THE RESPONSES OF TWO SAMPLES (Cont.)

The U.S. should give economic aid to poorer countries even if it means higher prices at home	11.2	36.7	31.2	18.4	1.4	1.1	100.0	45
Even though it probably means higher food prices here at home, it is worth selling grain to the Soviet Union since it may improve our relations with Russia	4.9	31.5	31.5	27.5	2.7	1.9	100.0	33
The U.S. has a moral obligation to prevent the destruction of the State of Israel	32.4	35.9	17.6	11.2	1.7	1.1	99.9	61
We shouldn't think so much in international terms but concentrate more on our own national problems	10.7	26.1	28.7	32.6	0.9	1.1	100.1	47

*Percentage of respondents answering "Agree Strongly" or "Agree Somewhat"

**In the Harvard-*Washington Post* survey this question was worded somewhat differently: "There is nothing wrong with using the CIA to help support governments friendly to the U.S. and to try to undermine hostile governments."

TABLE 10. AMERICA'S ROLE IN THE WORLD: ANTICOMMUNIST LEADER [MEAN SCORES FOR SEVEN GROUPS OF RESPONDENTS CLASSIFIED BY THEIR POSITIONS ON VIETNAM DURING THE EARLY AND LATE STAGES OF THE WAR]*

Please indicate how strongly you agree or disagree with each of the following statements concerning America's role in the world.	All Respondents [N=2,282]**	Supporters [N=363]	Converted Supporters [N=128]	Ambivalent Supporters [N=346]	Ambivalents [N=128]	Ambivalent Critics [N=63]	Converted Critics [N=867]	Critics [N=378]
***There is nothing wrong with using the C.I.A. to try to undermine hostile governments (F=84.27)	−0.04	0.94	0.56	0.69	0.02	−0.41	−0.30	−1.21
***The U.S. should take all steps including the use of force to prevent the spread of Communism (F=123.79)	−0.58	0.71	0.02	−0.07	−0.56	−1.21	−0.95	−1.56
***It is not in our interest to have better relations with the Soviet Union because we are getting less than we are giving to them (F=36.59)	−0.65	0.17	−0.20	−0.49	−0.92	−0.73	−0.87	−1.17

*The mean scores were computed by scoring a response of "Agree Strongly" as 2.00, "Agree Somewhat" as 1.00, "Disagree Somewhat" as −1.00, and "Disagree Strongly" as −2.00.

**Includes nine respondents who failed to state their positions on Vietnam and thus could not be classified among the seven groups.

***Differences among groups significant at the .001 level, whether computed according to parametric (analysis of variance) or nonparametric (chi-square) statistics. F ratio (given in parentheses immediately following each item) exceeding 3.47 are significantly at the .001 level.

253

stronger endorsement of an international role of leadership against communism. Differences between the groups are exceptionally large and in the predicted direction. Whereas 45.1% of the Supporters agreed strongly that there is nothing wrong with using the C.I.A. to undermine hostile governments, only 5.1% of the Critics did so. And the comparable figures on the question of using all means to contain communism are 32 and 1%. On the latter issue over two-thirds of the Critics expressed strong disagreement, compared to only 8% of the Supporters who did so. The value of better relations with the Soviet Union gave rise to a somewhat narrower range of responses, but the differences among the groups are substantial and in the predicted direction.

Providing Economic Assistance

Two items asked the respondents to assess United States policies in the context of a trade-off between foreign assistance and domestic inflation levels (Table 9). The issue of economic assistance to poorer countries resulted in an almost even division among our respondents. Grain sales to the U.S.S.R. that might also result in higher food prices at home received less support, as almost 60% of the respondents expressed opposition to such exports.

The hypothesis that the Critics would be more inclined than the Supporters to agree with economic assistance programs receives support when the data are disaggregated (Table 11). The difference among the seven groups of respondents are statistically significant on both issues and they are in the predicted direction. But whereas four groups supported economic aid to poorer countries, none of the groups was, on balance, in favor of grain exports to the Soviet Union; the differences among them are essentially in varying degrees of opposition to such exports.

Other Roles

Two additional questions deal with broad aspects of the United States role—whether more attention should be focused on the agenda of domestic problems and the very specific issue of guaranteeing Israel's existence.

Over two-thirds of the respondents agreed that the United States had a moral obligation to prevent the destruction of Israel (Table 9). Fears that disillusionment with the results of the commitment to preserve the independence of South Vietnam would ultimately endanger all international commitments appear to have been exaggerated or premature, at least insofar as Israel is concerned. And, by a margin of approximately three-to-two, the leaders in our sample rejected the proposition that attention and energies should be turned away from international problems to domestic ones.

TABLE 11. AMERICA'S ROLE IN THE WORLD: PROVIDING ECONOMIC ASSISTANCE [MEAN SCORES FOR SEVEN GROUPS OF RESPONDENTS CLASSIFIED BY THEIR POSITIONS ON VIETNAM DURING THE EARLY AND LATE STAGES OF THE WAR] *

Please indicate how strongly you agree or disagree with each of the following statements concerning America's role in the world.	All Respondents [N=2,282]**	Supporters [N=363]	Converted Supporters [N=128]	Ambivalent Supporters [N=346]	Ambivalents [N=128]	Ambivalent Critics [N=63]	Converted Critics [N=867]	Critics [N=378]
***The U.S. should give economic aid to poorer countries even if it means higher prices at home (F=27.73)	-0.09	-0.71	-0.68	-0.28	0.19	0.02	0.05	0.46
***Even though it probably means higher food prices here at home, it is worth selling grain to the Soviet Union since it may improve our relations with Russia (F=7.58)	-0.46	-0.79	-0.76	-0.52	-0.20	-0.47	-0.40	-0.20

*The mean scores were computed by scoring a response of "Agree Strongly" as 2.00, "Agree Somewhat" as 1.00, "Disagree Somewhat" as -1.00, and "Disagree Strongly" as -2.00.

**Includes nine respondents who failed to state their positions on Vietnam and thus could not be classified among the seven groups.

***Differences among groups significant at the .001 level, whether computed according to parametric (analysis of variance) or nonparametric (chi-square) statistics. F ratio (given in parentheses immediately following each item) exceeding 3.47 are significantly at the .001 level.

255

TABLE 12. AMERICA'S ROLE IN THE WORLD: OTHER ROLES ([MEAN SCORES FOR SEVEN GROUPS OF RESPONDENTS CLASSIFIED BY THEIR POSITIONS ON VIETNAM DURING THE EARLY AND LATE STAGES OF THE WAR] *

Please indicate how strongly you agree or disagree with each of the following statements concerning America's role in the world.	All Respondents [N=2,282] **	Supporters [N=363]	Converted Supporters [N=128]	Ambivalent Supporters [N=346]	Ambivalents [N=128]	Ambivalent Critics [N=63]	Converted Critics [N=867]	Critics [N=378]
The U.S. has a moral obligation to prevent the destruction of the State of Israel (F=2.42)	0.61	0.56	0.37	0.67	0.80	0.29	0.69	0.53
We shouldn't think so much in international terms but concentrate more on our own national problems (F=4.69)	−0.47	−0.29	−0.30	−0.49	−1.05	−0.10	−0.49	−0.50

*The mean scores were computed by scoring a response of "Agree Strongly" as 2.00, "Agree Somewhat" as 1.00, "Disagree Somewhat" as −1.00, and "Disagree Strongly" as −2.00.

**Includes nine respondents who failed to state their positions on Vietnam and thus could not be classified among the seven groups.

The expectation of significantly greater opposition to external commitments by the Critics was not borne out by the data (Table 12). On balance, all the groups agreed that a moral obligation exists to support Israel, and the differences among them were not significant. Nor did the respondents in the seven groups differ significantly on the proposal for a more isolationist role for the United States.

Conclusion

Table 13 provides further testimony to the strikingly different perspectives among the seven groups of respondents on a proper international role for the United States. Beyond a degree of similarity in their responses to the question of a commitment to Israel, there are few shared priorities among the groups. For example, sanctioning C.I.A. activities against hostile governments and preventing the spread of communism received the highest priority among the three groups at the Supporter end of the scale, but these ranked as the two least worthy undertakings for the Critics. A similar lack of consensus exists with respect to the other roles as well.

AMERICAN POLICY OBJECTIVES IN UNDERDEVELOPED COUNTRIES

A set of questions borrowed from the Russett-Hanson (1975) study of business executives and military officers asked the respondents to rank in order of importance a series of possible objectives for the United States to pursue among the less developed nations. Mean rank scores for the entire sample of 2,282 respondents, as well as for persons in each of the seven groups, are given in Table 14.

The overall results from the Vietnam survey parallel some of those achieved in the Russett-Hanson study. In both surveys the goals of governments in underdeveloped countries that are stable, that respect civil liberties, and that will not commit aggression ranked at the top, whereas governments that allow opportunities for American business investments were, by a very substantial margin, accorded the least importance. It may be worthy noting, however, that the importance of governments that maintain civil liberties fared somewhat better in our survey than in the Russett-Hanson study. Perhaps the difference reflects the fact that our questionnaire reached respondents at the beginning of a presidential campaign in which the alleged indifference of President Ford and Secretary Kissinger to human rights was one of the more visible issues. Alternatively, this result may simply reflect the different composition of the two samples; Russett and Hanson surveyed only

TABLE 13. AMERICA'S ROLE IN THE WORLD AS RANKED BY SEVEN GROUPS*

	Supporters [N=363]	Converted Supporters [N=128]	Ambivalent Supporters [N=346]	Ambivalents [N=128]	Ambivalent Critics [N=63]	Converted Critics [N=867]	Critics [N=378]
There is nothing wrong with using the C.I.A. to try to undermine hostile governments	1	1	1	3	4	3	6
The U.S. should take all steps including the use of force to prevent the spread of Communism	2	3	3	5	7	7	7
The U.S. has a moral obligation to prevent the destruction of the State of Israel	3	2	2	1	*1*	*1*	*1*
It is not in our interest to have better relations with the Soviet Union because we are getting less than we are giving to them	4	4	5**	6	6	6	5
We shouldn't think so much in international terms but concentrate more on our own national problems	5	5	5**	7	3	5	4
The U.S. should give economic aid to poorer countries even if it means higher prices at home	6	6	4	2	2	2	2
Even though it probably means higher food prices here at home, it is worth selling grain to the Soviet Union since it may improve our relations with Russia	7	7	7	4	5	4	3

*Rankings based on means scores for each group. Ranks in italics are for questionnaire items that received a favorable mean score (0.01 or higher).

**Tied ranks

258

TABLE 14. U.S. POLICY OBJECTIVES IN UNDEVELOPED COUNTRIES [MEAN RANKS FOR SEVEN GROUPS OF RESPONDENTS CLASSIFIED BY THEIR POSITIONS ON VIETNAM DURING THE EARLY AND LATE STAGES OF THE WAR]*

Please indicate the relative importance you believe the U.S. should attach, in general, to the following policy objectives in its involvement with underdeveloped countries. If a choice must be made, which ones should be considered most important? Use the numbers 1–7, with a 1 being the highest rank.	All Respondents |N=2,282|**	Supporters |N=363|	Converted Supporters |N=128|	Ambivalent Supporters |N=346|	Ambivalents |N=128|	Ambivalent Critics |N=63|	Converted Critics |N=867|	Critics |N=378|
***A stable government capable of preserving internal order (F=4.40)	2.55	2.43	2.31	2.35	2.67	2.54	2.53	2.91
***A government which is neutral or pro-American in its foreign policy (F=12.84)	3.72	3.31	3.48	3.37	3.59	4.27	3.81	4.27
***Rapid economic government (F=15.57)	4.38	4.83	4.58	4.85	4.42	4.31	4.27	3.72
***A government which maintains civil liberties (F=18.76)	2.83	3.36	3.43	3.09	3.02	2.37	2.71	2.17
***A government which retains the free enterprise system (F=15.22)	4.81	4.13	4.54	4.64	4.78	4.74	5.02	5.28

TABLE 14. U.S. POLICY OBJECTIVES IN UNDEVELOPED COUNTRIES [MEAN RANKS FOR SEVEN GROUPS OF RESPONDENTS CLASSIFIED BY THEIR POSITIONS ON VIETNAM DURING THE EARLY AND LATE STAGES OF THE WAR] * (Cont.)

Please indicate the relative importance you believe the U.S. should attach, in general, to the following policy objectives in its involvement with underdeveloped countries. If a choice must be made, which ones should be considered most important? Use the numbers 1–7, with a 1 being the highest rank.	*All Respondents [N=2,282] ***	*Supporters [N=363]*	*Converted Supporters [N=128]*	*Ambivalent Supporters [N=346]*	*Ambivalents [N=128]*	*Ambivalent Critics [N=63]*	*Converted Critics [N=867]*	*Critics [N=378]*
***A government which will not engage in unprovoked aggression against other nations (F=6.86)	2.95	3.35	3.03	3.09	2.52	3.10	2.92	2.56
A government which allows broad opportunities for American business investment (F=4.08)	5.90	5.62	5.73	5.79	5.89	5.70	6.03	6.08

*The mean scores were computed by scoring a response of "1" as 1, "2" as 2, and so on through the lowest rank of 7.

**Includes nine respondents who failed to state their position on Vietnam and thus could not be classified among the seven groups.

***Differences among groups significant at the .001 level whether computed according to parametric (analysis of variance) or nonparametric (chi-square) statistics. F ratios (given in parentheses immediately following each item) exceeding 3.47 are significant at the .001 level).

business executives and military officers, whereas our sample represents a more varied group of American leaders.[5]

Once again, however, a description of the entire sample masks considerable differences among persons in the seven groups of respondents. Without exception, all seven groups rated opportunities for American business investment as the least important policy goal. But priorities with respect to the other six objectives resulted in significant differences, all of which were in the predicted direction. Supporters ascribed greater importance to achievement of stable governments adhering to neutrality or pro-American policies and preserving free enterprise, whereas the Critics emphasized the importance of rapid economic development, maintenance of civil liberties, and governments that refrain from external aggression.

SUMMARY AND CONCLUSION

Results of the foregoing analyses are summarized in Table 15. The first three columns identify the hypotheses, and column four indicates the number of relevant questionnaire items for each hypothesis. The next two columns summarize results of statistical tests to determine whether there were significant differences among the seven groups of respondents. These tests do not, however, indicate whether the scores for the seven groups were arrayed in the order predicted by each hypothesis. Column seven presents rank-order correlations between the predicted and actual ordering of group scores. Hypothesis A.1(a), for example, predicted that the importance of American responsibilities for global security would receive the strongest rating from respondents in the Supporters group, followed in order by the Converted Supporters, Ambivalent Supporters, Ambivalents, Ambivalent Critics, Converted Critics, and Critics. Using the group rankings for each of the five items in Table 3, correlations between the actual and predicted scores were computed, resulting in coefficients of .93, .82, .82, .83, and .86.

Table 15 reveals consistently strong support for the hypotheses. Differences among the seven groups of respondents were significant and in the predicted direction for 26 of the 32 questionnaire items. Moreover, 23 of the 32 questionnaire items resulted in rank-order correlation coefficients between the predicted and actual sequences of group scores exceeding .80.

Consensus, Vietnam, and Belief Systems

The introduction identified three propositions underlying our specific hypotheses and data analysis: The consensus on American foreign policy that emerged in the period after World War II has been shattered; the war in

TABLE 15. TEST OF THE HYPOTHESES: A SUMMARY

Hypothesis Number	Table	Hypotheses	Number of Questionnaire Items: Total	Significant Differences:* ANOVA	Significant Differences:* X^2	Correlations, Predicted and Actual Rankings of Group Scores (r_s):**
		Foreign Policy Goals				
A.1a	3	Responsibilities for global security	5	5	5	.93, .82, .82, .83, .86
A.1b	4	Promoting U.S. economic interests	3	2	2	.68, .93, .67
A.2a	5	International cooperation: nonmilitary issues	5	5	5	.88, .86, .88, .89, .96
A.2b	6	International cooperation: security issues	2	1	1	.54, .96
A.2c-2e	7	Promoting American security and institutions	3	2	2	.86, .90, .31
		America's Role in the World				
B.1a	10	Anticommunist leader	3	3	3	.93, .96, .89
B.1b	12	Israel's protector	1	1	0	−.04
B.2a	11	Providing economic assistance	2	2	2	.89, .85
B.2b	12	A reduced international role	1	1	0	.42
C.1, C.2	14	*Policy Objectives in Underdeveloped Countries*	7	7	6	.75, .90, .89, .93, .96, .57, .79

*Of the total number of items relevant to each hypothesis, the number for which differences among groups were significant at the .001 level, as measured by analysis of variance (ANOVA) and *chi*-square (X^2).

**Spearman rank-order correlation between rankings of groups as predicted by hypotheses and actual group scores. Correlations for individual questionnaire items are given in the same order as in the tables presenting the group scores.

Vietnam has been a critical event in dissolving that consensus; and the resulting views on American foreign policy can appropriately be described as competing belief systems.

As earlier analysis, centering on the sources of failure in Vietnam, consequences of the war, and "lessons" to be drawn from that experience, revealed strong support for each of these propositions (Holsti and Rosenau, 1977b). To what extent do the present findings sustain or diverge from those of the earlier analysis?

The findings reported in Tables 3 to 15 provide substantial evidence in support of the first proposition. There are deep cleavages among the seven groups of respondents, and these differences extend across a broad spectrum of issues, ranging from the most fundamental purposes of American foreign policy to the appropriate strategies and tactics that might be used in the pursuit of external goals.

In order to test the second proposition—that Vietnam was a watershed experience with respect to basic American beliefs about international politics and foreign policy—we classified the respondents into seven groups *solely* on the basis of their policy preferences during the early and late stages of the war. Admittedly this is a rather simple classification scheme, but it serves our purposes well because it isolates views on the war from other variables such as age, education, occupation, ideology, and party identification.[6] Indeed, it is precisely because the classification scheme described in Table 1 is simple and based purely on the Vietnam issue that the results supporting the second proposition are so striking.

The third proposition postulated that responses to several clusters of issues—the goals of American diplomacy, the appropriate international role for the United States, and the objectives that should govern Washington's relations with underdeveloped nations—would form coherent and internally consistent belief systems. The hypotheses that guided our analysis of the issues represented, in effect, our conception of the beliefs that seemed logically to form a coherent system of thought. The results in Tables 3 to 15 yielded strong support for this line of reasoning, revealing strikingly different, almost mutually exclusive belief systems.

One of the belief systems is presented in the responses of persons in the Supporters group. Drawing upon the previously cited analysis, we can summarize their beliefs about the Vietnam war in the following terms. They are more likely to attribute failure in Vietnam to the manner in which the war was conducted (means) than to the nature of the undertaking itself (ends). The Supporters believe that the war should have resulted in victory and that it could have except for self-imposed restraints. They would, on the whole, agree with former President Ford's diagnosis: "I thought our motives were right. Our tactics were not the best tactics that could have been used" (*New York Times*, 1977:61). Further, they believe that the price of failure will be paid in the international arena; the consequences of the war will be an international system that is far less congenial to American interests and aspirations. Finally, the Supporters tend to adduce lessons from the Vietnam experience that are consistent with their diagnoses of failure and their prognoses of the consequences of Vietnam, emphasizing the bipolar structure of the international system, credibility, and the domino theory; doubts about the permanent fragmentation of the communist bloc; skepticism about the value of détente; and more effective management of military power.

Tables 3 to 15 reveal that respondents in the Supporters group also appear to maintain a consistent world view on issues other than those concerned directly with Vietnam, with emphasis on international security/military issues and such concepts as "balance of power" and "containment." With respect to means, they generally subscribe to a realpolitik position and are more prone than other groups of respondents to regard force and subversion as instruments of foreign policy that have not lost their utility. These beliefs are also consistent with the types of objectives that receive high priority among the Supporters: stable governments that will pursue pro-American, or at least neutral, foreign policies.

In contrast, respondents in the Critics group held to very different views of both the Vietnam experiences as well as the issues explored in the preceding pages. They regarded the Vietnam undertaking as an unwinnable one, tracing the American failure to unrealistic goals, to a lack of knowledge and understanding, and to shortcomings of the regime in Saigon. Unlike the Supporters, they tend to view the consequences of the war in terms of such domestic costs as inflation, loss of faith in American institutions, and a neglect of more critical issues. The Critics also derived lessons from the war that are consistent with their diagnoses of failure and their assessments of its consequences. They regard the international system as a multipolar one within which they tend to prescribe a reduced role for the United States in undertakings that involve, or might lead to, military intervention, and they are skeptical about the utility of military power in the conduct of foreign relations. And, most emphatically, the Critics find in the Vietnam experience ample evidence pointing to the need for decentralizing and demilitarizing the formulation and execution of foreign policy.

The Critics' assessment of the Vietnam experience thus appears to form a coherent and mutually supporting cluster of beliefs. This consistency also extends to their views on the types of issues described in Tables 3 to 15. Unlike their counterparts among the Supporters, the Critics rate international cooperation on such issues as arms control, inflation, hunger, resources, and living standards in underdeveloped countries as the most important goals for American foreign policy, and they assign significantly lower priority to such objectives as containment of communism and maintenance of a global balance of power. The Critics tend to be highly skeptical about the value of force in international affairs, placing greater emphasis on such instruments as foreign economic assistance. And the goals that they would pursue among underdeveloped nations seem consistent with their other views. Compared to respondents in the Supporters group, the Critics place greater value on efforts to establish or support governments that protect the civil liberties of their citizens, that live at peace with their neighbors, and that are capable of achieving rapid economic growth.

Although the data provide consistent support for the hypotheses, it is worth noting that no significant differences among the groups emerged on the proposition that, "We shouldn't think so much in international terms but concentrate more on our own national problems." Several students of American foreign policy have commented on an apparently persistent American tendency to swing from periods of isolationism to internationalism and back to isolationism (Klingberg, 1952; see also his chapter in this volume). That the war in Vietnam might provide a significant impetus for a period of greater concern with domestic issues has been a source of alarm for some and of hope for others. Our results reveal a tendency of respondents in all groups to be slightly opposed, on balance, to a "new isolationism." But the findings on this issue suggest the existence of a second dimension that is relatively independent of that described defined by policy preference on the Vietnam issue. A tentative hypothesis on this point, to be tested in a future paper, can be stated crudely in the form of a four-fold table (Table 16).[7]

Conclusion

The ability of the United States to cope with the challenges and opportunities of a global system in flux will depend, at least in part, on the absence or presence of a workable consensus among persons in leadership groups. By a workable consensus we mean broadly shared beliefs on what is desirable and what is feasible in foreign policy.[8] Even in its absence American administrations will be able to achieve some major foreign policy goals, but to do so will require significant expenditures of finite political resources for each undertaking.

If the data and our interpretations of them are valid, these findings may have significant implications for the task of rebuilding consensus in support of American foreign policy. One sign of possible difficulties in this respect is the finding of deep cleavages on such a wide range of issues. But perhaps the more significant point is that these differences are entwined in and supported

TABLE 16. SOME POSSIBLE DIFFERENCES WITHIN GROUPS OF RESPONDENTS: A HYPOTHESIS

	Supporters	Critics
Predominantly International Orientation	*Diagnosis: Primary threats to security* Dangers arising from the goals and policies of expansionist regimes, and uncertainties arising from doubts about U.S. security commitments. *Prescription: Preferred responses* Containment of expansionist nations, with an emphasis on cooperation with allies, actions to maintain the credibility of international commitments, etc.	*Diagnosis: Primary threats to security* Dangers arising from nonmilitary issues such as unchecked population growth, inadequate resources, maldistribution of resources, pollution, etc. *Prescription: Preferred response* Seek more extensive international cooperation to cope with these issues, none of which can be dealt with on a purely national basis. Strengthen international organizations. Foreign aid through international agencies.
Predominantly Domestic Orientation	*Diagnosis: Primary threat to security* Dangers arising from the goals and policies of expansionist regimes, *and* an overcommitment of U.S. resources to cope indiscriminately with all such threats. *Prescription: Preferred response* Strengthen American institutions, the U.S. economy, etc. as the necessary, if not sufficient, conditions to cope with military/security threats from abroad. Only take on international commitments that one is prepared to support to the hilt (e.g., avoid "no win" approaches).	*Diagnosis: Primary threat to security* Inadequate attention to and success in coping with domestic threats, including decay of cities, pollution, racial conflict, redistribution, etc. *Also,* a United States that indiscriminately attempts to impose its values on other nations. *Prescription: Preferred response* Place coping with urgent domestic issues at the top of the agenda. Scale down expectations about what the United States can achieve abroad, either in military/security or democratic development issues.

by well-defined clusters of supporting beliefs that extend from definitions of the proper role for the United States in the international system through issues of strategies and tactics. And because coherent and internally consistent belief systems tend to be self-perpetuating, these competing conceptions of international politics and foreign policy are unlikely to change soon or casually. In the absence of international developments of such dramatic proportions as to compel most persons to reexamine their central beliefs, such divisions within and outside Washington as have occurred recently on issues ranging from SALT to the Panama Canal may be the norm rather than exception for some time to come.

This is not to say that during the coming decade the United States will be unable to play a significant role in the world, nor that this nation will indeed become the "pitiful, helpless giant" that was sometimes proclaimed in Washington to be the inevitable result of a failure in Southeast Asia. Rather, these results suggest that manifestations of globalist foreign policy—whether in the form of interventions in the Third World, commitments to protect the weaker nations from aggression, massive economic assistance programs, or active promotion of American values and institutions abroad—are more likely to engender vigorous political controversy than unquestioning support from various sectors of American leadership. Thus, it is hard to imagine that any American administration will, in the near future, have sufficient political capital to gain necessary support for a range of major undertakings comparable in scope to those initiated, for example, during the period 1947-1950 (aid to Greece and Turkey, the Marshall Plan, formation of NATO, resistance to the aggression in Korea).

NOTES

1. For a more detailed description of the rationale for this project, sampling procedures, and the questionnaire, see Holsti and Rosenau, 1976a.

2. We do not present data about leadership beliefs prior to 1976; to gain some sense of changes, the interested reader may wish to compare our results with the "cold war axioms" described by Allison (1970-1971) and Halperin (1974).

3. At this point we are not in a position to rule out some obvious competing explanation for differences between our results and those of the Chicago leadership sample—for example, differences in the occupational, generational, or other attributes of the two samples.

4. For evidence on this point, see Holsti, 1970.

5. A future paper will explore in some detail the effects of occupation and other attributes on responses. For preliminary evidence on differences among respondents in various occupations, see Holsti and Rosenau, 1976b, 1977a.

6. This is not to imply, however, that analyses of these and other background attributes would not contribute to an understanding of policy preferences toward Vietnam, as well as other issues. A future paper will undertake such analyses of our data.

7. Table 16 provides a description of only the Supporters and Critics, the two groups at the ends of our scale. The hypothesis would further hold that the views of the other five groups would be arrayed in between the Supporters and Critics.

8. This discussion should not be read as an endorsement for the view that the correlation between consensus and the quality of foreign policy approaches 1.00. We are merely speculating on some implications of the findings, not trying to define the proper balance between the needs for consensus and for persistent questioning of fundamental premises.

REFERENCES

ALLISON, G.T. (1970-1971). "Cool it: The foreign policy of young America." Foreign Policy, 1:144-160.

CONVERSE, P.E. (1964). "The nature of belief systems in mass publics." Pp. 206-261 in D. Apter (ed.), Ideology and discontent. New York: Free Press.

HALPERIN, M. (1974). Bureaucratic politics and foreign policy. Washington, D.C.: Brookings Institution.

HOLSTI, K.J. (1970). "National role conceptions in the study of foreign policy." International Studies Quarterly, 14 (September):233-309.

HOLSTI, O.R., and ROSENAU, J.N. (1976a). "The 'lessons' of Vietnam: A study of American leadership." Paper presented at the 17th Annual Meeting of the International Studies Association, Toronto (February).

――― (1976b). "Vietnam revisited: Beliefs of foreign service and military officers about the sources of failure, consequences, and 'lessons' of the war." Paper presented at the Xth Congress of the International Political Science Association, Edinburgh (August).

――― (1977a). "The meaning of Vietnam: Belief systems of American leaders." International Journal, 32 (Summer):452-477.

――― (1977b). "Vietnam, consensus, and the belief systems of American leaders." Paper presented at the Hendricks Symposium on American Politics (October). Lincoln: University of Nebraska.

KLINGBERG, F.L. (1952). "Historical alternation of moods in American foreign policy." World Politics, IV (January):239-273.

MAY, E.R. (1973). "Lessons" of the past. New York: Oxford University Press.

MUELLER, J. (1973). War, presidents, and public opinion. New York: John Wiley.

――― (1977). "Changes in American public attitudes toward international involvement." Pp. 323-344 in E. Stern (ed.), The limits of international intervention. Beverly Hills, Cal.: Sage.

New York Times (1977). February 8.

REILLY, J.E. (1975). American public opinion and U.S. foreign policy. Chicago: Chicago Council on Foreign Relations.

RUSSETT, B.M., and HANSON, E. (1975). Interest and ideology. San Francisco: W.H. Freeman.

SUSSMAN, B. (1976). Elites in America. Washington, D.C.: The Washington Post.

Chapter 10

WHY NEW FOREIGN POLICY CHALLENGES MIGHT NOT BE MET: CONSTRAINTS ON DETECTING PROBLEMS AND SETTING AGENDAS

C H A R L E S F. H E R M A N N
Ohio State University

This chapter treats the United States government as an entity designed to solve problems. From this perspective the initial task of foreign policy agenda setting concerns the factors that influence whether and when a potential problem comes to the attention of officials with the authority to deal with it. Those agencies of government whose missions include foreign and national security issues attempt to cope with problems that pertain to the relationship between all or part of the nation and the world beyond America's political boundaries.

The beginning of all governmental action occurs with the establishment of a problem on the agenda of authoritative policy makers. How do foreign problems get the attention of such individuals? Why do some problems appear to be quickly addressed whereas others are ignored, receive consideration after much delay, or are recognized in a seemingly distorted manner?

EDITORS' NOTE: This version of the paper was received in April 1978.

AUTHOR'S NOTE: The author wishes to acknowledge the research support by the Mershon Center of Ohio State University. Appreciation is also due to Grant Hilliker who encouraged me to write an earlier version of this paper and to Charles Kegley and Mark Tompkins for their suggestions on its revision.

Part of the answer to these questions lies in the characteristics of the problems and the nature of the entities that monitor the environment searching for potential problems. The major portion of this essay will offer a general examination of the possible effects of situations and organizations. In the concluding section these general features will be applied to the circumstances that pose special difficulties for the United States in the 1980s. There is reason to believe that the types of problems America will increasingly face in the future are different in kind from those that have characterized much of the period since World War II. Our ability to monitor and make timely response to problems that do not fit into our familiar framework poses a major challenge for the 1980s.

For any problem-solving entity—whether it be an individual, a nation, a civilization, or any animal species—the failure to address a major problem in time can mean severe deprivation and even destruction. In the early post-World War II years a number of the members of the United States government believed that the Soviet Union posed a deadly military threat to our European and Asian allies and ultimately to America. They feared that the American democracy, lacking a strong tradition of a large and expensive peacetime military establishment, would fail to take adequate precautions and to respond to the problem in time. The governmental debates over the Marshall Plan, the Truman Doctrine, and NCS-68 reflected this profound concern on the part of these individuals and their efforts to mobilize the government and society.[1] More recently other individuals have described a series of interdependent problems resulting from the nature and rate of growth of homosapiens. They assert that unless the problems are recognized and effective corrections initiated soon, catastrophic events will ensue (Mesarovic and Pestel, 1974:69):

> Unless this lesson is learned in time, there will be a thousand desperadoes terrorizing those who are now "rich," and eventually nuclear blackmail and terror will paralyze further orderly development. Now is the time to draw up a master plan for organic sustainable growth and world development based on global allocation of all finite resources and a new global economic system. Ten or twenty years from today it will probably be too late.

In both examples, the individuals and groups who believed they had detected dangers feared that the government would fail to confront the problems—would fail to put the matters on their agenda in time. The groups believed that inadequate recognition would have dire consequences. These illustrations dramatize the need for understanding the foreign policy monitoring system and its relationship to the agenda-setting process. Of course, the foreign policy problems competing for the attention of the United States government vary greatly in the magnitude of their potential consequences.

The severity of the potential effects, however, do not necessarily determine whether a problem will be recognized and addressed. Among the factors that influence attention to a problem are the nature of the situation created by the problem and the organizations designed to deal with problem solving. After offering several basic definitions, this chapter will examine these features and discuss their implications for American foreign policy in the 1980s.

PROBLEMS, PROBLEM RECOGNITION, AND PROBLEM IDENTIFICATION

Problem

Three basic terms need clarification. They are "problem," "problem recognition," and "problem identification." A problem exists when there is a recognized discrepancy or imbalance between a preferred state of affairs and the present or possible future state of affairs. A number of implications follow from this definition. First, a problem requires that the actor be aware of one or more goals. If a government's foreign policy goals are poorly defined, then so are any problems that might pertain to them. Most governments share certain basic goals such as national physical survival, protection of citizens and their property abroad, continuation of the government in office, and so on. Beyond such basic national goals, however, governments differ in the degree to which goals pertaining to foreign policy are defined. To illustrate this point one might compare the Fourth and Fifth Republics of France. It can be argued that the Fourth Republic minimized goal definition and redefinition because to review and clarify national goals endangered the support of diverse political parties that formed the coalition essential to maintain politically unstable governments. Under Charles de Gaulle, however, with the increased powers of the President in the Fifth Republic, foreign policy goals became more clearly articulated. The fear was substantially less than in the Fourth Republic that explicit characterization of foreign policy goals would significantly reduce political support.

It should be noted that goals may be identified and refined in an interactive process with the emergence of potential problem-type events. A small child may not attach much value to a toy until another child shows interest in playing with it. Suddenly maintaining possession of the toy becomes an important goal and the interest displayed by another person in that object becomes a problem. After asserting ownership over the object, the child may lose interest in it entirely and even forget its whereabouts. In a more complex fashion, the analogy can reveal something about the behaviors of collective entities such as governments. Conditions or objects need not be continuously valued or valued at the same level of importance, but may emerge more or less suddenly in response to developing circumstances.

A second result of stipulating that the concept of problem depends on goals is that problems are relative. Whenever individuals or organizations have different goals or have assigned significantly different priorities to the same goal, then the possibility exists that a problem for one will not be a problem for another. It is apparent that different countries may have very different problems. (For example, the size of the Turkish or Mexican poppy crop may not be a problem for the United States unless it has the goal of controlling the heroin produced from these crops. Moreover, if the Turkish government does not share the American goal, then it may not be a problem for them.) Somewhat less frequently acknowledged is the idea that different departments, agencies, or bureaus within one government may have different—even competing—goals and, hence, different problems. The United States Commerce and Defense Departments may have goals that are advanced by the sale of sophisticated arms to an ally, but the same action creates a problem for the Arms Control and Disarmament Agency and the Department of State if they have a goal that involves restricting the distribution of certain armaments and maintaining an equilibrium in regional arms supplies. Thus, one of the first tasks in agenda setting may be convincing other governmental agencies of the importance of a particular goal.

A third consequence of the proposed definition of a problem is that the government must have some knowledge of present conditions and possible trends. In other words, for a problem-solver to identify a discrepancy, he must be aware not only of his goals but also of the existing or emerging conditions that seem likely to affect those goals. This intelligence about the environment and the interpretation of what effect it may have on the government's goals need not be accurate. The foreign policy literature as well as literature concerned with other kinds of problem-solving are filled with cases of misperception and erroneous estimates of cause and effect.[2] Of course, accuracy in the interpretation of the environment and its changes is essential for effective responses.

A fourth implication of the meaning assigned to the term problem involves the concept of discrepancy. Often we think of negative discrepancies that result from punishment or threats of punishment. Thus the deployment of MIRV warheads, which makes more difficult the goal of a verifiable arms agreement on strategic weapons, is a discrepancy between that goal and the existing state of affairs. Potential opportunities can also produce a discrepancy and, hence, a problem. Suppose the presence of an American military base has always obstructed the goal of improving diplomatic relations with another government. If changing world conditions and military technology are discovered by American officials to have substantially reduced the importance of the base to the United States, the opportunity exists for moving toward a goal of the United States. Unless a given development will transpire automatically without any government action, it remains only a potential opportunity. Recognizing a potential opportunity and the need for action to bring about its realization creates for the observer a discrepancy and a problem. Moreover, failure to realize the opportunity becomes a deprivation.

A final consequence, drawn from the manner in which a problem is defined, concerns attention. From the point of view of government action a problem does not exist until it is recognized by problem-solvers. Or, to state the matter more precisely, a problem does not exist as an occasion for decision until the discrepancy is identified by the governmental officials with the authority to act. An individual may have cancer and ultimately die from it if not successfully treated. Until the individual's condition is detected, however, it is not a problem in the sense that the undetected cancer is not an occasion for mobilization of resources for treatment. No discrepancy between the individual's preferred state of health and existing health has been recognized. In summary, the test of recognition becomes creating a state of awareness of those able to authorize attempts to reduce the discrepancy.

Problem Recognition

The requirement that an actor be aware of a discrepancy introduces another basic concept in need of definition—problem recognition. The human phenomena of selective attention and perception is well established (e.g., Tajfel, 1969; Tagiuri, 1969). Both individuals and organizations normally operate in environments so rich in stimuli that they cannot possibly attend to all of them, so they systematically screen out many signals—perhaps most— and select only a few to which they give conscious attention. Such recognition becomes the first analytic step necessary for coping with the problem.

For complex organizations, problem recognition is more demanding than for the individual. In the individual the same organism contains both problem recognition and problem coping capabilities (however, the latter may be inadequate under some circumstances). By contrast, the specialization and division of labor in any large complex organization or set of organizations, such as those that normally deal with foreign affairs, separate the function of recognition from the function of decision. It is at the lower "working level" of the State and Defense Departments, A.I.D., C.I.A., and so on that most of an organization's interaction with and monitoring of its environment occurs.

It is the political officer in an embassy, the military assistance officer in the field, the intelligence analyst, the arms control agency negotiator that often are the first members of the government to become aware of a problem. In most cases, however, such an official will not have the authority to resolve the problem and must confine his role to reporting to his organizational superiors. The studies of foreign policy are full of problems identified at the periphery of an organization only to be lost, discounted, or simply set aside until later by higher levels of the organization.[3] Nowhere has this organizational difficulty been more clearly highlighted than in the classic by Ogburn (1961) who relates the hypothetical case of the overthrow of a Western-oriented government in the Middle East. The coup is postulated to have occurred weeks after United States embassy personnel and the responsible desk officer had observed the government was in trouble and had recommended supportive measures. Their proposals simply were not attended to by the decision-making level, plagued by a myriad of seemingly more urgent problems, until too late.

The conclusion is clear. From the perspective of problem solving, organizational problem recognition occurs only when awareness of the problem reaches those within the organization with sufficient authority to decide whether any action is appropriate and, if so, to initiate the determined action. Studies of organizational problem recognition must include examination of those factors within government that can cause problem-identifying information to be mislaid.

Problem Definition

Analytically it is useful to distinguish problem recognition from problem definition. By problem definition is meant the meaning or interpretation that problem solvers attach to a problem. Snyder, Bruck and Sapin (1962) have referred to this as the "definition of the situation." In the practical world, it seems clear that an interpretation must be at least tentatively assigned to a problem when it is recognized. Thus, the question might arise as to why definition should be analytically separated from recognition. At least two reasons can be offered. Because meaning is subjective, the same problem may be defined quite differently for different observers. Furthermore, the definition of the problem is dynamic and can change dramatically across a period of months, weeks, days, or even hours.

We know that the same problem stimuli are defined differently by different individuals, organizations, and nations. The matter of definition of a problem is particularly acute in foreign affairs when cross-cultural differences, governmental motivations for keeping signals ambiguous or deceptive, and conflicting messages (e.g., Jervis, 1976) sent from different parts of a government or from nongovernmental sectors all make a discovered foreign policy problem subject to alternative definitions. For example, what meaning should the United States attach to the discovery that the Soviet Union is modifying its ICBM silos? Is it a long standing need to always improve defensive capabilities—in this case by hardening the sites of their retaliatory forces? Or, is it a provocative attempt to create a first-strike capability by deploying larger missiles? Or, to put the shoe on the other foot, what interpretation should the Soviets have attached to the Joint Resolution reached in SALT I concerning the interim agreement on ballistic missile launchers? Was it a domestic political ploy to maximize support for the agreement or was it a serious attempt to undermine the understandings reached between the two countries?

Not only must one contend with multiple interpretations by different individuals, agencies, and governments, but the same group's definition of the problem may vary through time. Paige (1968) illustrates the rapidity with which the problem can undergo change in his study of the Truman decision to enter the Korean War. At first, the President and his advisors believed the South Koreans could stop the invasion by themselves, but the American officials expected possible military probes elsewhere by other Communist nations to follow quickly. Within less than a week, their interpretation of the Korean situation had changed substantially and American ground forces were committed. In contrast to the Korean example, sometimes problems are redefined out of existence.

Considerable attention has been devoted here to definitions. This essay contends that the function of monitoring for potential problems in foreign affairs, as in other governmental problem solving, requires careful attention to the tasks revealed by these concepts. The implications that already have been drawn from these concepts should make the reader suspicious of simple proposals for improving the agenda-setting function of foreign policy machinery for the 1980s. For example, it should now be possible to recognize as inadequate such recommendations as: "Give me more diplomats, military officers, and intelligence analysts skilled in political observation and reporting and who know the national interests, and I will provide you with an improved foreign policy monitoring and agenda-setting capability." If the proposal had the primary effect of overloading those policy makers with decision-making authority, by producing more problems for them to cope with, the system could very well reduce the effectiveness of the agenda-setting function. Further insights into the requirements for improving this capability can be acquired by examining both characteristics of situations and organizational properties.

SITUATIONAL CHARACTERISTICS

The environment that the foreign policy agencies of the American government monitor for potential problems might be viewed as an endless strip of motion picture film composed of an infinite number of individual frames. Each frame freezes actors in time and space. The photographic frames are analogous to the analytical concept of situation in which the continuous interactions of international actors can be momentarily stopped (hypothetically) to reveal at a particular time the actions they are addressing to one another and their physical surroundings as well as their dispositions toward actors and their environment. Situations—or the configuration of actors, their actions, and their dispositions in a particular context—can be viewed as having various properties. Situational properties affect the likelihood of a problem being detected and the manner in which it will be interpreted. In this section we will consider the effect on detection of five situational properties—threat, opportunity, complexity, awareness, and time.

Threat

Individuals and organizations are more likely to recognize situations containing a problem stimulus if it poses a threat to some valued goal of the entity. Threats consist of future damage or obstruction to the desired object, activity, or state of affairs. Persons and organizations have a concern for the survival of their valued goals; therefore, the more a situation appears to threaten such a goal, the more likely it is to be recognized. In foreign policy and national security organizations, such as the Departments of State and Defense, threats are more likely to be channeled quickly to higher levels in the department and, thus, are ensured of being brought to the attention of people with the authorization to initiate action. Once recognized, the threat will mobilize the resources of the organization. The more widely shared the goal(s) that is threatened and the greater the magnitude of the threat, the less likely are major differences in problem definition to occur among bureaus within the organization and between bureaucratic organizations.

Threatening situations, however, can create difficulties in the accurate perception of changes in the definition of a problem. Any career officers or other persons highly dedicated to the mission of their organization or to one of its programs may transform the threat to organizational goals to a direct threat to themselves as individuals. The danger then becomes highly personalized and can lead to disruptive stress in the individual. Under such circumstances the individual's ability to discern changes in the environment pertaining to the threat may be seriously impaired. Personnel of large foreign policy organizations gain experience in handling threatening situations and the organization often has multiple individuals monitoring a situation. However, there remains a possibility that agenda setting will be affected if the threat is internalized by an individual who serves in a critical gatekeeping role. The potential adverse effects of stress may be offset by the information monitoring resources of the organization once a problem has been initially defined. Individuals and various resources that had been assigned to other tasks may be alerted or completely reassigned to follow the evolving situation.

Opportunity

Often the opposite of threat is opportunity or, more specifically the chance to move toward some goal. In the realm of foreign policy, opportunities to move on foreign policy goals usually involve occasions to exercise influence over or to direct change in some foreign nation, external entity, or part of the natural environment. For individuals, situations containing opportunities or visible means of exercising influence increase the chance of problem recognition. For organizations, such as the Departments of State and Defense, however, the opportunity to exercise influence may increase the likelihood of recognition only slightly, unless there is slack in the organization. If the policy makers with sufficient authority to seize the opportunity already are overloaded and no direct connection can be made between the new opportunity and the problems they currently are dealing with, then the chance may be lost even though subordinates within the department have perceived the significance of the situation.

Whereas threats frequently increase organizational consensus on the definition of the problem, opportunities may have the reverse effect. Given the existence of multiple agencies in the foreign policy sector with somewhat different missions (with occasional overlaps) and/or in control of different resources, the recognition of a situation offering an opportunity to exercise influence may invoke interagency competition. If the problem suggests activities central to the mission of more than one agency, each will tend to define the problem so as to increase the likelihood that their agency will be designated as the "action" agency. For example, given the sudden rise to power of a foreign government known to be favorably inclined toward the United States, the Navy may view the situation as a chance to establish a needed submarine base whereas the Department of State may view the very same situation as an opportunity to press for some substantial revision of the poor record in human rights demonstrated by the former regime. Each agency may regard the other's proposed initiative with the new government as reducing the likelihood of realizing the opportunity it sees.

Complexity

We will treat complexity as a situational characteristic, although one might argue that complexity is an interaction of a situation and the abilities of those that face the situation. (For the present purposes we will assume abilities are a constant.) For the individual, the more complex the situational characteristics, the less likely is the problem to be fully recognized. Although there may be some greater difficulty for an organization in recognizing a complex stimuli, it should not be as severe for an agency, such as State, Defense, U.S.I.A., A.I.D. and so on, as for the individual. An organization—particularly one continuously dealing with an extremely complex environment—will develop routines for dealing with complexity including specialists for this purpose. It will create some redundancy and integrative capability to cope more effectively with such potential situations. Discovering a complex problem, however, does not ensure its interpretation. For recognized problems with inherent complexity, a substantial lag may occur between the discovery of the problem and its accepted definition. It will be talked about and debated; more likely than not, divisions will emerge within the Executive Branch and among the Executive, Congress, and various nongovernmental groups over the most accurate interpretation. Because foreign situations are notorious for containing great uncertainty and incomplete information, these qualities will add to the complexity and make more difficult the elimination of one or more alternative definitions. Thus, complex problems increase the difficulty of problem recognition, but less so for a large organization than for isolated individuals. Complexity, though, can be expected to make problem definition more demanding for organizations.

Awareness

Situations also vary in the degree of foreknowledge or prior awareness available to agencies that monitor foreign affairs. Some situations are expected by policy makers before they occur; whereas others occur as a complete surprise. The general character of a situation may be anticipated, but not the specific details and, thus, a situation may present a greater or lesser degree of awareness. For both individuals and organizations, problems that are anticipated have an improved chance of being detected when they occur. Conversely, unexpected events are less likely to be detected unless they also have some other quality such as threat that encourages recognition. Foreknowledge or expectancy may be promoted by various factors. Regularity of occurrence, for example, offers a strong base for awareness. So also does a trend or sequence of ordered events. If it is known that representatives of country X have approached several of your nation's allies about aircraft purchases, it might not be difficult to anticipate that your government will also be approached. A sharp break or shift in the rate of change in a trend can be quite surprising, particularly if elaborate planning and sets of expectations were built on the stability of the trend. The sudden move by President Sadat of Egypt to visit Jerusalem in 1977 may constitute such a surprise break in a trend or pattern.

Problems that are anticipated are also likely to be interpreted a priori as well. Problem occurrence and problem definition are usually simultaneous. Internal debate over the meaning of an anticipated problem is minimal. This simultaneity of recognition and definition may create a serious problem in policy-making if the present situation in fact differs in some important way from what was expected. In other words, having once predicted the occurrence of some situation, an organization has a tendency to interpret a stimuli that does occur as the expected development as long as it has some of the anticipated qualities. Features of the actual problem situation that do not conform to the forecast may be ignored or misinterpreted.

Time

The time a situation allows for decision represents a fifth situational characteristic affecting problem recognition and discovery. Some situations appear open-ended. They contain no visible indications that the configuration of actors and objects that comprise the situation are likely to change in the foreseeable future in a manner unfavorable to the perceiving governmental representatives. By contrast, other situations contain identifiable characteristics that suggest the present situation is likely to change rapidly. Any situation involving a deadline or an ultimatum falls in the latter category as did the invasion of South Korea (American policy makers soon discovered that if the United States did not move quickly, the North Koreans would occupy the entire peninsula) or the 1962 emplacement of Soviet ballistic missiles in Cuba (once the missiles became operational, their removal would be more difficult).

Short decision time reduces the individual's probability of recognizing a problem. Again, foreign policy organizations live in an environment in which important problems often have short fuses and, therefore, they attempt to build some capability to offset the tendency that such problems will be missed. The problem of recognition then depends in part on the degree of organizational slack. If the policy makers who can authorize action are involved with several critical problems at the same time, then a new problem with short decision time probably will not be noted until it already has been transformed.

ORGANIZATIONAL FACTORS

The previous section did not attempt to apply an objective or observer perspective in delineating situational characteristics. Instead it dealt with the characteristics as they affected the perceiver of the situation (i.e., the foreign policy representatives of the government). As a consequence, the discussion of situational characteristics was relational in that the nature of a characteristic depended on the nature of the monitoring facility as well as the configuration of other actors and objects. For this reason, the previous section anticipated some of the observations in this section concerning the affects on monitoring problems and setting agendas of bureaucratic organizations. In general the theme of this section is that such organizations are potentially better able to recognize problem situations than individuals or small groups, but may encounter more difficulties in problem definition. Moreover, as we shall see in the last section even existing organizational capabilities may be inadequate for some possible types of foreign policy problems.

Organizational Restructuring

Problems can emerge from perceived changes in the foreign environment or from internal restructuring within the foreign policy machinery of the government. By restructuring, we mean the assembly, review, and/or new interpretation of information that the government already has acquired or the shift of organizational personnel so that people who hold different interpretations of existing information have new power to enable them to shape government action. An example of the former kind of restructuring is a National Security Study Memorandum (NSSM) such as that early in 1969 that involved a review of United States activities in Vietnam. As part of that exercise each agency of the government was required to respond to detailed questionnaires that sent officials throughout the government back to their files and discussion sessions. Information thus gathered was reviewed by an interdepartmental group, the National Security Council staff, and ultimately the NSC itself. The reexamination led to some new policy problems (recognition) and new interpretations of old ones (definition).

The reassignment of personnel offers another form of restructuring. A military officer who has been a field commander may have recognized a foreign policy problem, but been unable to get support from those in a position to address the issue. Suppose his next assignment is on one of the specialized staffs of the Joint Chiefs of Staff and he finds the new position gives him the authority to mobilize those policy makers able to deal with the problem he had identified previously. Assuming that the authority required to make most nonroutine choices resides at the middle and political levels of government, then the appointment of new individuals at these levels is apt to trigger new problem recognition through restructuring. With internal restructuring, changes in the foreign environment are not necessary to generate new problems for the policy agenda. The general conclusion is that the more foreign policy organizations reassign personnel—particularly across hierarchical levels of authority or recruit new personnel into the organization— the more likely are new problems to be recognized or old ones to be redefined.

Selective and Differential Search

The alternative means by which policy problems emerge is by changes in the organization's external environment. Foreign policy organizations must establish search routines to monitor any such possible environmental changes. Organizations by their nature involve specialization and role differentiation. Thus, specialists develop who search for a particular kind of problem or monitor a certain source of information. These specialists establish routines or standard operating procedures by which they search or monitor their assigned domains. For example, in the Department of State, as in most other foreign policy agencies, specialization involves a mix of geographical and functional categories for limiting and developing search capabilities. Facilities can be developed for monitoring special types of situations (e.g., the Crisis Communication Center, the Berlin Task Force) and procedures for transmitting information can be made systematic (e.g., under specified conditions cables of only a certain priority are to be transmitted; or instructions are given the watch officer to awake key individuals during the night if certain occurrences transpire).

The difficulty arises because search routines, decision rules, and standard operating procedures by definition focus the search for potential foreign policy problems toward some cues or particular kind of signals. The unavoidable question becomes: What about critical problems that do not have the characteristic established by the specialized search routines? Searching for the unexpected will always pose major challenges to foreign policy organizations, but they can at least avoid certain kinds of common biases. Pool and Kessler (1969:669-670) provide a convenient list of selective attention patterns that are applicable to bureaucratic specialists as well as isolated individuals:

1) People pay more attention to information that deals with them.
2) People pay less attention to facts that contradict their views.
3) People pay more attention to information from trusted, liked sources.

4) People pay more attention to information that they will have to act on or discuss because of the attention by others.
5) People will pay more attention to information bearing on actions they have already taken, i.e., action creates commitment.[4]

Internal Communication

Another consequence of organizational role specialization and task differentiation concerns the separation of the individuals and units engaged in the intelligence activities mentioned above from those able to make a decision as to whether action should be taken on detected problems. As has been noted previously, this is the reason that organizational problem recognition cannot be usefully defined as the perception of a problem stimuli by at least one member of the organization. The problem must be recognized by those individuals whose role specialization and level of authority enables them to mobilize the organization for action. Given the specialization of tasks, it is almost certain that the individual who first discovers a problem will not be the individual with authority to approve action. If the internal communication system between the initial perceiver of a problem and the occupant of the necessary authority role fails for any reason, then the organization's behavior will not reflect the discovery. In a meaningful sense the organization can be said not to have recognized the problem at all.

Problem Load

Not only weaknesses in the internal communication system of foreign policy organizations, but also the decision load on the middle and political levels of the organization can lead to failure of problem recognition. Study after study (e.g., Kissinger, 1966; Hoffman, 1968) has noted the decision overload on these policy makers in the making of American foreign policy. Given the broad scope of global activities that are assumed to pertain to American interests, many problems are stillborn because they fail to get out of the inbasket of the necessary policy maker. It is reasonable to speculate that the flatter the organization's authority structure and the greater the delegation of authority, the more likely are external problems to be recognized provided internal communication is well maintained.

A word of caution is required about the consequences of overloaded policy makers on the agenda-setting process. To capture a position on the overcrowded agenda of senior policy makers, earnest subordinates may attempt to mobilize support from other parts of the government, the media, the public, and foreign nations. In the process of gaining mass support, the characterization of the problem may become distorted and, frequently, the consequences of neglect will be exaggerated.

Organizational Goals

At the beginning of this chapter, a problem was stipulated as involving goals or preferred conditions. Goals, both formal and informal, bring us to a final organizational characteristic. The literature on bureaucratic organizations has made the point repeatedly that different organizations and different bureaus within an organization have different missions and different goals. To the extent that individuals identify with their particular bureau and organization and see their professional promotion and career dependent on excelling in that bureau and organization, then it will be natural for those persons to promote the goals of that agency. The result is that individuals in different locations will have a built-in diposition to interpret the same reported stimuli in terms of their organizational interests—its mission and goals.

Because various foreign policy organizations have different goals, individuals in these alternative organizations will tend to define problems differently. Moreover, those individuals who see their careers in terms of their own organization will have a strong incentive to advocate in a vigorous fashion the adoption of a definition of the problem consistent with their agency's mission and goals. Not only is this process at the heart of bureaucratic politics, it makes the task of reaching consensus on problem definition within the government difficult unless other factors intervene to minimize this process. Furthermore, once consensus on the definition of a problem has been reached, inertia sets in and works against the revision of that definition and the necessary task of mobilizing support in various units for a new interpretation. The evolution of a problem definition will tend to be more gradual for bureaucratic organizations than for individuals unless the top of an organization changes suddenly, a new administration comes to power, or the coalition, whose interpretation of the problem had prevailed, collapses.

IMPLICATIONS OF A SHIFT IN THE ARRAY OF PROBLEMS

In this final section we wish to examine how the characteristics of situations and properties of American governmental organizations could prove to be constraints in recognizing and defining the foreign policy problems of the 1980s. Basic to the discussion is the contention that the types of major foreign affairs problems in need of attention are undergoing a profound change.

Post-Cold War Problems

For much of the period since the end of World War II, most American foreign policy organizations concerned with foreign affairs have been greatly influenced in their monitoring of possible problem producing activities by the

Cold War. The protracted and intense antagonism between the United States and its associates on the one hand and the Soviet Union and its associates on the other have shaped what problems were recognized and how they were defined. Every person who was an adult before 1950 or became one in that decade or the next is familiar with the episodes, the issues, the policies that reflect this overriding concern—economic stagnation and political uncertainty in Western Europe after the war, the threat of Soviet military expansion into Europe, the aggression in South Korea, the fear of domestic infiltration of Communist sympathizers, the potential or actual emergence of Russian- or Chinese-oriented governments or ruling groups in Third World countries, the qualitative and quantitative buildup in strategic armaments, and so on. Even issues that in other periods might have been interpreted very differently were defined as Cold War problems—such as the end of colonialism, the emergence of nationalistic forces, the efforts at economic development, and the innovations in science and technology. Of course, not every problem became an adjunct of the Cold War (e.g., GATT) nor did every agency of the Federal government having some foreign affairs mission define its role primarily in Cold War terms (e.g., Agriculture Department treatment of surplus food). The budgets of major agencies, the time allocations of Presidents and other political level officials, and the foreign policy debates in Congress and the public, however, all suggest the prominence of the Cold War framework in foreign policy problem recognition and definition.

As the Vietnam experience recedes into history, more individuals inside and outside the American foreign policy community are identifying and debating problems that cannot be understood by reference to the Cold War antagonism. Of course, the politico-military problems stemming from the conflict between the Communist and Western powers have not disappeared as a set of problems for American foreign policy. These problems may even become more acute in the future. Difficulties could result from continued Soviet military buildup in some areas relative to the military strength of the United States and its Western allies. There could be an accelerated tendency on the part of the U.S.S.R. to engage in conflicts remote from its borders as its newer capabilities give it the ability to do so. Even if the loss of clear Western military superiority in certain areas in which we have been accustomed to being dominant does not create problems, and the Soviets exercise constraint, the coalitions that developed as a result of the Cold War may continue to underscore hypothetical problems that conform to their needs and experiences, regardless of their grounding in reality.

Having noted this continuing legacy, we must return to our observation that other types of foreign policy challenges seem to be altering the overall configuration of problems facing American policy makers. Even if Cold War problems continue, they may not be expected to dominate the foreign policy agenda as they have in the past. A study done for the Commission on the Organization of the Government for the Conduct of Foreign Policy ("the Murphy Commission") identified eight global problem areas that could have major adverse effects on the United States—and the rest of the world—after the year 2000 if not effectively handled before then. These problems, which were drawn exclusively from the area of global environmental and resource independence, included ocean pollution, atmospheric pollution, weather modification, resource satellites, communication satellites, nuclear reactors, food, and population (Koehane and Nye, 1975). Given the area this list canvassed for issues, it is understandable that energy did not surface as a more general problem than in its nuclear reactor form and that the entire range of economic problems was excluded. However, economic problems—ranging from trade deficits and widespread inflation to the calls for a new international economic order and the difficulties confronting various international economic institutions—illustrate the emergence of acute foreign policy problems with little or no direct relationship to the Cold War.

Only time will tell whether the Koehane and Nye (1975) list of emerging problems or some other enumeration (e.g., Platt, 1969) will accurately forecast the most demanding foreign policy problems of the future. Because we are interested in the recognition and definition of new international challenges, the particular itemization found on any given list is less important than the apparent shift from the predominant appearance of Cold War type problems. If there are likely to be significantly different types of problems threatening the well-being of the United States in the 1980s, how will situational characteristics and organizational properties influence their successful recognition and definition?

Situational and Organizational Effects

Let us first consider the situational properties discussed previously. With respect to threats, they may be directed not only at physical survival through possible war, but to a variety of social, political, and economic institutions and to ecological systems as well. As in the Cold War, threats may involve painful tradeoffs between several highly valued objects or states (e.g., individual freedom versus public order). Both threats and opportunities may well emerge from sources other than those to which we have grown accustomed to dealing. Not only may they involve states different from our familiar antagonists, but they also may originate from nonstate actors—such as terrorists, multinational corporations, nonterritorial states.

We noted earlier that complexity could be interpreted as an interaction between requirements of the problem and the capabilities of the problem solvers. The problem side of the equation might be expected to become more complex in several respects. First, the growth in interdependence between social and economic systems may complicate attempts at resolution by requiring coordination of more units inside and outside the United States. These units may not be particularly susceptible to American governmental influences. Interdependence may increase the likelihood that "solutions" to problems have more unanticipated secondary and tertiary effects which trigger new problems or confound the treatment of the original one. What may confuse detection of such problems is a breakdown in any clear idea of cause and effect. A second source of added complexity may result from an increased tendency for multiple, large, demanding problems to arise simultaneously. Platt (1969:1116) refers to this difficulty when he notes: "What finally makes all of our crises still more dangerous is that they are now coming on top of each other." The occurrence of one may mask the presence of others.

Awareness can be regarded as affecting the other side of the complexity equation—the ability of foreign policy agencies to cope with problems. For example, as dangerous as the repeated crises over West Berlin were, the United States in time gained familiarity with some recurrent features of the problem and of the adversary. This general awareness might not have prevented tactical surprise from developing in any particular crisis, but it made it easier for American policy makers to recognize the problem and define it within the context of the Cold War when critical situations suddenly arose. One of the difficulties of an emerging new array of foreign policy problems would be the absence of familiarity with them and with their associated indicators and danger signs.

Many of the problems of the Cold War emerged as crises in which decision time was extremely short such as in the Cuban missile crisis or the invasion of South Korea. Although one can conjecture about some future nuclear confrontation in which decision time is reduced to something less than the 30 minutes required for ICBMs to reach their targets, the Cold War problems of the past may have established benchmarks for acutely short decision time that are unlikely to be surpassed in the vast majority of new challenges. In fact, the emerging problems could be just the reverse in that they have long lead times before they become a major danger as in the case of ocean pollution. However, the time required for actions necessary to avert or correct these problems before they become irreversible may also be extremely protracted. Keohane and Nye (1975) discuss problems that they believe need prompt attention now if their major adverse effects are to be avoided when they materialize sometime between 2001 and 2020.

The previous paragraphs have tried to illustrate what might be the nature of situational characteristics for problems that would be different from those which have dominated American attention during the Cold War. Assuming that such different types of problems become more important for American foreign policy, how would the identified organizational characteristics affect recognition and identification of these new problems?

Perhaps the most critical organizational feature concerns the selective and differential search processes. We have suggested that governmental organizations, just as individuals, must be selective in their monitoring and in the domains they search. The Cold War provided a framework that for more than 25 years served as a structure for foreign policy organizations of the United States government. The framework or structure indicated what situations to monitor and what meaning to attach to problems that arose. These highly established search routines and interpretative processes may now become increasingly dysfunctional by not directing monitoring activities to situations that could pose new kinds of dangers or opportunities or by imposing a Cold War definition on a detected problem that may be inappropriate for effective response.

The organizational restructuring that regularly marks foreign policy agencies as new people assume key positions could aid in the more rapid erosion of the Cold War framework. The arrival at top posts of individuals who have not had firsthand experience in policy-making during the most extreme period of the Cold War could facilitate new patterns for monitoring international affairs. A darker side, however, also must be considered. If more of the foreign policy problems of the future demand extremely long lead times to avoid severe adverse effects, no leadership may find it desirable or politically feasible to attend to problems the outcomes of which may not be experienced until long after they have left office. The turnover of political leadership also may make it more difficult to construct coalitions with a shared definition of the problem. Just as agreement on the nature of the problem might seem to be within grasp, the chairman of a key Congressional Committee would be defeated or a needed deputy undersecretary would resign or the entire executive administration would be replaced.

Many agencies of the United States government participate in foreign policy decisions, but the Cold War gave certain agencies dominance—including the State and Defense Departments, the Joint Chiefs of Staff, the C.I.A., A.I.D. and its precursors, and, increasingly, the National Security Council staff. Established channels of communication, clearance processes, and inter-agency working groups have gradually evolved. Faced with different types of problems these internal channels of communication may not be the most salient ones, nor may these agencies be the most appropriate. Indeed, no agency may be charged with monitoring for a given set of problems. If they do engage in such monitoring, it may be unclear who has responsibility for communicating to whom about whether the problem merits attention on the agency's agenda. In other words, who should be alerted if a new problem is detected? Internal communications may need major revision.

What about problem overload? Any available organizational slack could be more than consumed in one of several ways. If problems are unfamiliar or seemingly more complex, it may take longer to agree on their definition and devise an acceptable response, thus other problems will have to be placed "on hold." Furthermore, if Platt (1969) is correct, the emerging challenge is not simply different kinds of problems, but more of them occurring concurrently.

Coping with a certain type of problem in foreign affairs has become part of the mission or goals of particular foreign policy organizations. The very names of some units indicate much about their assigned problems—for example, the Arms Control and Disarmament Agency, the Agency for International Development, or the former United States Information Agency. The difficulty arises when no agency regards coping with a particular class of problems as one of its primary goals. Until recently that was precisely the issue with respect to energy questions. If several organizations regard themselves as having only secondary responsibility for a given type of problem, it may be that none are devoting many resources to monitoring for particular outbreaks of it or its potential ramifications. The real possibility exists that the present array of organizational goals for American foreign policy bureaucracies excludes attention to potential problems of the future.

CONCLUSIONS

It can be argued that the picture sketched in this essay exaggerates the constraints and difficulties. The author hopes so, but perhaps more than hope is in order to make certain that the interaction of new situations and old organizational routines does not obstruct the recognition and definition of problems that need to get on the American national agenda and on the agenda of other parts of the world as well. The avoidance of these pitfalls partially entails modifying organization capabilities to meet the requirements of foreign policy in the 1980s and beyond.

Some might be tempted initially to regard substitution or replacement as the approach. The government, it could be argued, should shift from an East-West framework to one focused on North-South conflicts; from agencies concerned with military capability to economic capability; from crisis management to long-range planning. All indications are that such redistribution responses would be most inadequate and inappropriate. Few careful observers would claim that the older type of problems have been resolved or have faded away. The United States government must still attend to them. Even though various sources seek to dramatize presently emerging issues, relatively few responsible individuals or groups claim to have a clear and certain vision of what the total array of future foreign policy problems will be. Thus a greater sensitivity to the unusual in international affairs and its environment appears to be a watchword for monitoring rather than locking in on a given alternative domain of new problems.

Going beyond the heightened attention to various forms of activity, those persons responsible for foreign policy—and the government generally—may need to invest more in the exploration of new forms of social organization for collective problem recognition and management. McNeill (1963) argues that civilizations began to emerge when humankind developed primitive administrative and bureaucratic skills. Perhaps if we are to avert unpleasant future deprivations not only to our society but also to our civilization, we should devote significantly more resources and energy to the design of, and experimentation with, new forms of collective problem recognition and management.

N O T E S

1. The task of mobilizing support is well documented in the case of the Marshall Plan by Jones (1955), for the Truman Doctrine by Gaddis (1972), and for NSC-68 by Hammond (1962).

2. For a social psychological study of the mistaken belief in events and their anticipated effect, see Festinger, Riecken and Schachter (1956). In organizational theory, Thompson (1967) has made activities done on the basis of collective beliefs about cause and effect relationships an organization's core technology—regardless of whether the beliefs are correct or not. Misperception in international politics has been a major concern of Jervis (1976).

3. This difficulty in problem recognition is illustrated by the "loss" in the system of cues that might have alerted U.S. policy makers to the Pearl Harbor attack (see Wohlstetter, 1962) and by the failure to consider intelligence about the location of German Panzer Divisions prior to the beginning of Operation Market-Garden in 1944 (see Ryan, 1974).

4. It is possible to construct some plausible organizational parallels to the Pool and Kessler (1969) statements about selective perception of individuals. Consider these examples:

(a) An organization pays more attention to information pertaining to itself or its mission.

(b) An organization pays less attention or seeks to deny or to alter information that contradicts its objectives and that challenges its prior behavior.

(c) An organization pays more attention to information from its own members or from those to whom it is responsible.
(d) An organization pays more attention to information on which it will have to act.
(e) An organization pays more attention to information bearing on actions it has already taken or which appears to require action of the type the organization is ready to provide.

REFERENCES

FESTINGER, L., RIECKEN, H.W., and SCHACHTER, S. (1956). When prophecy fails. Minneapolis, Minn.: University of Minnesota Press.

GADDIS, J.L. (1972). The United States and the origins of the cold war. New York: Columbia University Press.

HAMMOND, P.Y. (1962). "NSC-68: Prologue to rearmament." Pp. 267-378 in W.R. Schilling, P.Y. Hammond, and G.H. Snyder, Strategy, politics, and defense budgets. New York: Columbia University Press.

HOFFMAN, S. (1968). Gulliver's troubles or the setting of American foreign policy. New York: McGraw-Hill.

JERVIS, R. (1976). Preception and misperception in international politics. Princeton: Princeton University Press.

JONES, J.N. (1955). The fifteen weeks. New York: Harcourt, Brace and World.

KEOHANE, R.O., and NYE, J.S. (1975). Organizing for global environmental and resource interdependence. Pp. 43-64 in Appendices for Commission on the Organization of the Government for the Conduct of Foreign Policy, Vol. 1, Appendix B. Washington, D.C.: U.S. Government Printing Office.

KISSINGER, H.A. (1966). Domestic structure and foreign policy. Daedalus, 95(2):503-529.

McNEILL, W.H. (1963). The rise of the west. New York: Mentor.

MESAROVIC, M., and PESTEL, E. (1974). Mankind at the turning point. New York: Dutton.

OGBURN, C. (1961). "The flow of policy-making in the Department of State." Pp. 229-233 in J.N. Rosenau (ed.), International politics and foreign policy. First edition. New York: Free Press.

PAIGE, G.D. (1968). The Korean decision. New York: Free Press.

PLATT, J. (1969). "What we must do." Science, 166 (November 28):1115-1120.

POOL, I.S., and KESSLER, A. (1969). "The Kaiser, the Tsar and the computer." Pp. 664-678 in J.N. Rosenau (ed.), International politics and foreign policy. Second Edition. New York: Free Press.

RYAN, C. (1974). A bridge too far. New York: Simon and Schuster.

SNYDER, R.C., BRUCK, H.W., and SAPIN, B. (eds.) (1962). Foreign policy decision-making. New York: Free Press.

TAGIURI, R. (1969). "Person perception." Pp. 395-449 in G. Lindzey and E. Aronson (eds.), Handbook of social psychology (vol. 3). Reading, Mass.: Addison-Wesley.

TAJFEL, H. (1969). "Social and cultural factors in perception. Pp. 305-394 in G. Lindzey and E. Aronson (eds.), Handbook of social psychology (vol. 3). Reading, Mass.: Addison-Wesley.

THOMPSON, J.D. (1967). Organizations in action. New York: McGraw-Hill.

WOHLSTETTER, R. (1962). Pearl Harbor: Warning and decision. Stanford: Stanford University Press.

PART IV.

BIBLIOGRAPHY

Chapter 11

BIBLIOGRAPHY OF RECENT COMPARATIVE FOREIGN POLICY STUDIES, 1974-1977

MARK W. DeLANCEY
University of South Carolina

THOMAS H. JOHNSON
University of Southern California

This is the fourth in a series of bibliographies on comparative foreign policy studies to appear in the *Yearbook*. This compilation consists primarily of studies which have been published since 1973, although earlier references are included if these have not been mentioned in the three previous bibliographies. To be included in this list, a publication must meet the following criteria. First, the study must be comparative, either examining two or more actors (national or subnational) or examining two or more instances of the international behavior of a single actor. Second, the study must attempt systematically to describe, explain, or predict foreign policy as either a dependent or an independent variable. Third, the study must be empirical; there must be an effort to operationalize foreign policy behavior. This is not

EDITORS' NOTE: The first draft of this bibliography, covering the 1974-1975 period, was submitted in April 1977. The expanded version published here was received in February 1978.

restricted to quantitative studies, as any comparative analysis that attempted to undertake controlled investigation was considered. Comparative case studies, quantitative analyses, and numerous types of research designs are included in the studies listed in the bibliography.

Comparison of this bibliographic list with those published previously in the series suggests that the study of comparative foreign policy studies is now well established but still undergoing rapid expansion. The number of studies per year is increasing, the number of journals publishing such items is increasing, and the number of doctoral dissertations is greatly increasing. Indeed, the latter fact and the additional point that the number of institutions accepting such dissertations is increasing suggest that continued growth in the number of publications can be expected during the next few years.

Since it is the Editors' intention to continue the inclusion of a similar bibliography in each addition of the *Yearbook,* corrections and additions are welcome. These should be addressed to the editors.

ABRAVANEL, M.D., and HUGHES, B. (1975). "Public attitudes and foreign policy behavior in Western democracies." Pp. 46-73 in W.O. Chittick (ed.), The analysis of foreign policy outputs. Columbus, Ohio: Merrill.

ADDO, H. (1974). "Structural basis of international communication." Papers of the Peace Science Society (International) 23:81-100.

AMSTRUP, N. (1976). "The perenial problem of small states: A survey of research efforts." Cooperation and Conflict, 11:163-182.

ANDRIOLE, S.J. (1976). "Resource scarcity and foreign policy: Implications for research and analysis." World Affairs, 139, 1 (Summer):17-26.

———, WILKENFELD, J., and HOPPLE, G.W. (1975). "A framework for the comparative analysis of foreign policy behavior." International Studies Quarterly, 19, 2 (June):160-198.

ANYANWU, R.A. (1976). "Great power intervention in small power conflicts (1945-1975): An investigation of international conflict outcomes. Ph.D. dissertation, University of Pennsylvania.

ASPIN, L.T. (1975). "An analysis of the relational determinants of international cooperation: United States cooperative behavior, 1959-1968." Ph.D. dissertation, Purdue University.

AXELROD, R. (1977). "Argumentation in foreign policy settings: Britain in 1918, Munich in 1938, and Japan in 1970." Journal of Conflict Resolution, 21 (December):727-744.

——— (1976a). "Decision for neoimperialism: The deliberations of the British Eastern Committee in 1918." Pp. 77-112 in R. Axelrod (ed.), Structure of decision: The cognitive maps of political elites. Princeton: Princeton University Press.

——— (ed.) (1976b). Structure of decision: The cognitive maps of political elites. Princeton: Princeton University Press.

AZAR, E.E. (1975). "Behavioral forecasts and policymaking: An events data approach." Pp. 215-239 in C.W. Kegley, Jr., et al. (eds.), International events and the comparative analysis of foreign policy. Columbia, S.C.: University of South Carolina Press.

——— (1972). "Conflict escalation and conflict reduction in an international crisis: Suez, 1956." Journal of Conflict Resolution, 16 (June):183-201.

——— (1970). "The dimensionality of violent conflict: A quantitative analysis." Peace Research Society Papers, 15:122-167.

——— and BEN-DAK, J. (eds.) (1975). Theory and practice of events research: Studies in inter-nation actions and interactions. New York: Gordon and Breach.

AZAR, E.E., BENNETT, J.P., and SLOAN, T.J. (1974). "Steps toward forecasting international interactions." Papers of the Peace Science Society (International) 23:27-67.

AZAR, E.E., and HAVENER, T.N. (1976). "Discontinuities in the symbolic environment: A problem in scaling." International Interactions, 2:231-246.

BAEHR, P.R. (1975). "Small states: A tool for analysis." World Politics, 18 (April): 456-466.

BAILIN, N. (1977). "Relationships between national role conceptions, national attributes, and foreign policy behavior." Ph.D. dissertation, Rutgers University.

BARSTON, R.P. (ed.) (1973). The other powers: Studies in the foreign policies of small states. London: Allen and Unwin.

BARTOS, O.J. (1977). "Simple model of negotiation: A sociological point of view." Journal of Conflict Resolution, 21 (December):565-579.

BEAL, R.S. (1977). "Systems analysis of international crises: Event analysis of nine pre-crises threat situations, 1948-1962." Ph.D. dissertation, University of Southern California.

BENNETT, J.P. (1975). "Foreign policy as maladaptive behavior: Operationalizing some implications." The Papers of the Peace Science Society (International) 25:85-104.

BIEL, H.S., and COX, K.R. (1976). "Dominance and dependence in an international context." International Interactions, 2:165-170.

BLONG, C.K. (1973). "A comparative study of the foreign policy behavior of political systems exhibiting high versus low levels of external penetration." Ph.D. dissertation, University of Maryland.

BOARDMAN, R. (1974). "Perception theory and the study of Chinese foreign policy." Pp. 321-352 in R.L. Dial (ed.), Advancing and contending approaches to the study of Chinese foreign policy. Halifax: Dalhousie Universtiy.

BONHAM, G.M., and SHAPIRO, M. (1976). "Explanation of the unexpected: The Syrian intervention in Jordan in 1970." Pp. 113-141 in R. Axelrod (ed.), Structure of decision: The cognitive maps of political elites. Princeton: Princeton University Press.

BRADY, L.P., and KEGLEY, C.W. (1977). "Bureaucratic determinants of foreign policy behavior: Some empirical evidence." International Interactions, 3:33-50.

BREWER, T.L. (1977). "Personality and policy preference: Attitudes in the Arms Control and Disarmament Agency and the State Department." International Interactions, 3, 1:83-89.

——— (1975). "Foreign policy process events: Problems of concept and data." Pp. 197-215 in E.E. Azar and J. Ben-Dak (eds.), Theory and practice of events research: Studies in inter-nation actions and interactions. New York: Gordon and Breach.

BRODY, R.A. (1975). "Problems in the measurement and analysis of international events." Pp. 120-131 in C.W. Kegley, Jr., et al. (eds.), International events and the comparative analysis of foreign policy. Columbia, S.C.: University of South Carolina Press.

BROWN, S.N., PRICE, D., and RAICHUR, S. (1976). "Public-good theory and bar-

gaining between large and small countries." International Studies Quarterly, 20, 3 (September):393-440.
BURGESS, P.M. (1970). "Nation-typing for foreign policy analysis: A partitioning procedure for constructing typologies." Pp. 3-66 in E.H. Fedder (ed.), Methodology of international relations. St. Louis: University of Missouri Center for International Studies Monograph Series.
——— and LAWTON, R.W. (1975). "Evaluating events data: Problems of conception, reliability, and validity." Pp. 106-119 in C.W. Kegley, Jr., et al. (eds.), International events and the comparative analysis of foreign policy. Columbia, S.C.: University of South Carolina Press.
BURROWES, R., and GARRIGA-PICO, J. (1974). "The road to the Six Day War: Relational analysis of conflict and cooperation." The Papers of the Peace Science Society (International) 22:47-74.
CALLAHAN, P.T. (1975). "Third party response behavior in foreign policy." Ph.D. dissertation, Ohio State University.
CHITTICK, W.O. (ed.) (1975). The analysis of foreign policy outputs. Columbus, Ohio: Merrill.
——— and JENKINS, J.B. (1976). "Reconceptualizing the sources of foreign policy behavior." Pp. 281-291 in J.N. Rosenau (ed.), In search of global patterns. New York: Free Press.
CHOUCRI, N. (1974a). "International nonalignment." Pp. 123-149 in M. Haas (ed.), International systems: A behavioral approach. New York: Chandler.
——— (1974b). Population dynamics and international violence: Propositions, insights, and evidence. Lexington, Mass.: Lexington.
——— (1973). "Applications of econometric analysis to forecasting in international relations." Papers of the Peace Science Society (International) 21:15-39.
———, LAIRD, M., and MEADOWS, D. (1972). Resource scarcity and foreign policy: A simulation model of international conflict. Cambridge, Mass.: M.I.T., Center for International Studies.
CHOUCRI, N., and NORTH, R.C. (1975). Nations in conflict: National growth and international violence. San Francisco: W.H. Freeman.
CHOUCRI, N., ROSS, D.S., and MEADOWS, D.L. (1976). "Towards a forecasting model of energy politics: International perspectives." Journal of Peace Science, 2, 1 (Spring):97-111.
CHUN, I.Y. (1977). "North Korea and the United States, 1955-1972: A study of North Korea's hostility toward the United States." Ph.D. dissertation, University of Cincinnati.
COLLINS, J. (1975). "Factor analysis and the groupings of events data: Problems and possible solutions." Pp. 121-128 in E.E. Azar and J. Ben-Dak (eds.), Theory and practice of events research: Studies in inter-nation actions and interactions. New York: Gordon and Breach.
COTTAM, R.W. (1977). Foreign policy motivation: A general theory and a case study. Pittsburgh: University of Pittsburgh Press.
DALY, J.A. (1976). "The superpowers: Perceptual, behavioral and capability dynamics, 1950-1965." Ph.D. dissertation, Georgetown University.
DIAL, R.L. (ed.) (1974). Advancing and contending approaches to the study of Chinese foreign policy. Halifax: Centre for Foreign Policy Studies, Dalhousie University.
DORAN, C.F. (1975). "Hierarchic regionalism from the core state perspective: The U.S. case." Pp. 210-236 in W.O. Chittick (ed.), The analysis of foreign policy outputs. Columbus, Ohio: Merrill.

DUNCAN, G.T., and SIVERSON, R.M. (1975). "Markov chain models for conflict analysis: Results from Sino-Indian relations, 1959-1964." International Studies Quarterly, 19 (September):344-374.

EAST, M.A. (1975). "Size and foreign policy behavior: A test of two models." Pp. 159-178 in C.W. Kegley, Jr., et al. (eds.), International events and the comparative analysis of foreign policy. Columbia, S.C.: University of South Carolina Press.

——— and WINTERS, B.K. (1976). "Targeting behavior: A new direction." Pp. 361-369 in J.N. Rosenau (ed.), In search of global patterns. New York: Free Press.

FALKOWSKI, L.S. (1976). "Foreign policy flexibility: A comparative analysis." Ph.D. dissertation, Rutgers University.

FARRELL, R.B. (1971). "East European foreign policy leadership, 1964-1970." Studies in Comparative Communism, 4, 1 (January):80-96.

FAURBY, I. (1976). "Premises, promises, and problems of comparative foreign policy." Cooperation and Conflict, 11:139-162.

FEIERABEND, I., FEIERABEND, R., and SCANLAND, F. (1972). "The relation between sources of systemic frustration, international conflict and political instability." Pp. 168-179 in I. Feierabend, R. Feierabend, and T. Gurr (eds.), Anger, violence and politics. Englewood Cliffs, N.J.: Prentice-Hall.

FEIFER, T. (1974). "An analysis of escalation in the Arab-Israeli conflict, 1949-1967." Ph.D. dissertation. College Park: University of Maryland.

FERRIS, E.G. (1976). "National support for the Andean Pact: A comparative study of Latin American foreign policy." Ph.D. dissertation, University of Florida.

FIELD, J.O. (1972). The Sino-Indian border conflict: An exploratory analysis of action and perception. Beverly Hills, Cal.: Sage Professional Papers in International Studies 02-002.

FREI, D. (1974). "Conflict reduction by mutual disengagement." International Interactions, 1:101-112.

FRIEDHEIM, R.L. (1970). "Quantitative content analyses of the United Nations seabed debate." International Organization, 24:479-502.

GALTUNG, J. (1975). "East-west interaction patterns." Pp. 95-120 in E.E. Azar and J. Ben-Dak (eds.), Theory and practice of events research: Studies in inter-nation actions and interactions. New York: Gordon and Breach.

GANTZEL, K.J. (1973). "Armament dynamics in the east-west conflict: An arms race?" Papers of the Peace Science Society (International) 20:1-24.

GELLER, D.S. (1977). "The prediction and explanation of foreign policy behavior: A multifactor analysis of internal/external attributes." Ph.D. dissertation, Rutgers University.

GEORGE, A.L. (1972). "The case for multiple advocacy in making foreign policy." American Political Science Review, 66 (September):751-785.

GILLESPIE, J.V. (1976). "Optimal control theory: A promising approach for future research." Pp. 235-246 in J.N. Rosenau (ed.), In search of global patterns. New York: Free Press.

——— et al. (1977). "An optimal control model of arms races." American Political Science Review, 71, 1 (March):226-244.

GILLESPIE, J.V., and ZINNES, D.A. (1977). Mathematical systems in international relations research. New York: Praeger.

——— and TAHIM, G.S. (1975). "Foreign military assistance and the armaments race: A differential game model with control." Papers of the Peace Science Society (International) 25:35-51.

GOCHMAN, C.S. (1975). "Status, conflict, and war: The major powers, 1820-1970." Ph.D. dissertation, University of Michigan.

GOLDSTEIN, M.E. (1975). "Congressional participation in foreign policy before and after Watergate." Political Science (Wellington) 27, 1/2 (July/December):111-116.

GOODMAN, R., HART, J., and ROSECRANCE, R. (1975). "Testing international theory: Methods and data in a situational analysis of international politics." Pp. 41-56 in E.E. Azar and J. Ben-Dak (eds.), Theory and practice of events research: Studies in inter-nation actions and interactions. New York: Gordon and Breach.

GUETZKOW, H. (1976). "Comment on Andriole, Wilkenfeld and Hopple." International Studies Quarterly, 20, 2 (June):331-334.

HAAS, M. (1975). "Survival decisionmaking." Pp. 146-176 in W.O. Chittick (ed.), The analysis of foreign policy outputs. Columbus, Ohio: Merrill.

––– (1974a). "International integration." Pp. 203-228 in M. Haas (ed.), International systems: A behavioral approach. New York: Chandler.

––– (ed.) (1974b). International systems: A behavioral approach. New York: Chandler.

HANSEN, P. (1977). "Explaining foreign policy attitudes: The case of Danish attitudes toward America." Cooperation and Conflict, 12:149-170.

HARBERT, J.R. (1976). "The behavior of the ministates in the United Nations, 1971-1972." International Organization, 30, 1 (Winter):109-127.

HARF, J.E., MOON, B.E., and THOMPSON, J.E. (1976). "Laws, explanation, and the X → Z syndrome." Pp. 271-281 in J.N. Rosenau (ed.), In search of global patterns. New York: Free Press.

HART, J.A. (1977). "Cognitive maps of three Latin American policy makers." World Politics, 30, 1:113-140.

––– (1976). "Comparative cognition: Politics of international control of the oceans." Pp. 180-217 in R. Axelrod (ed.), Structure of decision: The cognitive maps of political elites. Princeton: Princeton University Press.

––– (1974). "Structures of influence and cooperation-conflict." International Interactions, 1:141-162.

HART, T.G. (1976). "The cognitive dynamics of Swedish security elites: Beliefs about Swedish national security and how they change." Cooperation and Conflict, 11:201-219.

HATTIS ROLEF, S. (1975). "The politics of Britain, France and West Germany towards the Soviet Union 1955-75." Co-existence, 12 (May):58-86.

HAZLEWOOD, A., HAYES, J.J., and BROWNELL, J.R., JR. (1977). "Planning for problems in crisis management: An analysis of post-1945 behavior in the U.S. Department of Defense." International Studies Quarterly, 21, 1 (March):75-106.

HAZLEWOOD, L. (1975). "Diversion mechanisms and encapsulation processes: The domestic conflict-foreign conflict hypothesis reconsidered." Pp. 213-244 in P. J. McGowan (ed.), Sage international yearbook of foreign policy studies, III. Beverly Hills, Cal.: Sage.

HEINTZ, P. (1975). "Conformist and non-conformist behavior of developed nations." Journal of Peace Research, 12, 2:99-107.

HERMANN, C.F. (1976). Conceptualizing foreign policy behavior using events data." Pp. 354-360 in J.N. Rosenau (ed.), In search of global patterns. New York: Free Press.

––– (1975). "Comparing the foreign policy events of nations." Pp. 145-158 in C.W. Kegley, Jr., et al. (eds.), International events and the comparative analysis of foreign policy. Columbia, S.C.: University of South Carolina Press.

——— (1971). "What is a foreign policy event?" Pp. 295-321 in W.R. Hanrieder (ed.), Comparative foreign policy. New York: McKay.

———, et al. (1974). CREON: A foreign events data set. Beverly Hills, Cal.: Sage Professional Papers in International Studies.

HERMANN, M.G. (1976). "When leader personality will affect foreign policy: Some propositions." Pp. 326-333 in J.N. Rosenau (ed.), In search of global patterns. New York: Free Press.

HILL, G.A., and FENN, P.H. (1974). "Comparing event flows—*The New York Times* and *The Times* of London: Conceptual issues and case studies." International Interactions, 1:163-186.

HOGGARD, G.D. (1975). "An analysis of the 'real' data: Reflections on the uses and validity of international interaction data." Pp. 19-27 in E.E. Azar and J. Ben-Dak (eds.), Theory and practice of events research: Studies in inter-nation actions and interactions. New York: Gordon and Breach.

HOLLIST, W.L. (1977). "An analysis of arms processes in the United States and the Soviet Union." International Studies Quarterly, 21, 3:503-528.

——— (1974). "A transactional analysis of interstate cooperation: The United States/ Latin American example." Ph.D. dissertation, University of Denver.

HOLSTI, O.R. (1976a). "Cognitive process approaches to foreign-policy decision-making: A sketchy survey." In G.M. Bonham and M.J. Shapiro (eds.), Thought and action in foreign policy. Basel: Birkhauser Verlag.

——— (1976b). "Foreign policy formation viewed cognitively." Pp. 18-54 in R. Axelrod (ed.), Structure of decision: The cognitive maps of political elites. Princeton: Princeton University Press.

——— and ROSENAU, J.N. (1977). "The meaning of Vietnam: Belief systems of American leaders." International Journal, 32:452-474.

HOOLE, F.W., and ZINNES, D.A. (eds.) (1976). Quantitative international politics: An appraisal. New York: Praeger.

HOPMANN, P.T., and HUGHES, B.B. (1975). "The uses of events data for the measurement of cohesion in the international political coalitions: A validity study." Pp. 81-94 in E.E. Azar and J. Ben-Dak (eds.), Theory and practice of events research: Studies in inter-nation actions and interactions. New York: Gordon and Breach.

HOPMANN, P.T., and KING, T. (1976). "Interactions and perceptions in the test ban negotiations." International Studies Quarterly, 20, 1 (March):105-142.

HOPMANN, P.T., and SMITH, T.C. (1977). "An application of a Richardson process model: Soviet-American interactions in the test ban negotiations 1962-1963." Journal of Conflict Resolution, 21 (December):701-726.

HOPMANN, P.T., and WALCOTT, C. (1976). "The impact of international conflict and detente on bargaining in arms control: An experimental analysis." International Interactions, 2:189-206.

HUTCHINS, G.L. (1977). "The public policy behavior of heads of government: The character of leader behavior and its effect on the behavior of other decision-makers." Ph.D. dissertation, Ohio State University.

JENKINS, J.B. (1975). "Uncertainty and uncertainty-reduction in the global arena: Toward an integrated approach to international politics." Pp. 74-110 in W.O. Chittick (ed.), The analysis of foreign policy outputs. Columbus, Ohio: Merrill.

JENNINGS, R.M. (1975). "U.S./Soviet arms competition, 1945-1972: Aspects of its nature, control, and results." Ph.D. dissertation, Georgetown University.

JOHNS, D.H. (1975). "Diplomatic activity, power and integration in Africa." Pp. 85-105 in P.J. McGowan (ed.), Sage international yearbook of foreign policy studies, Ill. Beverly Hills, Cal.: Sage.

JOHNSTON, D.M. (1974). "Chinese treaty behavior: Experiments in analysis." Pp. 385-396 in R.L. Dial (ed.), Advancing and contending approaches to the study of Chinese foreign policy. Halifax: Dalhousie University.

KALELA, A. (1976). "Foreign policy elites, ideology and decision-making: A case study of the Finnish elites' image of the third world and their participation in decision-making." Cooperation and Conflict, 11:221-239.

KALICKI, H.H. (1974). "Theorizing about Chinese crisis behaviour: Two preliminary approaches." Pp. 233-252 in R.L. Dial (ed.), Advancing and contending approaches to the study of Chinese foreign policy. Halifax: Dalhousie University.

KAMINSKY, E.B.Z. (1975). "The French chief executive and foreign policy." Pp. 51-84 in P.J. McGowan (ed.), Sage international yearbook of foreign policy studies, III. Beverly Hills, Cal.: Sage.

KARL, C. (1975). "External penetration and foreign policy behavior." Ph.D. dissertation, University of Maryland.

KARNS, D.A. (1977). "The effect of interparliamentary meetings on the foreign policy attitudes of United States congressmen." International Organization, 31, 3 (Summer):496-513.

KATZENSTEIN, P.J. (1977). "Conclusion: Domestic structures and strategies of foreign economic policy." International Organization, 31, 4 (Autumn):879-920.

――― (1976). "International relations and domestic structures: Foreign economic policies of advanced industrial states." International Organization, 30, 1 (Winter):1-45.

KEGLEY, C.W. (1976a). "The pattern of foreign policy interactions in Asia: A quantitative comparison." Asian Forum, 8:1-22.

――― (1976b). "Selective attention: A general characteristic of the interactive behavior of nations." International Interactions, 2:113-116.

――― (1975). "A circumplex model of international interactions." Pp. 217-232 in E.E. Azar and J. Ben-Dak (eds.), Theory and practice of events research: Studies in inter-nation actions and interactions. New York: Gordon and Breach.

――― (1974). "Chinese behaviour in the context of the pattern of foreign policy interactions in Asia: A quantitative assessment." Pp. 197-224 in R.L. Dial (ed.), Advancing and contending approaches to the study of Chinese foreign policy. Halifax: Dalhousie University.

――― and HOLCOMB, P.A. (1976). "U.S. national security policy, 1950-73: A quantitative description." Armed Forces and Society, 2:573-594.

KEGLEY, C.W., and SKINNER, R.A. (1976). "The case-for-analysis problem." Pp. 303-318 in J.N. Rosenau (ed.), In search of global patterns. New York: Free Press.

KEGLEY, C.W., and WITTKOPF, E.R. (1976). "Structural characteristics of international influence relationships: A replication study." International Studies Quarterly, 20:261-300.

KENT, G. (1970). "Perceptions of foreign policies: Middle East." Papers of the Peace Research Society, 15 (June):99-121.

KIM, S. (1975). "A synthetic theory of actor objectives for the comparative study of foreign policy." Ph.D. dissertation, University of Maryland.

KÖHLER, G. (1977). "Exponential military growth." Peace Research, 9, 4 (October): 165-175.

――― (1975a). "Imperialism as a level of analysis in correlates-of-war research." Journal of Conflict Resolution, 19:48-62.

――― (1975b). "Le probleme de la définition d'une échelle d'hostilité pour le mesure des tensions." Études Internationales, 6, 1 (March):30-46.

――― (1974). Events research and war/peace prediction. Oakville, Ontario: Canadian Peace Research Institute Press.

KORANY, B. (1976). "Hypothèse marxiste et méthodologie behaviouriste: une analyse empirique." Études Internationales, 7, 1 (March):51-66.

――― (1974). "Foreign-policy models and their empirical relevance to third-world actors: A critique and an alternative." International Social Science Journal, 26, 1:70-94.

LAMBELET, J.C. (1975). "A numerical model of the Anglo-German dreadnought race, 1905-1914." Papers of the Peace Science Society (International) 24:29-48.

――― (1974). "The Anglo-German dreadnought race, 1905-1914." Papers of the Peace Science Society (International) 22:1-45.

LAMBERT, G. (1974). "The utility of elite aggregate data analysis in the explanation of Chinese foreign policy." Pp. 397-412 in R.L. Dial (ed.), Advancing and contending approaches to the study of Chinese foreign policy. Halifax: Dalhousie University.

LANPHIER, V.A. (1975). "Foreign relations indicator project (FRIP)." Pp. 161-174 in E.E. Azar and J. Ben-Dak (eds.), Theory and practice of events research: Studies in inter-nation actions and interactions. New York: Gordon and Breach.

LAURANCE, E.J. (1976). "The changing role of Congress in defence policy making." Journal of Conflict Resolution, 20, 2 (June):213-253.

LEVI, W. (1974). "International statecraft." Pp. 151-175 in M. Haas (ed.), International systems: A behavioral approach. New York: Chandler.

LISKE, C. (1975). "Changing patterns of partisanship in senate voting on defense and foreign policy, 1946-1969." Pp. 135-176 in P.J. McGowan (ed.), Sage international yearbook of foreign policy studies, III. Beverly Hills, Cal.: Sage.

LOOMIS, C.A. (1977). "The action international system 1966-7: Empirical description." International Interactions, 3, 1:21-26.

LUTERBACKER, U. (1975). "Bipolarity and generation factors in major power military activity 1900-1965." Journal of Peace Research, 12, 2:129-138.

MAHONEY, R.B., Jr. (1974). "Predicting the foreign behaviors of nations: A comparison of internal and external determinants." Ph.D. dissertation, Northwestern University.

MANDEL, R.M. (1976). "Political gaming and crisis foreign policymaking." Ph.D. dissertation, Yale University.

McCLELLAND, C.A. (1972). "The beginning, duration, and abatement of international crises: Comparisons in two conflict arenas." Pp. 83-105 in C.F. Hermann (ed.), International crises. New York: Free Press.

McGOWAN, P.J. (1976). "The future of comparative studies: An evangelical plea." Pp. 217-235 in J.N. Rosenau (ed.), In search of global patterns. New York: Free Press.

――― (1975). "Meaningful comparisons in the study of foreign policy: A methodological discussion of objectives, techniques, and research designs." Pp. 52-87 in C.W. Kegley, Jr., et al. (eds.), International events and the comparative analysis of foreign policy. Columbia, S.C.: University of South Carolina Press.

――― and GOTTWALD, K.P. (1975). "Small state foreign policies: A comparative study of participation, conflict, and political and economic dependence in Black Africa." International Studies Quarterly, 19 (December):469-500.

McKINLAY, R.D., and LITTLE, R. (1977). "A foreign policy model of U.S. bilateral aid allocation." World Politics, 30, 1:58-86.

MOORE, D.W. (1975). "Repredicting, voting patterns in the General Assembly: A methodological note." International Studies Quarterly, 19 (June):199-211.

MUNTON, D. (1976). "Comparative foreign policy: Fads, fantasies, orthodoxies, perversities." Pp. 257-271 in J.N. Rosenau (ed.), In search of global patterns. New York: Free Press.

MYKLETUN J. (1976). "Norwegian policy elites' attitudes toward the UN: A functionalist perspective." Cooperation and Conflict, 11:241-258.

NEWCOMBE, A.G., and ANDRIGHETTI, R. (1977). "Nations at risk: A prediction of nations likely to be in war in the years 1974-1978." International Interactions, 3, 2:135-160.

NEWCOMBE, A.G., NEWCOMBE, N.S., and LANDRUS, G.D. (1974). "The development of an inter-nation tensiometer." International Interactions, 1:3-18.

NEWCOMBE, A.G., and WERT, J. (1973). "The use of an inter-nation tensiometer for the prediction of war." Papers of the Peace Science Society (International) 21:73-83.

——— (1972). An inter-nation tensiometer for the prediction of war. Oakville, Ontario: Canadian Peace Research Institute.

NEWCOMBE, H. et al. (1976). "Patterns of nations: Interactions in the United Nations 1946-1971." International Interactions, 2:83-92.

NINCIC, M. (1975). "Determinants of third world hostility toward the United States: An exploratory analysis." Journal of Conflict Resolution, 19:620-642.

NOMIKOS, E.V., and NORTH, R.C. (1975). International crisis: The outbreak of World War I. New York: McGill-Queens.

ØBERG, J. (1975). "Arms trade with the third world as an aspect of imperialism." Journal of Peace Research, 12, 3:213-234.

ODELL, J.S. (1975). "The hostility of United States external behavior: An exploration." Pp. 107-134 in P.J. McGowan (ed.), Sage international yearbook of foreign policy studies, III. Beverly Hills, Cal.: Sage.

O'LEARY, M.K. (1976). "The role of issues." Pp. 318-326 in J.N. Rosenau (ed.), In search of global patterns. New York: Free Press.

——— and COPLIN, W.D. (1975). Quantitative techniques in foreign policy analysis and forecasting. New York: Praeger.

OLIVER, J., BOARDMAN, R., and DIAL, R. (1974). "A quantitative measure of causal and consequential explanation in the literature on Chinese foreign policy." Pp. 51-92 in R.L. Dial (ed.), Advancing and contending approaches to the study of Chinese foreign policy. Halifax: Dalhousie University.

OSTROM, C.W., Jr. (1977). "Evaluating alternative foreign policy decision-making models: An empirical test between an arms race model and an organizational politics model." Journal of Conflict Resolution, 21, 2 (June):235-266.

PARK, T.-W., ABOLFATHI, F., and WARD, M. (1976). "Resource nationalism in the foreign policy behavior of oil exporting countries (1947-1974)." International Interactions, 2:247-262.

PARK, Y.-O. (1975). "The structural balance of the international system: 1950-1965." Ph.D. dissertation, University of Hawaii.

PEARCE, D.L. (1975). "United States military aid and recipient nation defense expenditure: A quantitative analysis." Ph.D. dissertation, Syracuse University.

PEARSON, F.C., and BAUMANN, R. (1977). "Foreign military intervention and changes in United States business activity." Journal of Political and Military Sociology, 5:79-97.

PEARSON, F.S. (1976). "Policies, priorities, and event-interactions: The need for distinctions in foreign policy research." International Interactions, 2:159-164.

PENDERGAST, W.R. (1976). "Roles and attitudes of French and Italian delegates to the European community." International Organization, 30, 4 (Autumn):669-677.

PHILLIPS, W.R. (1975a). "The theoretical approaches in the events data movement." International Interactions, 2:3-18.

——— (1975b). "Two views of foreign policy interaction." Pp. 245-260 in E.E. Azar and J. Ben-Dak (eds.), Theory and practice of events research: Studies in inter-nation actions and interactions. New York: Gordon and Breach.

——— (1973). "The conflict environment of nations: A study of conflict inputs to nations in 1963." Pp. 124-147 in J. Wilkenfeld (ed.), Conflict behavior and linkage politics. New York: David McKay.

———, CALLAHAN, P.T., and CRAIN, R.C. (1977). "Simulated foreign policy exchanges: A formal theory of foreign policy interaction." International Interactions, 3, 4:345-368.

——— (1974). "Simulated foreign policy exchanges: The rationale underlying a theory of foreign policy interaction." International Interactions, 1:237-254.

PISANO, J.G. (1972). "Policy-making and policy types: Six cases of U.S. African policy." Ph.D. dissertation, Johns Hopkins University.

POTTER, W.C. (1976). "Continuity and change in the foreign relations of the Warsaw pact states, 1948-1973: A study of national adaptation to internal and external demands." Ph.D. dissertation, University of Michigan.

POWELL, C.A. et al. (1976). "Epistemology, theory, data, and the future." Pp. 291-303 in J.N. Rosenau (ed.), In search of global patterns. New York: Free Press.

PRINTUP, R.O. (1976). "Indo-Pakistan relations: 1962-1967, an events-data approach to analyzing dyadic international conflict." Ph.D. dissertation, Syracuse University.

QUISTGARD, J.E. (1977). "Distance change in foreign policy: A comparative analysis of relations between hegemons and members of their subsystems." Ph.D. dissertation, University of Arizona.

RAMBERG, B. (1977). "Tactical advantages of opening positioning strategies: Lessons from the seabed arms control talks 1967-1970." Journal of Conflict Resolution, 21 (December):685-700.

RATTINGER, H. (1976). "From war to war to war: Arms races in the Middle East." International Studies Quarterly, 20, 4 (December):501-531.

——— (1975). "Armaments, detente, and bureaucracy: The case of the arms race in Europe." Journal of Conflict Resolution, 19:571-595.

RAY, J.L. (1974). "Status inconsistency and war involvement in Europe, 1816-1970." Papers of the Peace Science Society (International) 23:69-80.

RHEE, S.-W. (1974). "China's co-operation, conflict, and interaction behaviour: Viewed from Rummel's field theoretic perspective." Pp. 111-196 in R.L. Dial (ed.), Advancing and contending approaches to the study of Chinese foreign policy. Halifax: Dalhousie University.

RICHMAN, A. (1975). "Issues in the conceptualization and measurement of events data." International Interactions, 2:19-32.

ROSENAU, J.N. (ed.) (1976a). In search of global patterns. New York: Free Press.

——— (1976b). "Restlessness, change, and foreign policy analysis." Pp. 369-376 in J.N. Rosenau (ed.), In search of global patterns. New York: Free Press.

——— (1975). "Comparative foreign policy: One-time fad, realized fantasy, and normal field." Pp. 3-38 in C.W. Kegley, Jr., et al. (eds.), International events and the comparative analysis of foreign policy. Columbia, S.C.: University of South Carolina Press.

——— (ed.) (1974). Comparing foreign policy: Theories, findings, and methods. Beverly Hills, Cal.: Sage.

——— (1973). "Theorizing across systems: Linkage politics revisited." Pp. 25-56 in J. Wilkenfeld (ed.), Conflict behavior and linkage politics. New York: David McKay.

———, BURGESS, P.M., and HERMANN, C.F. (1973). "The adaptation of foreign policy research: A case study of an anti-case study project." International Studies Quarterly, 17 (March):119-44.

ROSENAU, J.N., and RAMSEY, G.H. (1975). "External and internal typologies of foreign policy behavior: Testing the stability of an intriguing set of findings." Pp. 245-262 in P.J. McGowan (ed.), Sage international yearbook of foreign policy studies, III. Beverly Hills, Cal.: Sage.

ROSENBERG, S.W., and WOLFSFELD, G. (1977). "International conflict and the problem of attribution." Journal of Conflict Resolution, 21, 1 (March):75-103.

ROSS, M.E., and HOMER, E. (1976). "Galton's problem in cross-national research." World Politics, 29, 1 (October):1-28.

RUBNER, M. (1975). "Israel and Latin America: The politics of bilateral economic aid." Ph.D. dissertation, University of California, Berkeley.

RUMMEL, R.J. (1975). Understanding conflict and war: The dynamic psychological field. Beverly Hills, Cal.: Sage.

RUSSETT, B.M. (1975a). "The Americans' retreat from world power." Political Science Quarterly, 90, 1 (Spring):1-21.

——— (1975b). "The opportunity costs of American defense." Pp. 188-209 in W.O. Chittick (ed.), The analysis of foreign policy outputs. Columbus, Ohio: Merrill.

SABROSKY, A.N. (1975). "From Bosnia to Sarajevo: A comparative discussion of interstate crises." Journal of Conflict Resolution, 19:3-24.

SAETER, M. (1975). "The Nordic area and European integration: The Nordic countries in the area of overlap between great-power interests and regional European projects for cooperation." Cooperation and Conflict (no 1/2):77-89.

Sampson, M.W. (1976). "Policy zone: Where policies work." Pp. 348-375 in D.A. Zinnes and J.V. Gillespie (eds.), Mathematical models in international relations. New York: Praeger.

Schechter, M.G. (1976). "Processes of transnational policy-making: A comparison of economic and environmental issue-areas." Ph.D. dissertation, Columbia University.

SCHICK, J.M. (1974). "Crisis studies and the Near East: The cases of Lebanon and Cyprus." International Interactions, 1:187-192.

SCOLNICK, J.M. (1974). "An appraisal of studies of the linkage between domestic and international conflict." Comparative Political Studies, 6, 4 (January):485-509.

SHYAM, M. (1976). "International seabed regime: An empirical analysis of state preferences." Cooperation and Conflict, 11:111-134.

SIMMONS, R.R. (1974). "The concept of 'alliance' as a tool in the study of Chinese foreign policy." Pp. 253-290 in R.L. Dial (ed.), Advancing and contending approaches to the study of Chinese foreign policy. Halifax: Dalhousie University.

SINGER, J.D. (1973). "The peace researcher and foreign policy prediction." Papers of the Peace Science Society (International) 21:1-13.

SKINNER, R.A. (1975). "Impact analysis and the responsive stage of foreign policy: A study of the consequences of military intervention." Ph.D. dissertation, University of South Carolina.

SOROOS, M. (1977). "Behavior between nations." Peace Research Reviews, 7, 2:1-107.

——— (1975). "Patterns of cross-national activities in the international process simulation and a real world reference system." Pp. 143-160 in E.E. Azar and J. Ben-Dak (eds.),

Theory and practice of events research: Studies in inter-nation actions and interactions. New York: Gordon and Breach.

STARR, H. (1977). "Physical variables and foreign policy decision making: Daily temperature and the pre-World War I crisis." International Interactions, 3, 2:97-108.

STASSEN, G.H. (1972). "Individual preferences versus role-constraint in policy-making: Senatorial response to secretaries Acheson and Dulles." World Politics, 25 (October): 96-119.

STOHL, M. (1973). "Linkage between war and domestic political violence in the United States, 1890-1923." Pp. 156-179 in J. Caporaso and L. Roos (eds.), Quasi-experimental approaches: Testing theory and evaluating policy. Evanston: Northwestern University Press.

SUEDFELD, P., and TETLOCK, P. (1977). "Integrative complexity of communications in international crises." Journal of Conflict Resolution, 21, 1 (March):169-184.

——— and RAMIREZ, C. (1977). "War, peace, and integrative complexity: UN speeches on the Middle East problem, 1947-1976." Journal of Conflict Resolution, 21, 3 (September):427-441.

SULLIVAN, J.D. (1976). "Resources in comparative analysis." Pp. 333-338 in J.N. Rosenau (ed.), In search of global patterns. New York: Free Press.

SWANSON, D.E. (1976). "Degree of specificity: Actor expectations in foreign policy behavior." Ph.D. dissertation, Ohio State University.

TANTER, R., and POTTER, W. (1973). "Modelling alliance behavior: East-west conflict over Berlin." Papers of the Peace Science Society (International) 20:25-41.

THOMAS, S.T. (1975). "Domestic instability and war behavior: An empirical study of national political units, 1946-1965." Ph.D. dissertation, University of Colorado.

THOMPSON, W.R., and MODELSKI, G. (1977). "Global conflict intensity and great power summitry behavior." Journal of Conflict Resolution, 21, 2 (June):339-376.

THORSON, S.J. (1976). "Some conceptual problems in constructing theories of foreign policy behavior." Pp. 246-256 in J.N. Rosenau (ed.), In search of global patterns. New York: Free Press.

TOMLIN, B.W., and BUHLMAN, M.A. (1977). "Relative status and foreign policy: Status partitioning and the analysis of relations in black Africa." Journal of Conflict Resolution, 21, 2 (June):187-216.

TOMLINSON, R.G. (1977). "Analyzing the change characteristics and patterns in the international event flow over the years, 1966-1975." Ph.D. dissertation, University of Southern California.

TRICE, R.H. (1977). "Congress and the Arab-Israeli conflict: Support for Israel in the U.S. Senate, 1970-73." Political Science Quarterly, 92, 3 (fall):443-463.

VALENZUELA, J. (1973). "U.S. manufacturing investment, political instability and patterns of international cooperation and conflict, in Argentina and Chile, 1955-1971." Ph.D. dissertation, University of North Carolina.

VAN ATTA, R., and RUMMEL, R.J. (1971). "Testing field theory on 1963 behavior space of nations." Peace Research Society (International) Papers, 16:23-45.

VENGROFF, R. (1976). "Instability and foreign policy behavior: Black Africa in the U.N." American Journal of Political Science, 20, 3 (August):425-438.

VINCENT, J.E. (1977). "Analyzing international conflict and cooperation flows: An application of attribute theory." Social Science Quarterly, 58, 1 (June):111-117.

——— (1973). "An application of attribute theory to General Assembly voting patterns and some implications." International Organization, 16 (Summer):551-582.

――――, VOLGY, T.J., and KENSKI, H.C. (1976). "Toward an exploration of comparative foreign policy distance between the United States and Latin America." International Studies Quarterly, 20, 1 (March):143-166.

WAGNER, A.R. (1975). "A rational choice model of aggression: The case of the Six Day War." Pp. 15-49 in P.J. McGowan (ed.), Sage international yearbook of foreign policy studies, III. Beverly Hills, Cal.: Sage.

WALKER, S.G. (1977). "The interface between beliefs and behavior: Henry Kissinger's operational code and the Vietnam War." Journal of Conflict Resolution, 21, 1 (March):129-168.

WALLACE M.D. (1973). "Alliance polarization, cross-cutting, and international war, 1815-1964: A measurement process and some preliminary evidence." Journal of Conflict Resolution, 17:575-604.

WEEDE, E. (1973). "Nation-environment relations as determinants of hostilities among nations." The Papers of the Peace Science Society (International) 20:67-90.

WEIL, H.M. (1975). "Can bureaucracies be rational actors?: Foreign policy decision-making in North Vietnam." International Studies Quarterly, 19 (December):432-468.

WEISENBLOOM, M.V. (1977). "Chinese foreign conflict behavior: A test of the stimulus-response model." Ph.D. dissertation, University of Arizona.

WILKENFELD, J. (1975). "A time-series perspective on conflict behavior in the Middle East." Pp. 177-212 in P.J. McGowan (ed.), Sage international yearbook of foreign policy studies, III. Beverly Hills, Cal.: Sage.

―――― (ed.) (1973). Conflict behavior and linkage politics. New York: David McKay.

――――, LUSSIER, V.L., and TAHTINEN, D. (1972). "Conflict interactions in the middle East, 1949-67." Journal of Conflict Resolution, 16 (June):135-154.

WITTKOPF, E. (1976). "Politics and ecology, Easton and Rosenau: An alternative research priority." Pp. 338-354 in J.N. Rosenau (ed.), In search of global patterns. New York: Free Press.

―――― (1975). "Soviet and American political success in the United Nations General Assembly, 1946-1970." Pp. 179-204 in C.W. Kegley, Jr., et al. (eds.), International events and the comparative analysis of foreign policy. Columbia, S.C.: University of South Carolina Press.

YEE, H.S.-J. (1976). "Decisions to establish diplomatic relations with China: Environmental variables in foreign policy decision-making." Ph.D. dissertation, University of Hawaii.

YOUNG, R.A. (1975). "A classification of nations according to foreign policy output." Pp. 175-195 in E.E. Azar and J. Ben-Dak (eds.), Theory and practice of events research: Studies in inter-nation actions and interactions. New York: Gordon and Breach.

ZAGARE, F.C. (1977). "A game-theoretic analysis of the Vietnam negotiations: Preferences and strategies 1968-1973." Journal of Conflict Resolution, 21 (December): 663-684.

ZARTMAN, I.W. (1977). "Negotiation as a joint decision-making process." Journal of Conflict Resolution, 21 (December):619-638.

ZINNES, D.A., and GILLESPIE, J.V. (1976). Mathematical models in international relations. New York: Praeger.

ABOUT THE AUTHORS

FARID ABOLFATHI received his undergraduate education at the University of Oregon and his masters and doctoral degrees from Northwestern University. Currently he is a Senior Research Associate in the Policy Sciences Division of CACI, Inc.-Federal and is involved in a research project to forecast the future prospects of less-developed countries. His recent publications include *The OPEC Market to 1985* (1977), "Military Spending in the Third World" (1974), "The Origin and Consequences of Military Involvement in Defense and Foreign Policy" (1974), "Resource Nationalism in the Foreign Policy Behavior of Oil Exporting Countries" (1976), "The Absorptive Capacity of Arab Members of OPEC" (1978), "The Potential for Technology Transfer in the Future Development of Saudi Arabia's Energy Sector" (1978), and "Defense Expenditures in the Persian Gulf" (1978).

JAMES A. CAPORASO received his B.A. from Pennsylvania State University and his Ph.D. from the University of Pennsylvania. He is coeditor of *Quasi-Experimental Approaches: Testing Theory and Evaluating Policy, The Structure and Function of European Integration* and articles in the *American Political Science Review, International Studies Quarterly,* and *International Organization.* He has currently edited a special issue of *International Organization* on dependence and dependency in the global system (Winter, 1978). He is now Mellon Professor of International Studies at the Graduate School of International Studies, University of Denver.

MARK W. DELANCEY received his Ph.D. from Indiana University in 1973. He is now Associate Professor in the Department of Government and International Studies, University of South Carolina, and he recently served as Visiting Reader in the Department of Political Science, University of Nigeria. He specializes in the study of African comparative and international politics. Currently, he is involved in studies of the constitutional debate in Nigeria and a comparison of the foreign policies of Nigerian civilian and military regimes. Among his publications are articles in *Journal of Developing Areas, Journal of Modern African Studies,* and *Africa.*

CHARLES F. DORAN has written broadly in two major areas, resource and environmental politics at the international level and the analysis of political conflict, both foreign and domestic. Major research in the former area includes *Myth, Oil and Politics* (1977) and *Umweltschutz—Politik des peripheren Eingriffs: Eine Einfuhrung in die politische Ökologia* (1974) coauthored with P.C. Mayer-Tasch and Manfred Hinz. In the latter area his contributions include *The Politics of Assimilation: Hegemony and Its Aftermath* (1971) and *Domestic Conflict in State Relations* (1976). Educated at Harvard and Johns Hopkins Universities, he is currently Associate Professor of Political Science at Rice University and Director of International Programs in the Jones School of Administration.

WERNER J. FELD received his legal education at the University of Berlin (Referendar) and his Ph.D. from Tulane University. He is currently Professor of Political Science at the University of New Orleans. His publications include *Reunification and West German-Soviet Relations* (1963), *The Court of the European Communities: New Dimension in International Adjudication* (1964), *The European Common Market and the World* (1967), *Transnational Business Collaboration Among Common Market Countries: Implications for Political Integration* (1970), *Nongovernmental Forces and World Politics* (1972), *The European Community in World Affairs* (1976), and *Domestic Political Realities and European Unification* (with John K. Wildgen) (1977). In addition he has contributed chapters to a number of edited books and articles to journals including *International Organization, Political Science Quarterly, The Journal of Common Market Studies,* and *Orbis.*

MG JOHN J. HAYES (USA, Ret) joined the staff of CACI, Inc.-Federal as a Senior Associate in 1974. Since then, he has performed research in the areas of crisis management, effective performance of military forces, decision-making, forecasting critical events, and the application of logistics analysis to policy problems such as the future of the Panama Canal. His experience extends to participation in staff support decision-making for several international crises, some of which were analyzed for this volume. His doctoral studies at Washington University were in the field of social and public welfare administration. Since joining CACI, he has authored or coauthored a number of technical reports and published in *International Studies Quarterly.*

RICHARD E. HAYES is Manager of the Policy Sciences Division at CACI, Inc.-Federal, a multidisciplinary private research, development, and consulting corporation. He did his undergraduate work in the School of Foreign Service at Georgetown University and his doctoral work at Indiana University. Prior to joining CACI in 1974, Dr. Hayes spent two years on a joint appointment in the Center for International Studies and the Political Science Department for the University of Missouri-St. Louis. While his current duties focus on development and direction of multidisciplinary research projects, he has contributed to several edited volumes in the field of political science as well as the *Western Political Quarterly* and *International Studies Quarterly.*

CHARLES F. HERMANN serves as Associate Director of the Mershon Center and Professor of Political Science at Ohio State University. Among his publications are *Crises in Foreign Policy, International Crises, CREON: An Events Data Set, Why Nations Act,* and a number of articles. He received his Ph.D. from Northwestern University and then taught at Princeton University. Before coming to Ohio State, he received a Council on Foreign Relations International Affairs Fellowship which resulted in his working on Henry Kissinger's NSC staff for a year.

OLE R. HOLSTI, currently George V. Allen Professor of Political Science at Duke University, taught previously at Stanford and the University of British Columbia, and he has been a Fellow at the Center for Advanced Study in the Behavioral Sciences. He received his undergraduate education at Stanford, his M.A. from Wesleyan, and his doctoral degree from Stanford. His publications include *Content Analysis for the Social Sciences and Humanities* (1969), *Crisis, Escalation, War* (1972), coauthorship of *International Alliances* (1973), and he has contributed to *The Handbook of Social Psychology, The American Political Science Review, Journal of Politics, International Social Science Journal, Journal of Conflict Resolution* and several other books and journals.

THOMAS H. JOHNSON is a Ph.D. candidate in international relations at the University of Southern California. His areas of specialization include international relations theory and methodology, conflict analysis and peace research, computer simulation and modeling, and African international affairs. Publications include coauthorship of "The AFRICA Project and the Comparative Study of African Foreign Policy Behavior," in *African International Relations.*

CHARLES W. KEGLEY, Jr. received his undergraduate education at the School of International Service, The American University, and his doctoral degree from the International Relations Program at Syracuse University. Currently Associate Professor of Comparative Foreign Policy at the University of South Carolina, he has taught previously at Georgetown University and the University of Texas. His publications include coeditorship of *Analyzing International Relations* (1975), *International Events and the Comparative Analysis of Foreign Policy* (1975), and *After Vietnam* (1971), coauthorship of *American Foreign Policy: Pattern and Process* (1979); and he has contributed to a number of edited books and journals, including *International Studies Quarterly, International Organization, Armed Forces and Society, Simulation and Games, International Interactions,* and *The Journal of Politics.*

FRANK L. KLINGBERG received his A.B. and A.M. degrees at the University of Kansas, and his Ph.D. at the University of Chicago. After teaching at James Millikin University and Knox College, he served in the Department of Political Science at Southern Illinois University-Carbondale from 1946 to 1976, and is now Professor Emeritus. He pioneered in three areas: psychometric methods and factor analysis in international relations ("Studies in Measurement of the Relations Among Sovereign States," *Psychometrika,* December 1941); the relation of casualties to the ending of wars ("Predicting the Termination of War: Battle Casualties and Population Losses," *Journal of Conflict Resolution,* June 1966—based largely on research in the Department of War in 1945); and the study of cyclical trends in American foreign policy (articles in *World Politics,* January 1952, and *Journal of Conflict Resolution,* December 1970).

PATRICK J. McGOWAN received his Ph.D. from Northwestern in 1970 and is now an Associate Professor of International Relations and Political Science at the University of Southern California. He has edited *The Sage Yearbook* since 1973. Among his publications is coauthorship of *The Comparative Study of Foreign Policy: A Survey of Scientific Findings* (1973). His current research interests are in the areas of international political economy and the comparative study of foreign policy, with particular reference to Africa.

ALVIN RICHMAN received his undergraduate education in engineering at MIT, and his graduate work in international relations from Columbia University (M.I.A.) and the University of Pennsylvania (Ph.D.). Currently Associate Public Opinion Analyst in the Department of State, he has been with the Office of Research, International Communications Agency, and previously taught at Purdue University and Villanova University. His publications include two monographs on events data scaling and contributions to several edited books and journals, including the *Journal of International Affairs, International Interactions,* and *Communication in International Politics.*

JAMES N. ROSENAU is Director, School of International Relations and Institute for Transnational Studies, University of Southern California, and has taught previously at Rutgers University and at Ohio State University. His recent publications include authorship of *Citizenship Between Elections: An Inquiry into the Mobilizable American* (1974) and *The Dramas of Politics: An Introduction to the Joys of Inquiry* (1973), as well as editorship of *In Search of Global Patterns* (1976).

J. DAVID SINGER received his B.A. from Duke University, and his doctorate from New York University. He is currently Professor in the Political Science Department at the University of Michigan, having been Coordinator of the World Politics Program from 1969-1975. He has previously held teaching positions at New York University, Vassar College, and Harvard, and been a Visiting Faculty Member at the University of Oslo and Institute for Social Research, Norway; the Carnegie Endowment for International Peace and Graduate Institute of International Studies, Geneva, Switzerland; and ZUMA and the University of Mannheim, West Germany. His publications include *The Study of International Politics: A Guide to Sources for the Student, Teacher, and Researcher* (with Dorothy LaBarr) (1976), *Beyond Conjecture in International Politics: Abstracts of Data-Based Research* (with Susan Jones) (1972), *The Wages of War, 1816-1965: A Statistical Handbook* (with Melvin Small) (1972), *Deterrence, Arms Control, and Disarmament: Toward a Synthesis in National Security Policy* (1962), *Financing International-Organization: The United Nations Budget Process* (1961), as well as numerous articles in such journals as *American Political Science Review, International Security, British Journal of International Studies, Journal of Conflict Resolution.*

MELVIN SMALL is Professor in the History Department of Wayne State University and co-investigator in the Correlates of War Project. He received his B.A. degree from Dartmouth College (1960) and his M.A. and Ph.D. (1965) degrees from the University of Michigan. A recipient of an American Council of Learned Societies Study Fellowship in 1969, Small was a fellow at the Center for Advanced Studies in the Behavioral Sciences. He has been a visiting professor at the University of Michigan, Marygrove College, the University of Windsor, and Aarhus University in Denmark. Editor of *Public Opinion and Historians* (1970) and coauthor of *The Wages of War* (1972), Small has published articles on diplomatic history and world politics in, among other journals, *The Historian, Journal of Peace Research, Journal of Conflict Resolution, Historical Methods Newsletter,* and *Film and History.*

MICHAEL D. WARD received his B.A. degree from Indiana University and his Ph.D. from Northwestern University. He is Research Associate with the Gordon Scott Fulcher Chair of Decision-Making, Department of Political Science, Northwestern University. His interests in international affairs, centering on political economy, include coalitions and alliances, stratification and inequality, and energy policy. His publications include *The Political Economy of Distribution: Equality versus Inequality* (1978). Current research involves construction of models in the areas of alliance behavior and international stratification which are being integrated into comprehensive global simulations of international affairs.